KB016159

제물포 각국 조계지 회의록 2

인천학자료총서 25

제물포 각국 조계지 회의록 2

이영미 역

본서는 미국국립문서보관소 소장 「제물포 각국 조계 회의록 제2권(Chemulpo Minutes, Vol. II)」과 「제물포 각국 조계 기타 문서(Miscellaneous Chemulpo Papers)」를 국립중앙도서관이 2009년 영인한 자료를 바탕으로 하였으며, 사용된 이미지는 국립중앙도서관 소장 자료임.

역자 서문

15~16세기 이른바 '지리적 발견(Geographical Discoveries)'의 시대를 기점으로 유럽인들은 자신들이 살던 세계 밖으로 세력을 넓혀 나가기 시작하였다. 국내에서 조계(租界) 또는 거류지(居留地)로 번역되는 '세틀먼트(settlement)'는 그들이 해외에 건설한 유럽인 전용 거주지를 가리킨다. 시간이 지남에 따라 그들은 토지 매매부터 징세와 미화, 치안에 이르는 많은 일들을 처리할 기구의 필요성을 절감하고, 이에 '자치 의회(municipal council)'를 구성하여 거주지 제반 사무의 의결과 집행을 담당하였다. 이상의 일들은 중국과 일본을 거쳐 개항기 조선에서도 비슷하게 일어났다. 1883년 11월 26일 체결된 조영수호통상조약 제4관에는 조계에 대한 설명과 함께 '관리조계사무신동공사(管理租界事務紳董公司)'라는 용어가 처음으로 등장하였다. 이는 조계 사무를 관리하는 유지들의 공회 즉, '자치 의회'를 지칭하는 것이었다.

제물포 각국 조계는 일본 조계와 청국 조계에 이어 1884년 10월 설정되었고, 이 조계의 자치 의회였던 이른바 '신동공사'는 1888년 12월 5일 제물포주재일본영사관에서 첫 번째 모임을 가졌다. 신동공사는 당연직 위원 6명과 선출직 위원 3명으로 구성되었다. 전자는 각국 조계 장정 체약국인 미국, 독일, 영국, 중국, 일본, 한국의 대표들로, 한국 대표를 제외한 나머지는 서울이나 제물포에 주재하던 외교관이었다. 후자는 정식으로 토지를 조차한 사람들(등록된 토지소유주)이 투표로 뽑은 임기제 대표였다. 또한 당연직과 선출직을 막론하고 제물포에 거주하는 위원 중 3명을 매년 집행위원회로 임명하여 신동공사에서 결의된 안건의 집행을 맡겼다. 한편 제물포보다 먼저 개항한 부산과 원산에는 각국 조계가 들어서지 않았다. 1880년대에 내한한 서양인들은 대부분 서울이나 제물포에 정착하였다.

1890년대 말 전국의 여러 지역이 개항장과 개시장으로 지정되면서 진남포, 목포, 군산, 성진, 마산, 절영도 등지에도 각국 조계가 세워졌다. 이들 후발 각국 조계에 관하여는 알려진 바가 많지 않으나 서양인이 적었던 것은 확실하다. 1905년 자료에 따르면 이곳들의 신동공사는 대개 감리와 2~3인의 일본인으로 구성되었으며 회장은 거의 일본 영사였다. 반면 제물포 각국 조계의 경우에는 한국을 제외하고도 5~6개국 사람들이 신동공사에 참여하였으며, 회장으로는 당연직 위원 중에서도 직급이 높은 미국 또는 독일 대표가 선출되는 경우가 많았다. 이러한 점에서 제물포 각국 조계는 국내 모든 각국 조계를 통틀어 '각국'이라는 명칭이 어울리는 거의 유일한 조계였다.

이 책은 2009년 국립중앙도서관이 미국국립문서보관소(NARA)에서 영인한 「제물포 각국 조계 회의록 제2권」과 「제물포 각국 조계 기타 문서」를 판독 및 번역한 것으로,[1] 인천학자료총서 제17권으로 발간된 『제물포 각국 조계지 회의록 1』(박진빈 역, 2017)의 후편이다. 전편의 저본

이 신동공사가 출범한 1888년 12월 5일부터 1892년 5월 11일까지의 회의록을 담은 136페이지 분량의 공책이었다면,[2] 역자의 첫 번째 자료 「제물포 각국 조계 회의록 제2권」은 1892년 5월 11일부터 1895년 3월 7일까지의 회의록과 선거록을 담은 82페이지짜리 공책이었다. 이 기록은 서기에 의하여 비교적 알아보기 쉬운 필기체로 작성되었다. 반면 두 번째 자료 「제물포 각국 조계 기타 문서」는 한 편의 자료가 아니라 편지, 도표, 도면, 회의록이 뒤죽박죽 섞여 있는 문서철로, 1898~1900년과 1913년 회의록처럼 역자에게 꼭 필요한 것도 있고 그렇지 않은 것도 있었다. 그 중에는 역자의 수고를 덜어 주는 타자 문서도 있었지만, 필기체 문서의 경우에는 다양한 사람들이 각자의 필체로 작성하였기 때문에 첫 번째 자료보다 난이도가 높았다.

역자는 『제물포 각국 조계지 회의록 1』을 따라 앞부분에는 번역문과 원문을 싣고 뒷부분에는 영인본을 실었으나, 「제물포 각국 조계 회의록 제2권」과 「제물포 각국 조계 기타 문서」를 차례대로 수록하지는 않았다. 그 대신 앞부분에는 전자와 후자의 회의록과 선거록을 수합하여 날짜순으로 실었으며 뒷부분에는 후자의 문서들을 종류와 날짜에 따라 재배치하였다. 원본에 문단이 제대로 구분되어 있지 않은 경우가 많았으므로 안건별로 문단을 구분하였고, 번역문과 원문을 함께 검토하기

1) 전자는 국립중앙도서관 해외한국관련기록물 〈Foreign Settlements in Korea (6)〉, 후자는 〈Chemulpo General Foreing [sic.] Settlements〉를 가리킨다. 이렇게 적절하지 못한 제목이 붙은 것은 근본적으로는 자료 표지에 2개 이상의 구절이 적혀 있기 때문일 것이다. 역자는 그 중 "Chemulpo Minutes, Vol. II"와 "Msc. Chemulpo Papers"를 선택하여 「제물포 각국 조계 회의록 제2권」과 「제물포 각국 조계 기타 문서」로 명명하였다.

2) 국립중앙도서관 해외한국관련기록물 〈Foreign Settlements, Chemulpo Minutes Vol. 1〉을 가리킨다.

수월하도록 각 문단 앞에 번호(①, ②, ③)를 넣었다. 또한 필요하다고 생각되는 부분에는 각주를 달았다. 용어는 전편에서 사용된 것을 가급적 따르려고 했으나 결과적으로는 많이 바꾸었다. 예를 들면 '세관 위원(Commissioner of Customs)'은 '해관장', '공식 회원(official member)'은 '당연직 위원', '행정위원회(Executive Committee)'는 '집행위원회', '재무관(treasurer)'은 '회계', '무역감독관(Superintendent of Trade)'은 '감리'로 변경하였다. 각국 조계에 토지를 조차한 사람들은 전편과 마찬가지로 '토지소유주'로, 그들이 자신의 토지에 대하여 납부한 돈은 '세금'으로 번역하였다. 독자들께서 너그러이 이해해 주시기를 바란다. 아울러 여러 번 원고를 검토하였음에도 불구하고 부족한 점이 있을 줄 안다. 그 부분은 전적으로 역자의 책임이다.

귀중한 자료를 번역서로 낼 수 있게 해 주신 인천학연구원 조봉래 원장님 이하 여러 선생님들께 감사의 말씀을 드린다. 작업 과정 내내 신경 써 주신 남동걸 선생님, 작업을 제때 마칠 수 있도록 때때마다 연락 주신 신미혜 선생님께도 감사한다. 오랜 시간 역자를 지도해 주신 인하대학교 사학과의 모든 선생님들께 지면을 빌어 감사의 인사를 올린다. 특히 보이는 곳에서나 보이지 않는 곳에서나 변함없이 제자를 지지해 주시는 이영호 선생님께 날이 갈수록 커지는 감사의 마음을 표하고 싶다. 『극동의 유럽인 거류지(European Settlements in the Far East)』(1900)의 번역 작업에 역자를 참여시켜 값진 경험을 쌓게 해 주신 윤승준 선생님께도 머리 숙여 감사드린다. 다음으로는 건양대학교의 김현숙 선생님께 감사의 말씀을 드리고 싶다. 역자가 필기체 영문 자료를 비교적 큰 어려움 없이 읽어낼 수 있었던 것은 선생님 밑에서 3년간 연구 과제를 수행하며 배운 덕분이었다. 더불어 인하대학교 한국학연구소의 장윤희 소장님과 여러 선생님들께, 여러 가지로 부족한 역자를 응원해 주시고 번역 과정에서도 크고 작은 도움을 주신 선후배들께 마음 다하여 감사드린다. 편집으로 힘써 주신 보고사 이순민 선생님께도 감사의 말씀을 전한다.

대단한 연구 성과를 발표하는 것도 아니라서 마지막까지 망설였지만, 쑥스럽다는 이유로 가장 가까운 사람들께 드리는 감사 인사를 생략하면 안 될 것 같다. 변변찮은 장녀를 자랑스럽게 여기고 늘 기도해 주시는 부모님께, 그리고 역자의 좋은 친구인 두 동생과 그들의 가족께 감사드린다. 공부하는 며느리를 딸처럼 생각하며 배려해 주시는 시부모님께도 깊은 감사의 말씀을 드린다. 마지막으로 짧다면 짧고 길다면 긴 시간 동안 함께 걸어 준 남편 김상영 목사에게 글로는 표현할 수 없는 사랑의 마음을 전한다.

2020년 2월

인하대학교 한국학연구소에서 역자 씀

차례

◆ 기타 문서(번역문 / 원문) · 189

◆ 부록 · 255

◆ 국립중앙도서관 영인본 · 279

회의록·선거록

1892년 5월 11일 회의록

··– 번역문 –··

① 회의를 속개하였다. 오전과 마찬가지로 크린 씨(의장), 노세 씨, 볼터 씨, 스트리플링 씨, 니시와키 씨가 참석하였다.[1)]

② 참석자 전원이 D39~B2 구역의 도로를 살펴보았다. D39 구역 앞의 도로를 상당 부분 깎아야 한다는 것이 중론이었으나 정확히 얼마를 깎아야 할지는 결정하지 않았다. 크린 씨는 이 문제를 각국 외교 대표들에게 제출하기로 했다.[2)]

③ 노세 씨가 발의하고 니시와키 씨가 재청하였다. "서기께 요청합니다. 감리에게 편지를 써서 각국 조계, 특히 공원과 묘지에 있는 한국인들의 무덤을 3주 안에 옮겨 달라고 하되, 3주 후에는 신동공사가 별도의 통지 없이 옮기겠다고도 전해 주십시오."

---

1) 1892년 5월 11일 오전 10시에 개회하고 잠시 휴식한 후 오후 3시에 속개한 회의이다. 오전 회의의 회의록은 『제물포 각국 조계지 회의록 1』 260~263쪽에 수록되어 있다. 독일 대표 겸 신동공사 부회장으로서 서울주재독일총영사 크린, 일본 대표로서 제물포주재일본부영사 노세, 선출직 위원 겸 회계 겸 집행 위원으로서 독일인 볼터, 선출직 위원 겸 집행 위원으로서 영국인 스트리플링과 일본인 니시와키가 참석하였다. 미국 대표 겸 회장이었던 주한미국공사 허드, 영국 대표 겸 서기였던 제물포주재영국대리부영사 스캇, 중국 대표였던 제물포주재중국부영사 홍즈빈은 참석하지 않았다. 한편 인천해관장대리였던 영국인 존스턴은 1889년 12월부터 한국 대표로 참석하였으나, 해관에서 물러나게 되었으므로 1892년 5월 9일 회의부터는 참석하지 않았다.

2) '각국 외교 대표들(Foreign Representatives)'이란 서울에 주재하는 각국 공사들과 총영사들을 가리킨다. 원문 그대로 번역하면 '각국 대표'이지만 신동공사의 각국 대표와 혼동할 수 있으므로 '각국 외교 대표'라고 번역하였다.

④ 볼터 씨는 B4, D2, D4 구역의 1891년도 세금 문제를 제기하였다. 그는 존스턴 씨가 자신에게 세금을 전달하지 않았다며 작년 세금이 왜 아직도 미납 상태인지 이해할 수 없다고 이야기하였다. 그가 받아야 할 돈은 이 구역들에 부과된 세금 총액 243.99달러 중 한국 정부에 내야 할 47.76달러를 뺀 196.23달러이다. 스트리플링 씨는 자신이 3월 초에 세금을 납부하였다고 밝혔다.[3] 최종적으로 볼터 씨가 발의하고 스트리플링 씨가 재청하였다. "존스턴 씨께 편지를 써서 신동공사가 세금 수령을 기다리고 있으니 196.23달러를 보내 달라고 합시다." 만장일치로 통과되었다.

⑤ 노세 씨는 각국 조계에 교도소를 두는 것이 괜찮은지, 각국 조계 당국이 사람을 구금할 권리를 가지는지 문의하였다. 크린 씨는 제물포에서는 일본 조계와 중국 조계만이 교도소를 두고 있다고 언급하였다. 만일 누군가 범죄를 저지르면 어떻게 해야 할까? 고베 각국 조계에는 신동공사 회관 인근에 훌륭한 교도소가 있을 뿐 아니라 수감자들을 위한 규정과 일과도 있다고 한다. 크린 씨는 신동공사 회관에 하룻밤 이상 범죄자를 가둘 수 있는 견고한 공간이 있어야 한다는 뜻을 확실히 밝혔다. 범죄자를 가두는 것은 당연히 신동공사의 권한이 아니지만, 적절한 당국이 인계할 때까지 범죄자를 구금하는 것은 신동공사의 권리이자 의무라는 것이었다.[4]

⑥ 노세 씨는 홍콩상하이은행 상하이 지점에 맡긴 신동공사 기금을

---

3) B4, D2, D4 구역은 모두 스트리플링의 땅이었다. 1892년 3월 스트리플링이 존스턴에게 전년도 세금을 납부하였으나, 존스턴이 회계 볼터에게 그것을 전달하지 않고 가지고 있었던 듯하다.

4) 여기까지의 내용은 『제물포 각국 조계지 회의록 1』 264~265쪽에 수록되어 있다.

인출하는 문제에 대하여 논의하기를 희망하였으나, 이는 매우 중요한 문제이므로 모든 위원들에게 제대로 고지되어야 한다는 것이 중론이었다. 그는 회의록에 다음을 기록해 달라고 요청하였다. "노세 씨는 현재 홍콩상하이은행에 있는 5,000달러를 인출하여 제물포의 현지 은행에 맡기는 문제를 모든 위원들에게 고지해야 한다고 발언하였다. 그는 이 방법이 보다 합리적이고 편리하다고 생각할 뿐 아니라 굳이 상하이에 그 돈을 맡길 필요가 없다고 확신한다. 이곳에 있는 몇몇 은행이 상하이의 어떤 은행 못지않게 훌륭하기 때문이다."

⑦ 볼터 씨는 자신과 스트리플링 씨가 존스턴 씨를 만나 방파제 공사를 하루빨리 시작해 달라고 부탁하면서 방파제 바깥쪽 가장자리에 매끈한 돌을 써 달라고 요청한 사실을 알렸다. 그들은 이 일이 반드시 필요하다고 판단하였는데, 그 이유는 현재 그 부분이 매끈하지 않아 모든 선박들의 뱃머리가 손상되었기 때문이다. 만일 매끈한 돌을 쓰지 않을 경우, 그들은 한국 정부가 그곳에 완충재 대용의 나무더미라도 가져다 놓아야 한다고 이야기하였다. 크린 씨는 이 문제를 각국 외교 대표들에게 제출하기로 했다.

⑧ 노세 씨가 발의하고 스트리플링 씨가 재청하였다. "다음 회의는 6월 첫째 주에 개최하되 날짜는 현지 위원들의 결정에 따릅시다."[5] 만장일치로 통과되었다. 회의를 마쳤다.

---

5) '현지 위원들(local members)'이란 제물포에 거주하는 위원 즉, 한국·중국·일본·영국 대표들과 선출직 위원들을 가리킨다.

부회장 겸 의장 대행 크린 (서명)

서기 스캇 (서명)

·· – **원문** – ··

① Adjourned Meeting of 11th May, 1892. Present: same members.

② Road leading from D39 to B2: All members having gone over this road, it was the general opinion that the same ought to be cut down a good deal more at D39, the depth was however left an open question. Mr. Krien kindly undertook to bring this matter before the Foreign Representatives.

③ Corean Graves: Proposed by Mr. Nosse and seconded by Mr. Nishiwaki: "that a letter be addressed by the Hon. Secretary to the Kamni asking him to have the Graves in the G. F. S. especially those in the Public Garden and the cemetery removed within 3 weeks or else the M. C. would have them removed without further notice after the expiration of that period."

④ Taxes on Lots B4, D2 & 4 for 1891: Mr. Wolter raised the question of taxes for [18]91 on Lots B4, D2 & D4 which, so far he had not yet received from Mr. Johnston; he wanted money and he could not understand why it had not been paid yet. The taxes were for these lots $243.99, of which the Cor. Government kept $47.76, so he ought to have received $196.23. Mr. Stripling mentioned that the amount had been paid at the beginning of March. Finally Mr. Wolter proposed and Mr. Stripling seconded: "That a letter be written to Mr. Johnston asking him to send the amount of $196.23 to the Hon. Treasurer as the Council wanted money." Carried unanimously.

⑤ Prison: The question was raised by Mr. Nosse whether it was advisable to have any prison at all in the G. F. S. and whether the Municipality had a right to imprison any body. Mr. Krien mentioned that with the exception of the Japanese and Chinese Authorities no other ones had a prison here in Chemulpo. What should they do if somebody committed a crime? In Kobe in the Foreign Settlement they had a proper prison adjoining the Municipal Buildings, prison regulations and daily charges for the keeping of prisoners were made out. He would certainly like to see the Council building a proper prison; what name they gave to the place was quite immaterial but they ought to have a good and strong room where a prisoner could be kept for a night or for a longer period if the proper Authorities should wish it. In his opinion the Council had of course not the right to imprison offenders, but they had certainly the right and not only the right but it was their duty to detain such offenders until taken over by the proper Authorities.

⑥ Funds of Hong Kong & Shanghai Bank, Shanghai: Mr. Nosse wished to discuss the question of withdrawal of money now in this bank but as this was a very important question, it was generally thought that proper notice should be given to all members. Mr. Nosse then asked to have the following inserted with the Minutes of this meeting. "Mr. Nosse expressed his wished that notice be given to the members to the effect that the Municipal fund accounting to something to something Five Thousand Dollars at present deposited with the Hg kg & Shai Bank shall be withdrawn and deposited with the local Bank in Chemulpo. He deems this course be more reasonable and convenient: besides he does not see any necessity of depositing the money at Shanghai while there are several Banks here which are as good as any Bank in Shanghai."

⑦ Seawall & Jetty: Mr. Wolter said that Mr. Stripling and he had called on Mr. Johnston and asked him to begin the work that was still to be done at an early date: they had also asked Mr. Johnston to use when building the outer edge of the seawall, well dressed stones. They thought this absolutely necessary, as in the present state of this outer edge all boats got their bows swashed in, if there were only a moderate sea, if no dressed stones were used, there the Government ought to put wooden bulks as fenders in front. Mr. Krien kindly undertook to mention as a meeting of the For. Repps. the necessity of having dressed stones at the outer edge of seawall and jetty.

⑧ Next Meeting: Mr. Nosse proposed and Mr. Stripling seconded; "that the next meeting be held some time in the first week of June on a day to be decided upon by the local members of the Council." — carried unanimously. The meeting there adjourned.

(signed) F. Krien, Vice President and Chairman, p. t.

(signed) J. Scott, Hon. Secretary.

1892년 8월 25일 회의록

··– **번역문** –··

① 1892년 8월 25일 현지 위원들끼리 신동공사 회의를 개회하였다. 6월 7일에 낸 신동공사 회관 건축 입찰 공고와 관련하여 견적서를 선정하기 위해서였다. 홍즈빈 씨, 노세 씨, 볼터 씨, 스트리플링 씨, 스캇 씨가 참석하였다.[6)]

② 첫 번째 견적서는 구로다의 4,273.608달러, 두 번째는 요시다 와주의 3,985.40달러, 세 번째는 아사이다 류우치의 5,271달러, 네 번째는 아사오카의 3,442.25달러, 다섯 번째는 루이리링의 3,200달러였다. 3,200달러를 적어 낸 루이리링의 견적서를 선정하였다. 최종 계약을 위한 합의를 마무리해 달라고 집행위원회에 요청하였다.

③ 신동공사 경찰국은 7월 11일 밤 어떤 한국인이 보낸 의심스러운 문서를 되찾았다. 개봉한 결과 야와시타의 것으로 밝혀져 문서와 문서함을 노세 씨에게 전달하였다.

---

6) 이 회의는 제물포에 거주하는 한국·중국·일본·영국 대표들과 선출직 위원들의 회의였다. 제물포주재중국부영사 홍즈빈, 제물포주재일본부영사 노세, 제물포주재영국대리부영사 스캇, 선출직 위원 볼터와 스트리플링이 참석하였다. 한국 대표는 인천해관장대리 존스턴이었으나 그가 해관에서 물러난 후 공석이 되었다. 또 다른 선출직 위원 니시와키는 참석하지 않았다.

의장 대행 노세 (서명)

서기 스캇 (서명)

1892년 8월 25일

·· – **원문** – ··

① Meeting of local members of Municipal Council 25th Aug. 1892. For the purpose of considering and accepting estimates for erection of Municipal Building in terms of Municipal recruit of 7th June 1892. Present: Messrs. Hung, Nosse, Wolter, Stripling & Scott.

② First estimate by Y. Kurota $4273.608. Second estimate by Yoshida Waju $3985.40. Third estimate by Asayida Riuchi $5271. Fourth estimate by Asaoka $3442.25. Fifth estimate by Lui Li Ling $3200. The estimate of $3200 by Lui Li Ling accepted and executive Committee requested to complete arrangement for the final contract unanimously.

③ While despatch had recovered by Police from Corean under suspicious circumstances on night of 11th July was opened and as is was found to belong to R. Yawashita the hod and contents were handed to Mr. Nosse.

(signed) Nosse, Chairman p. t.

(signed) James Scott, Hon. Secr.

Chemulpo 25th, 1892, Aug.

1892년 9월 23일 회의록

·· – **번역문** – ··

① 1892년 9월 23일 신동공사 회의를 개회하였다. 노세 씨, 볼터 씨, 스트리플링 씨, 스캇 씨가 참석하였다. 정족수가 부족하여 28일 오전 10시에 속개하기로 하고 휴회하였다.[7)]

의장 대행 노세 (서명)
서기 스캇 (서명)

·· – **원문** – ··

① Meeting of Municipal Council of 23, Sept. 1892. Present: Messrs. Nosse, Wolter, Stripling & Scott, but not being a quorum the meeting was adjourned from day to day until 28th Sept. 1892 at 10 a. m.

(signed) J. Nosse Chairman, p. t.
(signed) James Scott Hon. Secr.

---

7) 제물포 각국 조계 신동공사는 당연직 위원 6명과 선출직 위원 3명, 총 9명으로 구성되었다. 회의 진행 및 의결에 필요한 정족수는 5명이었다.

1892년 9월 27일 회의록

·· – 번역문 – ··

① 1892년 9월 27일 신동공사 회의를 개최하였다. 스트리플링 씨, 스캇 씨, 볼터 씨가 참석하였다. 정족수가 부족하여 다음 주에 속개하되 날짜는 현지 위원들의 뜻에 따르기로 결정하였다. 한국인 경찰관 우경선이 뒤늦게 왔다.[8)]

의장 대행 노세 (서명)

서기 스캇 (서명)

·· – 원문 – ··

① Meeting of M. C. of 27th, Sept. 1892. Present: Messrs. Stripling, Scott and Wolter but there being no quorum the meeting was further adjourned from day to day until next week for a date to be afterwards fixed by the Local Members. Woo, the Corean Magistrate afterwards appeared.

(signed) J. Nosse, Chairman, p. t.

(signed) James Scott, Hon. Secretary.

8) 제물포주재영국대리부영사 스캇은 이 날을 끝으로 부영사직에서 물러났다. 인천항 경찰관 우경선(禹慶善)은 인천해관장대리 존스턴을 이어 한국 대표로 참석하였다. 한국 대표는 처음에는 김씨 성을 가진 경찰관이었다가 1889년 12월 존스턴으로 바뀌었다. 『제물포 각국 조계지 회의록 1』 48쪽과 109쪽을 참고할 것.

1892년 10월 5일 회의록

·· – **번역문** – ··

① 1892년 10월 5일 신동공사 회의를 개최하였다. 스트리플링 씨, 노세 씨, 존슨 씨, 볼터 씨가 참석하였다.[9] 정족수가 부족하여 6일 오후 3시에 속개하기로 하고 휴회하였다.

의장 대행 노세 (서명)

서기 존슨 (서명)

·· – **원문** – ··

① Meeting of Municipal Council of 5th Oct. 1892. Present: Messrs. Stripling, Nosse, Johnson, Wolter but there being no quorum the meeting was further adjourned until the 6th inst. at 3 p. m.

(signed) J. Nosse, Chairman, p. t.

(signed) Oct. Johnson, Hon. Secretary.

---

9) 존슨은 스캇의 후임이다. 1892년 9월 27일부터 1893년 7월 24일까지 제물포주재영국 대리부영사로 복무하였다.

1892년 10월 6일 회의록

·· – **번역문** – ··

① 1892년 10월 6일 신동공사 회의를 개회하였다. 스트리플링 씨, 니시와키 씨, 존슨 씨, 볼터 씨가 참석하였다. 정족수가 부족하여 7일 오후 3시에 속개하기로 하고 휴회하였다.

의장 대행 노세 (서명)

서기 존슨 (서명)

·· – **원문** – ··

① Meeting of Municipal Council of 6th Oct. 1892. Present: Messrs. Stripling, Nishiwaki, Johnson, and Wolter but there being no quorum the meeting was further adjourned until the 7th inst. at 3 p. m.

(signed) J. Nosse, Chairman, p. t.

(signed) Oct. Johnson, Hon. Secr.

1892년 10월 7일 회의록

·· – **번역문** – ··

① 1892년 10월 7일 신동공사 회의를 개회하였다. 스트리플링 씨, 니시와키 씨, 노세 씨, 존슨 씨, 볼터 씨가 참석하였다.[10] 정족수가 부족하였던 지난 번 회의록을 낭독하고 승인하였다.

② 노세 씨는 존슨 씨를 서기로 선출하자고 발의하였다. 니시와키 씨가 재청하였으며 통과되었다. 노세 씨가 또 발의하였다. "서기께 요청합니다. 신동공사를 위하여 그의 임기 동안 봉사해 준 전임 서기 스캇 씨께 공식적인 감사 인사를 전해 주십시오." 볼터 씨가 재청하였으며 통과되었다.

③ 볼터 씨가 신동공사 회관 건축을 위한 계약서를 제출하였다. 그는 신동공사가 지불하기로 결의한 계획서 작성 비용 100달러를 자신이 미리 지불하였다고 밝히고, 신동공사가 자신의 지불 조치를 승인해 줄 수 있는지 문의하였다. 스트리플링 씨가 승인하자고 발의하였다. 니시와키 씨가 재청하였으며 통과되었다.

④ 노세 씨가 발의하고 니시와키 씨가 재청하였다. "D2 구역과 B4 구역의 낡은 부동산 권리증을 폐기하고 새 권리증을 발행하는 데 영사 수수료 20달러를 징수합시다."

---

10) 주한미국공사 허드, 서울주재독일총영사 크린, 제물포주재중국부영사 홍즈빈, 인천항 경찰관 우경선은 참석하지 않았다. 회장 허드와 부회장 크린이 모두 불참하였으므로 노세가 의장직을 대행하였다.

⑤ 스트리플링 씨는 신동공사가 자신의 땅 일부에 도로를 건설하였으므로 그에 해당하는 세금 106.04달러를 환불해 달라는 편지를 제출하였다. 노세 씨는 이 일이 사실이라면 회계가 세금을 돌려줘야 한다고 발의하였다. 니시와키 씨가 재청하였으며 통과되었다.

⑥ 각국 조계 서쪽 끝에 부지를 편성하고 도로를 평탄화하는 문제에 대하여 오랫동안 의논하였다. 스트리플링 씨는 조계 서쪽 끝 전역에 부지를 편성하고 구역을 획정할 수 있도록 신동공사가 조치를 취하자고 발의하였다. 재청하는 사람이 없었다. 최종적으로 볼터 씨가 발의하였다. "서기께 요청합니다. 서울의 각국 외교 대표들께 편지를 써서 한국 정부에 압력을 행사해 달라고 촉구해 주십시오. 한국 정부는 각국 조계의 더 많은 도로를 하루빨리 평탄화하고 신동공사가 이를 위하여 이미 지출한 금액을 돌려줘야 합니다. 그렇지 않으면 신동공사는 한국 정부에 매년 납부하던 세금(100제곱미터당 30센트)을 내지 않고 토지소유주들이 신동공사에 납부하는 세금(같은 액수)도 임의로 사용할 것입니다." 노세 씨가 재청하였으며 통과되었다.

⑦ 스트리플링 씨가 다음 제안서를 제출하였다. "저는 D1, D7, D8, D9 구역과 D2 구역 사이를 통과하는 남북 방향 공용 도로의 평탄화 작업을 하루빨리 시작하자고 제안합니다.[11] 1892년 10월 6일 스트리플링(서명)." 볼터 씨가 재청하였으며 통과되었다. 그는 현재 신동공사가 도로 평탄화 작업에 쓸 수 있는 인력과 재정을 갖추고 있음을 고려한 것이라면서, 자신이 재청한 이유를 회의록에 기록해 주기를 희망하였다.

11) D1 구역은 볼터, D7~D9 구역은 독일인 브링크마이어, D2 구역은 스트리플링의 땅이었다.

⑧ 볼터 씨는 어떤 사람이 자신에게 와서 부두에 석탄을 임의로 두어도 되는지 문의하였다고 보고하였다. 만장일치로 불허하였다.

⑨ 내일 오후 3시에 속개하기로 하고 휴회하였다.

·· – **원문** – ··

① Meeting of Municipal Council of 7th Oct. 1892. Present: Messrs. Stripling, Nishiwaki, Nosse, Johnson and C. Wolter. Minutes of last meeting & of no quorum meetings read and signed.

② Proposed by Mr. Nosse, by Mr. Nishiwaki that Mr. Johnson be elected secretary for the current year — carried. Proposed by Mr. Nosse, seconded by Mr. Wolter, that the secretary be asked to convey a warm vote of thanks to Mr. James Scott, for service rendered to the Council during his term of office as Secretary — carried.

③ Mr. Wolter handed in the contract for erection of Municipal building and stated that the sum of $100, for drawing out the plans for the sum as ready voted by the Council had been paid although the work was not get completed he asked that the approval of the Council to this early payment might be given. Mr. Stripling proposed that this early payment be approved & Mr. Nishiwaki seconded carried.

④ On the motion of Mr. Nosse, seconded by Mr. Nishiwaki the sum of $20.00 Consular fees for cancelling old and issuing new title deeds for lots D2 & B4.

⑤ A letter was handed in by Mr. Stripling requesting a refund of $106.04 taxes paid by him on land fencing past of his property which had been utilized by the Council for making a road. Proposed by Mr. Nosse seconded by Mr.

Nishiwaki, that the treasurer be authorized to pay this sum if found correct. Carried.

⑥ A long discussion took place with regard to laying out the Western end of the settlement in lots and grading road therein. Mr. Stripling proposed that steps should be taken by the Council to lay out in lots and mark on the place of the General Foreign Settlement the whole of the Western end of the same, but this found no seconds. Eventually Mr. Wolter having proposed and Mr. Nosse seconded it was carried that the Secretary should be asked to write to the Doyen of Diplomatic Body at Seoul urging him to press the Corean Government to begin grading more roads in the General Foreign Settlement at once and also to refund the Council for expenses already incurred under this head. If the Corean Government refuse this it is to be suggested that the sum of 30 cents per 100 meters annual ground rent at present paid to the Corean Government be withheld and the same sum paid by the lot proprietor to this Consul to be kept by the latter at the disposal of the Council.

⑦ Mr. Stripling handed in the following proposition, signed. "I beg to propose that the grading of Public Road leading south to north dividing D2 from D1. and D 7, 8, 9 be proceeded with without further delay. Signed. Alfred B. Stripling. Oct. 6th, 1892." This was seconded by Mr. Wolter who at the same time wished it to be recorded that he did so in consideration of the fact that there were men & material at present at the disposal of the Council that might be employed for the purpose. — Carried.

⑧ Mr. Wolter reported that a man applied to be allowed to shove coal on jetty. Council unanimously disapproved.

⑨ The meeting there adjourned until the 8th inst. at 3 p. m.

1892년 10월 8일 회의록

·· - **번역문** - ··

① 1892년 10월 8일 신동공사 회의를 개최하였다. 스트리플링 씨, 니시와키 씨, 노세 씨, 존슨 씨, 볼터 씨가 참석하였다.12)

② 5월 10일 신동공사 회의 때 통과된 결의안과 관련하여, 존슨 씨는 신동공사 회관 건축 계획이 완성되었으며 공원의 위치는 집행위원회의 결정에 맡기자고 발의하였다. 노세 씨가 재청하였으며 통과되었다.13)

③ D39~B2 구역의 도로 중에서도 중국 조계에 접한 도로(B4~B2 구역)의 불만족스러운 상태가 또 다시 거론되었다. 노세 씨는 제물포주재중국부영사를 방문하여 이 문제를 의논하는 한편 제물포주재중국부영사관 언덕 북동쪽 모퉁와 B2 구역 사이에 도로 건설을 촉구하기로 했다.14)

④ 스트리플링 씨는 다음 회의를 4주 후에 개최한다는 안내문을 발송할 수 있는지 문의하였다. 그는 각국 조계 서쪽을 개발하기 위해서 신동공사가 600달러를 지출하여 B 부지 앞에 부두를 건설하자고 발의할 예정이다.

---

12) 주한미국공사 허드, 서울주재독일총영사 크린, 제물포주재중국부영사 홍즈빈, 인천항 경찰관 우경선은 참석하지 않았다. 회장 허드와 부회장 크린이 모두 불참하였으므로 노세가 의장직을 대행하였다.

13) 1892년 5월 10일 통과된 신동공사 회관 건축 계획에 대해서는 『제물포 각국 조계지 회의록 1』 250~255쪽을 참고할 것.

14) D39~B2 구역의 도로는 북쪽의 각국 조계와 남쪽의 중국 조계 사이를 통과하는 동서 방향의 공용 도로였다.

·· — 원문 — ··

① 8th Oct. 1892. Present: Messrs. Stripling, Nishiwaki, Nosse, Johnson & Wolter.

② Proposed by Mr. Johnson, in continuation of the resolution carried by the Council on the subject at the meeting of 10th May last, that the plans having now been completed, the position of the Public Gardens in the Municipal lot be left to the decision of the Executive Committee, seconded by Mr. Nosse. — Carried.

③ Road leading from D39 to B2, specially from B4 to B2: The unsatisfactory condition of the Chinese side of this road was again mentioned and Mr. Nosse kindly consented to call on the Chinese Consul and speak with him on the subject and also urge the necessity of a road in front of Chinese Settlement from B2 to N. W. corner of Consular Hill.

④ Mr. Stripling asked that notices might be sent out calling for a general meeting to be held within four weeks of this date at which he would propose that "in order to open up the western part of the settlement the Council authorize the expenditure of $600.00 for the purpose of building a jetty in front of lots B."

1892년 11월 8일 회의록

·· – **번역문** – ··

① 1892년 11월 8일 신동공사 회의를 개회하였다. 크린 씨, 홍즈빈 씨, 우경선 씨, 스트리플링 씨, 볼터 씨, 존슨 씨가 참석하였다.[15] 개회 선언 후 지난 번 회의록을 낭독하고 승인하였다.

② 존슨 씨는 홍즈빈 씨에게 노세 씨와 도로 문제를 의논하였는지 질문하였다.[16] 홍즈빈 씨는 그렇다고 대답하였다. 그는 제물포주재중국부영사관 뒤 도로가 지금은 불편하지만 내년에는 정비할 것이고 이 문제의 결정권이 자신에게 있다고 이야기하였다. 또한 그는 제물포주재중국부영사관 언덕 북동쪽 모퉁이와 B2 구역 사이에 도로를 건설하는 것은 전적으로 중국의 관할이며 무역이 번창한다면 충분히 가능한 일이라고 답변하였다. 볼터 씨는 신동공사가 도로 건설을 위하여 재정을 지원할 수 있을 것이라고 발언하였으나, 홍즈빈 씨는 돈 문제가 아니라 자신이 그 일을 원하느냐 원치 않느냐의 문제라고 응수하였다. 크린 씨는 홍즈빈 씨에게 제물포주재중국부영사관 뒤 도로 중 중국 조계에 접한 경사면을 깎아도 되는지 문의하였다. 이는 각국 조계에 접한 쪽으

---

15) 주한미국공사 허드, 제물포주재일본부영사 노세, 선출직 위원 겸 집행 위원 니시와키는 불참하였다. 허드는 1891년 12월 신동공사 회장으로 선출되었으나 임기 동안 한 번도 회의에 참석하지 않았다.

16) 1892년 10월 8일 노세는 제물포주재중국부영사 홍즈빈을 찾아가 B4~B2 구역의 도로를 정비하는 일, 제물포주재중국부영사관 언덕 북동쪽 모퉁이와 B2 구역 사이에 도로를 건설하는 일을 의논하기로 했다.

로 흙더미가 떨어져 내리는 것을 막기 위해서였으나 홍즈빈 씨는 승인하지 않았다. 그는 해당 도로에 접한 중국 조계 전역이 정리되면 올해나 내년에 중국인들이 그 일을 처리할 것이며, 도로가 제물포주재중국부영사관의 주춧돌 아래로 꺼지면 자신이 꺼진 도로를 메우겠다고 대답하였다.

③ 허드 씨가 보내 온 편지를 낭독하였다. 총세무사에게 신동공사 회의록 사본을 보내는 문제를 다룬 내용이었다. 존슨 씨는 앞으로 총세무사에게 회의록을 보내야 하는지 질문하였다. 스트리플링 씨가 발의하였다. "총세무사께 회의록을 보내지 않되 그가 점검할 경우에는 회의록을 공개하고, 서기의 편의를 고려하여 모든 토지소유주들에게도 공개해야 합니다." 볼터 씨가 재청하였다. 그는 신동공사는 해관에 대하여 의무가 없으며 오히려 해관이 신동공사에 대하여 의무를 진다고 생각하였다. 스트리플링 씨의 제안은 통과되었다.[17)]

④ 홍즈빈 씨가 편지를 제출하였다. 부두 근처에서 노 젓는 배를 탈 경우 집행위원회에 알려야 하는지 문의하는 내용이었다.

⑤ 노세 씨가 보내 온 편지를 낭독하였다. 회의에 불참한 일과 관련하여 양해를 구하는 내용이었다.

⑥ 홍즈빈 씨는 다른 업무가 있어 양해를 구하고 회의장을 떠났다.

⑦ 스트리플링 씨는 각국 조계 서쪽을 개발하기 위해서 신동공사가 600달러를 지출하여 B 부지 앞에 부두를 건설해야 한다고 발의하였다

---

17) 국립중앙도서관은 1889년 3월 23일부터 1893년 2월 7일까지의 회의록 사본을 소장하고 있다. 대부분은 인천해관장대리 존스턴이 필사하였고 그가 물러난 후에는 다른 해관원들이 필사하여 총세무사에게 전달하였다.

(서명한 제안서를 제출하였다). 볼터 씨가 재청하였다.[18] 논의 후 오후 3시에 속개하기로 하고 휴회하였다.

⑧ 크린 씨, 볼터 씨, 존슨 씨, 스트리플링 씨가 참석하였다. 정족수가 부족하여 현지 위원들이 정하는 날짜에 속개하기로 하고 휴회하였다.

부회장 겸 의장 대행 크린 (서명)

서기 존슨 (서명)

·· – **원문** – ··

① Meeting of Nov. 8, 1892. Present: Messrs. Krien, Hung, Ou, Stripling, Wolter, Johnson. The notice calling the meeting was read. Minutes of last meeting read and confirmed.

② Mr. Johnson asked Mr. Hung whether Mr. Nosse had called on him with reference to the roads as promised. Mr. Hung said he had called and discussed the matter. Mr. Hung said that present the road could not be put in proper order so it would not be convenient for the Chinese Consular Premises, but it would be done next year. He said that the decision in the matter rested with him. About the road from the Chinese Settlement to the corner of Consular Hill, Mr. Hung said it was entirely a Chinese matter and when trade was flourishing enough no doubt it would be done. Mr. Wolter suggested that perhaps

18) 각국 조계 서쪽 끝에 자리한 B 부지는 4개 구역으로 구분되어 있었다. 1891년 1월 12일 구역별 토지 매각 목록에 따르면 B1과 B2 구역은 볼터의 동료였던 독일인 뤼어스(최초 소유주는 볼터), B4 구역은 스트리플링의 땅이었다. B3 구역은 1891년 말 영국인 로저스가 매입하였다.

the M. C. might help with regard to funds in making this road. Mr. Hung said it was not a matter of money only nor of any other particular consideration, but of the wishes of the Chinese Consul. Mr. Krien asked if Mr. Hung would allow the — slope of the Chinese half of the road behind the Chinese Consulate to be sloped off so that the earth would not fall with the Gen. For. Settlement part of the road. He answered No; he would not, but it would be done by Chinese if not this year then, next year, when the whole of the Chinese part of the road would be put in order; if the road sank below the level of the Chinese Consulate foundation he would have it filled up again.

③ Mr. Heard's letter relative to the sending of the minute-book to the Commissioner of Customs to be copied was read. Mr. Johnson asked whether the book was to be sent in future or not. Mr. Stripling proposed that the book should not be sent to the Commissioner of Customs but should be open to his inspection, or any landowners, at the convenience of the Hon. Sec. — Seconded by Mr. Wolter. Mr. Wolter said that he thought the M. C. was under no obligations to the Customs, but rather the contrary. The proposition being put to the meeting was carried.

④ The letter of Mr. Hung referring to a row on the jetty & asking that the matter might be brought to the notice of the Ex. Com. was read.

⑤ Mr. Nosse's letter excusing himself from attending at this meeting was read.

⑥ Mr. Hung having other business to attend to excused himself and left.

⑦ Mr. Stripling proposed that in order to open up the Western part of the Settlement the M. C. authorize the expenditure of $600.00 for the purpose of building a jetty in front of lots B (Prop. put in voting signed) — seconded by Mr. Wolter: After some discussion, meeting adjourned till 3 p. m. Nov. 8, 3 p. m.

⑧ Present: Messrs. Krien, Wolter, Johnson, Stripling. Then being no quorum, meeting adjourned until a day to be afterward fixed by the local members.

(signed) F. Krien, Vice Pres. & Chairman pro. tem.
(signed) Octavius Johnson, Hon. Sec.

1892년 12월 6일 회의록

·· – 번역문 – ··

① 1892년 12월 6일 신동공사 회의를 개최하였다. 크린 씨, 홍즈빈 씨, 우경선 씨, 스트리플링 씨, 노세 씨, 존슨 씨, 알렌 씨가 참석하였다.[19] 지난 번 회의록을 낭독하고 승인하였다. 개회를 선언하였다.

② 볼터 씨가 회계직을 사임하였다는 것이 대다수 위원들에게 알려졌다.[20] 신동공사는 이 문제와 관련하여 어떤 편지도 받지 못하였으나 그의 사임을 수리하였다. 스트리플링 씨는 볼터 씨의 사임이 매우 유감이며 그의 봉사에 공식적인 감사 인사를 전하자고 발의하였다. 노세 씨가 재청하였으며 통과되었다. 볼터 씨를 대신할 임시 선출직 위원을 뽑았다. 뤼어스 씨가 5표, 타운젠드 씨가 2표를 얻었으므로 뤼어스 씨를 선출하였다.[21]

③ 감리가 제물포주재영국부영사에게 보내 온 편지를 낭독하였다. 도로를 다시 경사지게 만들 때 들어가는 경비에 대한 내용이었다. 지난 번 회의 이후 해관장과 브링크마이어 씨, 허치슨 씨가 신동공사에 보내 온 편지를 낭독하였다.[22]

---

19) 미국 대표 겸 신동공사 회장이었던 주한미국공사 허드를 대신하여 주한미국공사관 서기관 알렌이 참석하였다. 회계 겸 선출직 위원 겸 집행 위원 볼터와 선출직 위원 겸 집행 위원 니시와키는 참석하지 않았다.

20) 볼터는 1889년 12월 4일 3년 임기의 선출직 위원으로 뽑혔다. 1891년 말에는 회계와 집행 위원으로도 선출되어 약 1년간 복무하였다.

21) 임시 선출직 위원 뤼어스의 임기는 1892년 12월 31일까지였다.

22) 해관장이란 1892년 11월 4일 인천해관장대리로 부임한 영국인 오스본을 가리킨다.

④ 알렌 씨가 발의하였다. “뤼어스 씨에게 볼터 씨를 대신하여 임시 회계가 되어 달라고 부탁합시다.” 노세 씨가 재청하였으며 만장일치로 통과되었다.

⑤ 스트리플링 씨가 발의하였다. “외국인 묘지 둘레에 튼튼한 옹벽을 세워 하루빨리 적절한 상태로 만듭시다. 토지소유주들의 특별 요청에 따라 이를 발의합니다.” 뤼어스 씨가 재청하였으며 통과되었다. 오후 2시 30분에 속개하기로 하고 휴회하였다.

⑥ 크린 씨, 뤼어스 씨, 홍즈빈 씨, 노세 씨, 스트리플링 씨, 알렌 씨, 존슨 씨가 참석하였다.[23)]

⑦ 존슨 씨는 내일 오전 10시 30분부터 오후 12시 30분까지 실시되는 선출직 위원 선거에 당연직 위원 3명이 참석해야 한다는 사실을 환기시켰다.

⑧ 우경선 씨는 회의에 불참한 일과 관련하여 양해를 구하는 내용의 엽서를 보내 왔다.

⑨ 스트리플링 씨가 발의하였다. “유능한 인물을 고용하여 즉시 각국 조계 서쪽을 조사하고 부지를 편성합시다. 그리고 허치슨 씨가 그의 편지에서 회장께 제안한 것처럼 모든 구역의 경계와 도로를 공식 도면에 분명하게 표시합시다. 토지소유주들의 강력한 지지에 힘입어 이를 발의합니다.” 노세 씨가 재청하였으며 통과되었다.

⑩ 뤼어스 씨를 집행 위원으로 임명하자는 의견이 위원들의 박수와 당사자의 수락에 따라 통과되었다.

---

23) 오전에 결정된 사항에 따라 뤼어스가 임시 회계 겸 임시 선출직 위원으로서 참석하였다. 오전에 참석하였던 우경선은 불참하였다.

⑪ 알렌 박사가 발의하였다. "집행위원회에 요청합니다. 각국 조계 서쪽 끝에 부지를 편성하는 일과 관련하여 사바친 씨의 보수가 얼마인지 알아보고 다음 회의 때 보고해 주십시오."[24] 뤄어스 씨가 재청하였으며 통과되었다.

⑫ 존슨 씨는 뤄어스 씨를 감사로 임명하여 전임 회계 볼터 씨의 회계 내역을 감사하게 하자고 발의하였다. 알렌 박사가 재청하였으며 통과되었다.

⑬ 중국 조계 앞 도로를 메우는 일에 대하여 의논하였다. 훙즈빈 씨는 중국 조계에 관한 모든 문제는 자신이 결정할 일이라고 단언하였다. 누구도 그에게 영향을 끼치지 못했다.

⑭ 지난 번 회의 때 통과된 스트리플링 씨의 부두 건설 제안과 관련하여, 존슨 씨는 부두 건설이 허가를 받으려면 적절한 견적서를 신동공사에 제출해야 한다는 수정안을 발의하였다. 알렌 박사가 재청하였다. 논의 후 스트리플링 씨가 현지 신문에 입찰 공고를 내자고 제안하였다. 존슨 씨의 수정안은 통과되었다.

⑮ 알렌 박사는 락스데일 씨의 봉급 840달러(월 70달러)와 6개월치 집세 90달러, 경찰관 6명의 봉급 864달러(월 12달러)와 제복 180달러, 청소부 4명의 봉급 192달러(월 16달러), 도로 정비 400달러, 가로등 10개 90달러, 예비비 344달러, 합계 3,000달러를 내년도 신동공사 기금으로 책정하자고 발의하였다.[25] 훙즈빈 씨가 재청하였으며 통과되었다.

---

24) 이렇게 하여 각국 조계 서쪽 끝을 개발하는 일은 우크라이나(당시는 러시아) 출신의 사바친에게 맡겨졌다.

25) 미국인 락스데일은 신동공사가 조계의 치안을 위하여 고용한 경찰국장이었다.

⑯ 해관장 자택 앞과 제물포주재일본부영사관 뒤를 통과하는 동서 방향의 도로에 대하여 의논하였다.[26] 스트리플링 씨가 발의하였다. "각국 조계 동쪽과 서쪽 끝을 연결하는 대로 즉, 해관장 자택 앞과 제물포주재일본부영사관 뒤를 통과하는 도로를 하루빨리 평탄화합시다." 뤼어스 씨가 재청하였다. 노세 씨는 평탄화 작업에 착수하기 전에 유능한 인물이 도로를 조사하여 신동공사에 보고해야 한다는 수정안을 발의하였다. 존슨 씨가 재청하였다. 스트리플링 씨는 노세 씨의 수정안과 관련하여 락스데일 씨가 그동안 모든 도로를 건설하였으니 이번에도 그에게 맡기자고 발의하였다. 통과되었다. 서기는 이 일과 관련하여 서울의 사바친 씨에게 편지를 보내라는 지시를 받았다.

⑰ 스트리플링 씨가 손수레, 수레, 선박을 비치하는 문제를 꺼냈으나 추후에 좀더 의논하기로 했다. 그는 소방대에 대해서도 이야기하였다. 노세 씨는 일본인 및 외국인 주택에 발생한 화재를 담당하는 일본인 소방대가 있다고 이야기하였다. 오후 6시에 휴회하고 내일 오후 2시 30분에 속개하기로 결정하였다.

·· – **원문** – ··

① Dec. 6, 1892. Present: - Messrs. Krien, Hung, Ou, Stripling, Nossé, Johnson, Allen. Minutes of last meeting read and confirmed. Notice calling meeting read.

---

26) 해관장 자택 앞과 제물포주재일본부영사관 뒤를 통과하는 동서 방향의 도로란 각국 조계와 중국 및 일본 조계 사이에 놓인 도로를 가리킨다. 앞에서 몇 차례 언급되었던 D39~B2 구역의 도로는 이 도로의 서쪽 부분이다.

② The fact that Mr. Wolter had resigned the treasurership being known to most members his resignation was accepted although no letter to that effect had been received to place before the meeting. Mr. Stripling proposed & Mr. Nossé seconded that Mr. Wolter's resignation be accepted with great regret & that a hearty vote of thanks for his services to the Council be accorded him. — Carried. Election of a member pro. tem. caused by resignation of Mr. Wolter. Result, C. Lührs, 5 votes, W. D. Townsend, 2 votes. Lührs declared elected.

③ Letter to the British Vice-Consul from the Kamni regarding payment of expenses of regrading roads read. Correspondence received since last meeting — Letters from Commissioner of Customs, Brinckmeier & Hutchison — were read.

④ Proposed by Mr. Allen, sec. by Nossé, that Mr. Lührs be asked to act as Treasurer pro. tem. & so fill the vacancy caused by resignation of Mr. Wolter. Carried unanimously.

⑤ Cemetery: Proposed by Mr. Stripling "that a strong wall be put around the foreign cemetery & that the ground be put & left in proper condition without delay. This proposal is made by special request of a member of landholders who are very anxious to see the ground put in proper condition." Seconded by Mr. Lührs. Carried. Meeting adj. till 2:30 p. m. Adjourned meeting 2:30 p. m.

⑥ Present: Messrs. Krien, Lührs, Hung, Nossé, Stripling, Allen, Johnson.

⑦ Mr. Johnson called attention to the fact that tomorrow between 10:30 a. m. & 0:30 p. m. the presence of 3 official members is necessary for the election of one member.

⑧ Mr. Ou sent his card excusing himself.

⑨ Proposed by Mr. Stripling "That the western end of the Settlement be at once surveyed & laid out in lots by a competent person — and that all lots boundaries & roads be distinctly marked on the official plan of the settlement as suggested by Mr. Hutchison in his letter to the President. This proposal is strongly supported by the land-holders." Seconded by Mr. Nossé & carried.

⑩ By acclamation and consent of Mr. Lührs, Mr. Lührs was appointed member of the Exec. Com.

⑪ Proposed by Dr. Allen & seconded by Mr. Lührs "That the Exec. Com. be instructed to confer with Mr. Sabatin & ascertain for what compensation he will lay out that portion of the western end of settlement not yet laid out in conformity with the plan. So report at next meeting." Carried.

⑫ Proposed by Mr. Johnson & sec. by Dr. Allen that Mr. Lührs be appointed auditor of the last Treasurer's (Mr. Wolter) accounts. — Carried.

⑬ Discussion about filling in in front of Chinese Settlement. Mr. Hung said that all matters connected with the Chinese Settlement were for him to decide; no one could influence him.

⑭ In pursuance of Mr. Stripling's proposal concerning jetty at last meeting:- Proposed as an amendment by Mr. Johnson, sec. by Dr. Allen, that with a proper estimate of the cost of the building of same can be brought before the M. C. the building of it cannot be sanctioned. Discussion:- Mr. Stripling suggested that advertisement be put in local paper inviting tenders for the work. Amended as above, carried.

⑮ Appropriation of funds:- Ragsdale's pay @ $70 a month $840. Rent of Ragsdale's house for 6 months $90. Six police at $12 per month $864. Six Uniforms $180. Four scavengers $16 per month $192. Repairs to roads $400. Ten lamps $90. Contingencies $344. (Total) $3,000. Proposed by Dr. Allen, sec. by Mr. Hung, that the sum of $3,000, as above particularized, be appropriated from the funds for the next year's expenses. — Carried.

⑯ Discussion with regard to road from east to west passing behind Japanese Consulate in front of Commissioner of Custom's House:- Proposed by Mr. Stripling:- "That the main road connecting the eastern with the western end of settlement, i. e., the road running past the back of Japanese Consulate & in front of the Commissioner of Custom's house, be graded & made without unnecessary delay." Sec. by Mr. Lührs. Amended by Mr. Nossé:- "a competent man should be engaged to inspect the road and report to the M. C. before commencing work." Sec. by Mr. Johnson. Discussion on Amendment:- "Mr. Stripling said that roads had always hitherto been made by Mr. Ragsdale; why should they not be done by him again?" Amendment carried. The President requested the Sec. to write to Mr. S. Sabatin of Seoul on the subject.

⑰ Mr. Stripling brought up the matter of laying wheelbarrows, carts, boats:- decided that the matter should be left for further consideration. Mr. Stripling brought up the matter of fire brigade. Mr. Nossé said that there was a Japanese fire brigade that would be willing to assist at a fire in any house in Chemulpo — Japanese or foreign. Meeting adjourned at 6 p. m. till to-morrow at 2:30 p. m.

1892년 12월 7일 선거록

·· – **번역문** – ··

1892년 12월 7일 제물포 각국 조계의 등록된 토지소유주 명단27)

순서	성명	토지
2	영국 정부	D38
7	스트리플링	D2, D4, B4, D33
8	허치슨	D11, D12
13	홀링스워스	D15
12	홉킨스	D10, D24
1	복음전도협회	D43
	영국국교회 한국선교부 책임자	각국 조계 밖
부재	로저스	B3
17	모스타운젠드상사	
부재	마이어(A)	C1, C2, C3, C4, D25, D26, D27, D28, D37
〃	볼터	C5, C6, C7, C8, D1, D19, D33
3	뤼어스	B1, B2
부재	마이어(B)	C10, C11, D42
16	브링크마이어	D7, D8, D9
부재	알마허	D31, D32
10	뫼르젤	C17, C20, C22, C29, C30, C31, D13
4	고르샬키	D3
15	니시와키(A)	C25

27) 원본에는 '1893년 12월 7일(Dec. 7. 1893)'로 잘못 쓰여 있다. 마이어상사(세창양행) 사장 마이어는 마이어(A), 시그널 호(S. S. Signal) 선장 마이어는 마이어(B), 선출직 위원 니시와키는 니시와키(A), C13 구역 토지소유주는 니시와키(B)로 구분하였다.

거부	도미타	D14
부재	구마모토	C13
6	리키타케	C12
18	신도	C15, C16
	호리	C18, C26, C27
5	히구치	C19
14	스에나가	C21
부재	니시와키(B)	C13
9	기무라	D15
19	우리탕	C23, C24, C28, C32, D16, D17, D30
11	보리오니	D11
부재	리원눈	C9

1892년 12월 7일 투표자 명단[28)]

투표 순서	성명	투표 순서	성명
1	복음전도협회	9	기무라
2	영국 정부	10	뫼르젤
3	뤼어스	11	보리오니
4	고르샤키	12	홉킨스
5	히구치	13	홀링스워스
6	리키타케	14	스에나가
7	스트리플링	15	니시와키
8	허치슨	16	브링크마이어

28) 원본에는 '1893년 12월 7일(Dec. 7. 1893)'로 잘못 쓰여 있다. 이 표는 미국인 타운젠드가 11표, 독일인 뫼르젤이 7표, 뤼어스가 1표를 얻어 타운젠드가 선출되었음을 보여 준다. 그리하여 1893년에는 스트리플링, 니시와키, 타운젠드가 선출직 위원으로 복무하였다.

17	모스타운젠드상사	19	우리탕
18	신도		
		투표 결과	
		타운젠드	11
		뫼르젤	7
		뤼어스	1

··— **원문** —··

Registered Land-holders in the

Chemulpo General Foreign Settlement on Dec. 7, 1893.

Order of Voting	Name	Lots
2	H. B. M. Gov't	D38
7	Alfred Burt Stripling	D2
	〃	D4
	〃	B4
8	William Duflon Hutchison	D11 & 12
13	Thomas Hollingsworth	D15
12	Leonard Armstrong Hopkins	D10
1	The Society for the Propagation of the Gospel in Foreign Parts, London	D43
	Head for time being of Ch. of Eng. Mission in Korea	Outside Settlement
	Alfred Burt Stripling	D33
	Leonard Armstrong Hopkins	D24
Absent	Edward Rogers	B3
17	Morse, Townsend & Co.	

Absent	H. C. Edouard Meyer	C1, 2, 3, 4, D25, 26, D27, 28, 37
〃	Carl Wolter	C5, 7, 6, 8, D1, 19, 33
3	Carl Lührs	B1,2
Absent	Franz Meyer	C10, 11, D42
16	Robt. Brinckmeier	D7, 8, 9
Absent	Fr. Allmacher	D31, 32
10	F. H. Mörsel	C17, 20, 22, 29, 30, 31, D13
4	A. Gorschalki	D3
15	C. Nishiwaki	C25
Objected	S. Tomita	D14
Absent	E. Kumamoto	C13
6	H. Rikitake	C12
18	S. Shindo	C15, 16
	Hori Kintaro	C18, 26, 27
5	S. Higuchi	C19
14	J. Suyenaga	C21
Absent	Ko Nishiwaki	C13
9	J. Kimura	D15
19	Woolitang	C24
11	〃	C23
	〃	C32
	〃	C28
	〃	D16,17
	〃	D30
11	Romulo Borioni	D11
Absent	Li Yun-noon	C9

List of those Voting at election Dec. 7 '93

1	S. P. G.	10	Mörsel
2	H. B. M. Gt.	11	Borioni
3	Lührs	12	Hopkins
4	Gorschalki	13	Hollingsworth
5	Higuchi	14	Suyenaga
6	Rikitaki	15	Nishiwaki
7	Stripling	16	Brinckmeier
8	Hutchison	17	Morse, Townsend
9	Kimura	18	Shindo
		19	Woolitang
	Result of Voting		
	Townsend	11	
	Mörsel	7	
	Lührs	1	

1892년 12월 7일 회의록

-- 번역문 --

① 어제 오후 2시 30분에 개회한 신동공사 회의를 속개하였다. 크린 씨, 홍즈빈 씨, 노세 씨, 니시와키 씨, 존슨 씨, 뤼어스 씨, 스트리플링 씨가 참석하였다.[29)]

② 내년도 임원 선거 결과 회장에 허드 씨, 부회장에 크린 씨, 서기에 존슨 씨, 회계에 타운젠드 씨가 선출되었다.

③ 뤼어스 씨는 자신이 감사한 회계 내역을 신동공사에 제출하였다. 회계 내역은 정확한 것으로 판명되었다. 뤼어스 씨에게 공식적인 감사 인사를 전하자는 제안이 통과되었다.

④ 크린 씨는 그동안 신동공사가 방 하나를 쓸 수 있게 해 준 제물포 구락부에 공식적인 감사 인사를 전하자고 발의하였다. 존슨 씨가 재청하였으며 통과되었다. 스트리플링 씨는 그동안 집행위원회의 허락 아래 제물포 구락부를 이용하였으나 앞으로는 다이부츠 호텔에서 회의를 열자고 발의하였다. 크린 씨가 재청하였다. 존슨 씨가 다음과 같은 수정안을 발의하였다. "지금부터 신동공사 회관이 준비되기 전까지 가장 편리한 장소에서 회의를 개최하되 회의 장소는 서기가 확인하여 위원들에게 통지합시다." 뤼어스 씨가 재청하였으며 통과되었다.

⑤ 크린 씨가 발의하였다. "각국 조계 부지를 조사 및 편성하고 모든

---

29) 주한미국공사 허드와 인천항 경찰관 우경선은 불참하였다. 선출직 위원은 임시 위원 뤼어스를 포함하여 3명 모두 참석하였다.

구역의 규격과 경계를 공식 도면에 표시할 사람에게 최대 200달러의 보수를 책정합시다.[30] 또한 집행위원회는 조계의 동쪽과 서쪽을 연결하는 도로 즉, 해관장 자택 앞과 제물포주재일본부영사관 뒤를 통과하는 도로의 평탄화 작업을 최대한 좋은 조건으로 진행해 주십시오." 노세 씨가 재청하였으며 통과되었다.

⑥ 일본인 소방대에 돈을 기부하는 문제에 대하여 의논하였다. 노세 씨는 신동공사가 일본인 소방대에 돈을 기부하자고 발의하였으나 신동공사가 그 일을 할 권한이 없다는 말을 듣고 바로 철회하였다.

⑦ 다음과 같이 결의하였다. "서기께 요청합니다. 한국 정부 관계자가 각국 조계 토지소유주들의 완전한 명단과 모든 신규 매입 및 양도 내역을 서기에게 보낼 수 있도록 회장께 연락해 주십시오."

⑧ 다음 회의는 2월 첫째 주에 개최하되 날짜는 현지 위원들의 뜻에 따르기로 결정하였다. 의장에게 공식적인 감사 인사를 전하고 회의를 마쳤다.

부회장 존슨 (서명)

서기 존슨 (서명)

1893년 2월 7일[31]

---

30) 사바친을 가리킨다.

31) 회의록 하단에 의장과 서기가 서명하는 일은 회의 서두에 지난 번 회의록을 낭독하고 승인하는 과정에서 이루어졌다. 1892년 12월 7일 회의록 끝에 1893년 2월 7일 존슨의 서명이 들어간 것은 이러한 이유에서이다.

·· – 원문 – ··

① Dec. of 7th, 1892. Meeting adjourned from yesterday 2:30 p. m. Present: Messrs. Krien, Hung, Nossé, Nishiwaki, Johnson, Lührs, Stripling.

② Election of Officers for ensuing year:- President, Mr. A. Heard, Vice President, Mr. Krien, Secretary, Mr. Johnson, Treasurer, Mr. Townsend.

③ Accounts audited by Mr. Lührs & found correct, handed it to M. C. Vote of thanks to auditor carried with cordiality.

④ Proposed by Mr. Krien, sec. by Mr. Johnson, That a vote of thanks be tendered to the Chemulpo Club for allowing one of their rooms to be used by the Council. — Carried. Proposed by Mr. Stripling: "That in future M. C.'s meeting be held in Daibutsu Hotel instead of at the Club where the Committee hitherto have kindly allowed it to be held." Sec. by Mr. Krien. Amended by Mr. Johnson "That in future the meetings of M. C. be held in the room found most convenient until the M. C. building is ready, the most convenient room to be ascertained by the Sec. and notice given by him to members." Sec. by Mr. Lührs. — Carried.

⑤ Mr. Krien proposed, & Mr. Nossé seconded "that a sum not exceeding 200.00 should be appropriated as a remuneration for surveying and laying out into lots & marking on the plan of the G. F. S. the size and boundary of lots in that part of the G. F. S. that has not yet been laid out — and for inspecting and reporting about the grading & building of the road leading from the eastern to the western end of the G. F. S., i. e., the road passing the back of the Jap. Consulate & in front of the Commissioner of Custom's House — & that the Exec. Com. should arrange for the best terms possible." Carried.

⑥ Discussion about subscribing to the Jap. Fire Brigade. Mr. Nossé made a proposal that the M. C. should subscribe towards it, but subsequently withdraw it on being convinced that the M. C. had no power to do so.

⑦ Resolved that the Sec. be asked to with to the President asking him to call on the Korean authorities to provide the Sec. with a complete list of the land-holders in the G. F. S. & to inform him of all fresh purchases & transfers.

⑧ Resolved that the next meeting take place in the first week in Feby (　　) day to be appointed by local members. Vote of thanks to Chairman closed the meeting.

(signed) Oct. Johnson, Vice President.
(signed) Octavius Johnson, Hon. Sec.
7/2/1893.

1892년 12월 29일 회의록

– 번역문 –

① 규정에 따라 회장이 1892년 12월 29일 임시 회의를 소집하였다. 내년도 회장에 선출된 허드 씨가 직위를 사양하였으므로 새로운 회장을 선출하기 위해서였다. 그밖에도 집행위원회 선거와 내년 개회 전에 처리해야 할 기타 업무가 있었다. 홍즈빈 씨, 존슨 씨, 스트리플링 씨, 노세 씨, 뤼어스 씨, 니시와키 씨가 참석하였다.[32] 개회를 선언하였다.

② 회장 선거 결과 크린 씨가 6표를 얻어 만장일치로 선출되었다. 부회장 선거에서는 존슨 씨가 5표, 노세 씨가 1표를 얻어 존슨 씨가 선출되었다.[33] 집행위원회 선거에서는 타운젠드 씨 5표, 스트리플링 씨 6표, 노세 씨 5표, 니시와키 씨가 2표를 얻었으므로 타운젠드 씨, 스트리플링 씨, 노세 씨를 선출하였다.

③ 존슨 씨는 한국 정부가 제의한 내용 즉, 신동공사가 영사들에게 도로평탄화 작업의 책임을 묻는 문제를 거론하였다. 이 일에 대하여는 회의 전부터 상당한 논의가 있었다. 최종적으로 뤼어스 씨는 제물포 주재 영사관원인 홍즈빈 씨, 노세 씨, 존슨 씨가 감리와 해관장을 만나 비용 문제를 결정해야 한다고 발의하였다. 스트리플링 씨가 재청하였으며 통과되었다. 이를 위하여 적절한 때에 감리와 연락할 것이다.

---

32) 주한미국공사 허드, 서울주재독일총영사 크린, 인천항 경찰관 우경선은 불참하였다.

33) 이렇게 하여 1893년도 신동공사 임원은 회장 허드, 부회장 크린, 회계 타운젠드, 서기 존슨에서 회장 크린, 부회장 겸 서기 존슨, 회계 타운젠드로 바뀌었다.

④ 다음과 같이 결의하였다. “회계께 요청합니다. 도로평탄화 작업 비용과 관련하여 회계 내역을 작성하고 전표를 발행하고 당연직 위원들께 모든 정보를 제공해 주십시오.”

⑤ 뤼어스 씨는 내년 1월 1일부로 경찰국장의 월급을 5달러 인상하되 이 금액은 예비비에서 지출하자고 발의하였다. 노세 씨가 재청하였으며 통과하였다.

⑥ 감리가 보내 온 메모를 제출하였다. 신동공사가 납부해야 할 세금이 75.60달러라는 내용이었다. 스트리플링 씨가 발의하고 노세 씨가 재청하였다. “내년에 세금을 반액으로 절감하는 문제를 다루기 전까지, 신동공사는 내년 1월 1일 토지소유주들에게 받아야 할 세금을 받지 맙시다.” 존슨 씨가 다음과 같은 수정안을 발의하였다. “세금 관련 조항이 명시된 각국 조계 장정을 개정하지 않는 이상 신동공사는 세금 절감에 대하여 의논할 권한이 없습니다.” 노세 씨가 재청하였으며 통과되었다.

⑦ 홍즈빈 씨는 락스데일 씨의 일지 중 한 항목을 언급하였다. 그는 노세 씨에게 일본인들이 신동공사 중국인 경찰관들의 목숨을 위협한 것이 사실인지, 이와 관련하여 적절한 조치를 취하였는지 문의하였다. 노세 씨는 자신도 소문을 들었으나 현재 걱정할 만한 일은 없다고 답변하는 한편 사망한 중국인에 대하여 합당한 조치를 취하였음을 증명하는 문서를 작성하였다.

⑧ 오후 12시 30분쯤 회의를 마쳤다.

부회장 존슨 (서명)

서기 존슨 (서명)

등록된 토지소유주 명단은 158페이지를 볼 것.[34]

·· – **원문** – ··

① Meeting of Dec. 29, 1893. Extraordinary meeting called in accordance with the rules, by the President, Mr. A. Heard for the election of a President for the ensuing year. — Mr. Heard himself having declined to accept the office — & to elect an Exec. Com. & to transact such other business as might properly be brought before the meeting. Present: Messrs. Hung, Johnson, Stripling, Nossé, Lührs, Nishiwaki. Notice calling meeting read.

② Election of President:- Mr. Krien, 6, elected unanimously. Vice President, Mr. Johnson, 5, Mr. Noseé, 1, Mr. Johnson elected. Exec. Com. Mr. Townsend, 5, Stripling, 6, Noseé, 5, Nishiwaki 2, Messrs. Townsend, Stripling & Noseé elected.

③ Mr. Johnson brought the matter of the Korean Govt. offer to meet Consuls & decide liability regarding grading of roads. Before the meeting, considerable discussion ensued, at length it was: Proposed by Mr. Lührs, sec. by Mr. Stripling that the M. C. appoint the 3 local Consuls at Chemulpo, i. e., Messrs. Hung, Nossé & Johnson to meet the Kamni & the Commissioner of Customs in order to decide the amount due to the M. C. for grading roads. Carried. Communication in the sense of the above motion to be put in due course to the Kamni.

④ Resolved that the Treasurer be asked to make an account, produce vouchers & provide the official members with all information with regard to expenses of grading roads.

⑤ Proposed by Mr. Lührs, sec. by Mr. Nossé, that the salary of the Chief

34) 원본 158페이지에는 1892년 12월 7일 선거록의 일부로서 제물포 각국 조계의 등록된 토지소유주 명단이 수록되어 있다.

of Police be increased by $5.00 per month from Jan. 1, 1893, the amount to be paid out of the contingency appropriation. Carried.

⑥ Land-rent memo. from Kamni received & laid before the meeting. Amount $75.60. Mr. Stripling proposed, Mr. Nossé sec. that the annual ground rent for the Municipal lot be not paid on Jan. 1 & not until after the question of half taxes has been brought before a meeting of M. C. for 1893. Amendment by Mr. Johnson. That until the agreement has been altered the M. C. has no right to discuss the matter of reducing the amount of ground rent stipulated to be paid in that agreement. Sec. by Mr. Nossé. Carried.

⑦ Mr. Hung, referring to an entry in Ragsdale's occurrence book, asked Mr. Nossé whether it was true that the M. C.'s Chinese policemen's lives had been threatened by Japanese & if so, whether proper measures had been taken in the matter. Mr. Nossé replied that he had heard the rumor but that there was now no cause for alarm. Mr. Nossé produced a paper containing evidence that he had taken suitable steps regarding the late now between Jap. & Chinese policemen in the G. F. S.

⑧ Meeting closed at about 12:30.

(signed) Oct. Johnson, Vice-President.
(signed) Oct. Johnson, Hon. Sec.

See page 158 for List of Registered Land-holders.

1893년 2월 7일 회의록

-- 번역문 --

① 1893년 2월 7일 오전 10시 30분 신동공사 회의를 개회하였다. 니시와키 씨, 스트리플링 씨, 타운젠드 씨, 노세 씨, 존슨 씨(의장)가 참석하였다.[35] 작년도 마지막 정기 회의와 임시 회의의 회의록을 낭독하고 승인하였다.

② 중국일본무역상사가 보내 온 편지를 낭독하였다. B3 구역에 등유 저장 창고를 짓는 것을 반대하는지 알려 달라는 내용이었다. 논의 후 다음과 같이 답장을 보내기로 결의하였다. "등유 저장 창고를 가연성 소재로 짓지 않는다면 현재로서는 금지할 권한이 없으나, 그곳에 그러한 건물을 올리는 것이 신중한 처사는 아니라는 의견을 제시합니다."

③ 홍즈빈 씨는 회의에 참석하였다가 곧 양해를 구하고 회의장을 떠났다. 자신의 친구를 태운 중국 증기선이 막 도착하였고 그와 함께 중요한 업무를 봐야 한다는 이유였다.

④ 해관장 자택 앞의 도로에 대하여 의논하였다. 타운젠드 씨가 발의하였다. "해관장 자택 앞 도로에 쇄석을 깔고 배수 시설을 설치합시다." 스트리플링 씨가 재청하였으며 통과되었다.

⑤ 지난 몇 년간 신동공사를 위하여 봉사한 제물포주재영국부영사관 서기에게 사례금을 지급하기로 결의하였다.[36]

---

35) 선출직 위원들은 전원 참석하였으나 당연직 위원은 일본 대표 노세와 영국 대표 존슨만 참석하였다.

⑥ 타운젠드 씨가 발의하였다. "회계가 홍콩상하이은행 상하이 지점에 예치한 신동공사 기금을 인출하여 일본국립은행(십팔은행) 제물포 지점에 맡기는 것을 승인합시다." 노세 씨가 재청하였으며 통과되었다.[37]

⑦ 타운젠드 씨가 발의하였다. "서기께 요청합니다. 감리에게 편지를 써서 그가 받은 1892년도 세금을 달라고 하십시오." 노세 씨가 재청하였으며 통과되었다.

⑧ 사바친 씨가 와서 각국 조계 북서쪽 끝에 부지를 편성하는 문제와 관련하여 자신의 계획을 개괄적으로 설명하였다. 그는 도면에 도로를 표시해 왔으나 직선으로만 표시해 왔다. 신동공사는 지형에 어울리게 도로를 표시해 달라고 요청하였고 그는 내일(2월 8일) 아침까지 그렇게 하겠다고 답변하였다. 집행위원회는 내일 그를 만나 최종안을 확정하기로 결의하였다.

⑨ 다음 정기 회의의 날짜는 현지 위원들의 뜻에 따르기로 결정하였다. 오후 12시 30분에 회의를 마쳤다.

부회장 존슨 (서명)

서기 존슨 (서명)

---

36) 1894년 4월 23일 회의록을 참고할 때 한국인 방경희(方敬喜)를 가리키는 것으로 추정된다.

37) 1892년 5월 11일 노세가 이 일을 제안하였으나 중요한 문제이기 때문에 모든 위원들에게 고지되어야 한다는 이유로 보류된 바 있다.

-- 원문 --

① Meeting of the Municipal Council Feby 7, 1893, 10:30 a. m. Present: Messrs. Nishiwaki, Stripling, Townsend, Nosse, Johnson (in the chair). The minutes of the last regular meeting and of the subsequent extra-ordinary meeting were taken as read and confirmed.

② Letter from China & Japan Trading Co. read, requesting to be informed whether there was any objection to the erection of a building for storage of kerosene oil on Lot B3. After some discussion it was resolved that an answer be sent as follows: The Council at present have no power to prevent your erecting a building for the storage of kerosene oil on Lot B3, provided that it is not of an inflammable nature, but at the same time they express their opinion that it is not prudent to do so.

③ Mr. Hung was announced and joined the meeting, but excused himself at once as a friend had arrived by the Chinese steamer and he had important business with him.

④ Discussion with regard to road in front of Commissioner of Custom's house:- Proposed by Mr. Townsend and seconded by Mr. Stripling "That the road in front of the Commissioner of Custom's house be metalled and drained at present grade." Carried.

⑤ Resolved that the writer at the British Vice-Consulate be presented with the sum of the dollars in recognition of his service rendered to the Council during the last few years.

⑥ Proposed by Mr. Townsend and seconded by Mr. Nossé "That the Treasurer be authorized to withdraw the Council money now deposited in the Hongkong and Shanghai Bank, Shanghai and deposit same and other monies received by him in the 18th National Bank of Japan, Chemulpo Branch." Carried.

⑦ Proposed by Mr. Townsend and seconded by Mr. Nossé "That the Secretary be asked to write to the Kamni requesting him to pay over to the Municipal Council the rents collected by him in 1892." Carried.

⑧ Mr. Sabatin came forward and explained in general, the manner in which he proposed to lay out the N. W. end of the settlement. The roads were sketched out on the plan but in direct lines. He was accordingly requested to sketch them out as they would be if made to suit the conformation of the land. Mr. Sabatin said he would have such a sketch ready by the next day morning (Feby 8th) and it was resolved that the Executive Committee should meet him on that day and decide what the final plan should be.

⑨ Resolved that the date of the next regular meeting should be left to be decided by the local members. Meeting closed at 12:30 p. m.

(signed) Oct. Johnson, Vice-President.
(signed) Octavius Johnson, Hon. Sec.

1893년 4월 7일 회의록

-- 번역문 --

① 1893년 4월 7일 오전 10시 30분 제물포주재영국부영사관에서 신동공사 회의를 개최하였다. 스트리플링 씨, 류자충 씨(제물포주재중국부영사), 니시와키 씨, 노세 씨, 우경선 씨, 타운젠드 씨, 존슨 씨(의장)가 참석하였다.[38] 지난 번 회의록을 낭독하고 승인하였다.

② 감리가 보내 온 편지를 낭독하였다. 세금이 완납된 후에야 신동공사에 전달할 수 있다는 내용이었다. 타운젠드 씨는 해관에서 입수한 미납자 명단을 제출하였다. '스트리플링 487.98달러, 뫼르젤 347.70달러, 리키타케 60.90달러, 신도 87.12달러, 호리 222.48달러, 고르샬키 42.30달러, 신동공사 75.60달러'였다. 스트리플링 씨가 발의하였다. "서기께 요청합니다. 우경선 씨와 노세 씨가 감리를 설득하지 못할 경우 서울의 각국 외교 대표들께 이 문제를 알려 감리가 일주일 안에 세금을 내놓도록 조치해 주십시오." 타운젠드 씨가 재청하였으며 통과되었다. 타운젠드 씨는 1891년 신동공사가 지금처럼 자금난에 처하였을 때 존스턴 씨가 세금을 분할 납부한 적이 있다면서, 수중에 있는 신동공사 기금은 45일 남짓이면 동날 것이기 때문에 이 사안이 긴급하다고 이야기하였다.

③ 타운젠드 씨가 발의하였다. "서기께 요청합니다. 감리에게 편지를 써서 내일부터 열흘 안에 세금을 내지 않는 사람을 영사 법정에 고소해

38) 홍즈빈의 뒤를 이어 제물포주재중국부영사로 부임한 류자충이 중국 대표로서 처음 참석하였다. 서울주재독일총영사 크린과 주한미국공사 허드는 참석하지 않았다.

달라고 하십시오." 그는 자신이 이를 제안한 이유를 "지난 15개월간 세금을 내지 않은 이들에게 자주 납부를 요청하였습니다. 어떤 사람에게는 법정에서 살펴볼 만한 이유가 있었으나 이유 없이 미납한 사람도 있으니 강제로라도 내게 해야 합니다"라고 설명하였다. 존슨 씨가 재청하였으며 통과되었다.

④ 신동공사 회관 건축에 관하여 의논하였다. 집행위원회는 계약을 마무리하는 것과 관련하여 사바친 씨의 조언을 따르기로 결의하였다.

⑤ 타운젠드 씨가 발의하였다. "서기께 요청합니다. 도면에 표시된 도로가 신동공사의 승인을 받은 것임을 명시하기 위하여, 각국 외교 대표들께 편지를 써서 일본 조계와 부두를 잇는 도로 건설 문제를 신속히 조치해 달라고 하십시오. 초록색으로 표시된 해변 쪽에는 울타리를 두르면 안 되고, 갈색으로 표시된 부분은 추가 조사를 위하여 남겨두어야 합니다. 또한 도로에 쇄석을 까는 작업은 다른 일들을 결정하느라 지체하지 말고 즉각 이루어져야 합니다." 니시와키 씨가 재청하였으며 통과되었다. 스트리플링 씨는 각국 조계가 도로 건설 비용을 부담하는 데 반대하고, 일본 조계에 거주하는 상인들이 주로 사용하기 때문에 일본인들이 일부를 부담해야 한다고 주장하였다. 그는 자신의 의견을 회의록에 기록해 달라고 요청하였다.

⑥ 오후 1시 15분에 회의를 마쳤다.

의장 크린 (서명)

서기 존슨 (서명)

① Meeting of April 7, 1893. Vice-Consulate 10:30 a. m. Present: Messrs. Stripling, Liu (Chinese Consul), Nishiwaki, Nossé, Ou, Townsend & Johnson (in the chair). Minutes of last meeting read and confirmed.

② Letter from Kamni read, in reply to letter, requesting him to pay up as much as is due to the M. C. out of the tops as he has already received, at once, in which he says that he cannot pay up until the full amounts due by all land-renters have been received. Discussion on the subject: a list of landowners who had not paid was laid on the table by Mr. Townsend, procured by him from customs, as follows. Stripling $487.98, Mörsel 347.70, Rikitaki 60.90, Shindo 87.12, Hori 222.48, Gorschalki 42.30, M. C. 75.60. Proposed by Mr. Stripling, 2nd by Mr. Townsend "That in the event of Messrs. & Ou & Nossé failing to induce Kamni to pay in to the M. C. that portion of the taxes due to them already collected for 1892, the Sec. be instructed to bring the matter to the notice of the Representations in Seoul with a view to instructions being issued to the Kamni to pay over to the M. C. the taxes on each lot within a week often the amount is paid to him." — Carried. Mr. Townsend said during the discussion on the above proposal, that there was a precedent in 1891 when the M. C., being as at present, in want of funds, Mr. J. C. Johnston acting Commissioner of Customs, paid up amounts from the rents collected on account. He said the matter was at present urgent as the funds in hand would only last 45 days more.

③ Proposed by Mr. Townsend, 2nd by Mr. Johnson. That the Sec. be requested to write to the Kamni requesting him to bring suits for non-payment of rent against such land-renters as should not have paid up their rents within ten days from the 8th inst. in their respective Consular Courts. — Carried. Mr. Townsend explained that his reason for bringing forward was that during the last 15 months those that had not paid had been frequently asked to pay.

— some of the land-renters who have not paid have reasons which should be looked into by a law-court some have no reasons and should be forced to pay.

④ Discussion regarding Municipal Building — it was resolved that the Exec. Com. be requested to abide by Mr. Sabatin's advice as to the proper completion of the contract.

⑤ Proposed by Mr. Townsend, 2nd by Mr. Nishiwaki, that the Sec. be asked to write to the Body of Foreign Representatives at Seoul requesting that action be taken at once in the matter of laying out the road from the Jap. Settlement to the Jetty, to state that the plan sent herewith so far as regards the road meets the approbation of the M. C. that with regarding to the portions of the foreshore colored green the M. C. suggest that if the proposed scheme be adopted, these should not be fenced in, that with regard to the portions colored brown they suggest that these should be left for further inquiry, that at the same time they wish to lay weight on the fact that the metalling of the road should proceed at once, not being delayed for the decision of the other matters. Carried. Mr. Stripling requested that it should be noted that he objected on the ground that the expense of the road would have to be borne by the G. F. S. whereas seeing that it would be used mostly by the merchants living in the Jap. Settlement the Japanese should contribute a portion.

⑥ The meeting closed at 1:15 p. m.

(signed) F. Krien, President.

(signed) Oct. Johnson, Hon. Sec.

1893년 5월 20일 회의록

-- 번역문 --

① 1893년 5월 20일 신동공사 회의를 개최하였다. 크린 씨(의장), 존슨 씨, 노세 씨, 스트리플링 씨, 타운젠드 씨가 참석하였다.[39] 지난 번 회의록을 낭독하고 승인하였다.

② 존슨 씨는 예전의 한 회의 때 묘지 둘레에 옹벽을 세우자는 의견이 통과되었는데 왜 아직도 세우지 않았는지 질문하였다.[40] 타운젠드 씨가 대답하였다. "옹벽을 세우기 위하여 한 중국인과 계약을 맺었지만 공사에 착수하려면 한국인들의 무덤을 다른 곳으로 옮겨야 합니다. 감리에게 무덤을 옮겨 달라고 부탁하는 편지를 보냈으나, 그가 대답만 하고 아직까지 해 주지 않아 지연되고 있습니다." 스트리플링 씨는 감리가 무덤을 옮기지 않고 있는 것은 재정이 부족해서라고 언급하였다.

③ 타운젠드 씨는 허드 씨로부터 들은 이야기를 전달하였다. 한국 정부가 해관 창고 앞 토지에 대한 권리증을 받아들이지 않고 울타리 운운하였다는 내용이었다. 타운젠드 씨가 발의하였다. "한국 정부는 해관 창고 앞 토지를 항상 비워 놓겠다고 보증하기를 거부하였습니다. 서기께 요청합니다. 각국 외교 대표들께 편지를 써서 제방 도로에 대한 원래의 계획을 고수함으로써 이 문제를 해결해 달라고 하십시오. 도로

39) 주한미국공사 허드, 제물포주재중국부영사 류자충, 인천항 경찰관 우경선, 선출직 위원 니시와키는 불참하였다.

40) 묘지 둘레에 옹벽을 세우는 일은 1892년 12월 6일 스트리플링이 발의하고 뤼어스가 재청하여 통과된 사안이었다.

의 너비는 최소 15미터가 되어야 하고 수송용 국도는 해관 창고 때문에 있는 것이니 유지해야 합니다. 또한 각국 외교 대표들이 해관 창고 앞 토지에 와서 화물 수송을 방해하는 울타리가 둘러 있지 않음을 확인하게 합시다." 스트리플링 씨가 재청하였으며 만장일치로 통과되었다.

④ 회계 타운젠드 씨는 현재 수중에 있는 신동공사 기금이 1,500달러 정도인데 6월 1일경 신동공사 회관 건설업자에게 1,300달러, 사바친 씨에게 조사비 200달러, 경상비 170달러, 경찰관 숙소 집세와 연체료 40달러를 지출해야 한다고 보고하였다. 존슨 씨는 경상 지출과 부채 상환만으로도 빠듯한 사정을 고려하여 조례에 명시된 의무에 따라 경상비를 제외한 어떤 전표에도 연서(連署)하지 않겠다고 밝혔다. 그는 특별 지출 때문에 기금을 초과하는 것보다는 경찰관과 청소부, 가로등 같은 일상적 서비스를 유지하는 것이 더욱 필요하다고 판단한 것이다. 논의 후 존슨 씨에게 한국 정부와의 자금 문제를 해결할 때까지 연서 거부를 철회해 달라고 요청하였다.

⑤ 스트리플링 씨는 회계의 수중에 있는 모든 돈을 신동공사 회관 건축 공사를 맡은 중국인에게 지불해야 한다는 의견을 밝혔다. 존슨 씨는 만일 그렇게 하지 않으면 그가 제물포주재중국부영사에게 호소할 것이라고 이야기하였다.

⑥ 존슨 씨가 5월 8일자 허드 씨의 편지를 낭독하였다. 외아문 독판이 감리에게 편지를 써서 신동공사에 즉시 세금을 전달하고 앞으로 들어올 세금도 들어오는 즉시 전달하라고 지시하였다는 내용이었다. 스트리플링 씨가 이 편지와 관련하여 발의하였다. "감리는 1892년도 세금을 신동공사에 전달하지 않았습니다. 신동공사는 수중에 1,500달러밖에 없으

나 6월 1일 1,710달러를 지출해야 합니다. 따라서 서기께 요청합니다. 각국 외교 대표들께 또 한 번 편지를 써서 즉각 조치를 취해 달라고 하십시오." 크린 씨가 재청하였다. 논의 후 존슨 씨는 오늘 당장 감리를 만나 독촉하자고 제안하였다.

·· – **원문** – ··

① Meeting May 20, 1893. Present: Messrs. Krien (in chair), Johnson, Nossé, Stripling, Townsend. Minutes of last meeting read and confirmed.

② Mr. Johnson said that a resolution had been passed at a previous meeting to build a wall around the cemetery & wished to know why it had not been done. Mr. Townsend replied that a contract had been made in 1891 with a Chinese contractor to build the said wall but before beginning the desired work the Korean graves must be removed. A letter was sent to the Kamni asking him to have the graves removed & he replied that he would do so, but up to the present it has not been done therefore the building of the wall has been postponed. Mr. Stripling remarked that want of money prevented the work proceeding at present.

③ Mr. Townsend stated that Mr. Heard informed him that the Korean Govt. refused to accept title-deed for ground in front of present Customs Godowns with any limitations regarding fencing. Proposed by Mr. Townsend & seconded by Mr. Stripling: In view of the refusal of the Korean Govt. to guarantee that the ground along the sea-wall in front of the present Customs Godowns be always kept open that the Secretary be requested to write to the Foreign Representatives asking them to settle the matter of this ground by adhering to the original plan of a road along the sea-wall, but of a suitable width, not less than 15 metres, at the same time maintaining that the national road for traffic is by the present Customs Godowns that it would be better that the road be made that way, but that the Foreign Reps. be called on to see that the ground in front of the Customs Godowns be not inclosed by a fence at all, to interfere with the handling of cargo. Carried unanimously.

④ Mr. Townsend as Hon. Treasurer then stated that the amount of funds belonging to the M. C. now on hand was $1,500 odd whereas our liabilities on June 1 will be approximately. To Contractor of Municipal Building $1,300. To Mr. Sabatin for surveying 200. To Current Expenses 170, To arrears & rent of Constable's house 40. Mr. Johnson then said that in view of the funds being insufficient to meet the ordinary expenses & liabilities incurred he objected to counter-signing as by the By-laws it was his duty to do, any vouchers now except for ordinary expenses, holding that it was more necessary to keep up the ordinary services of the Settlement, i. e., police, scavengers, lighting, etc. than to overstep the limits of the funds by paying extraordinary sums rightly due. Discussion followed & Mr. Johnson having offered to resign was requested to withdraw same until it was seen whether money matters could be settled with the Korean Govt.

⑤ Mr. Stripling said that he thought we should pay the Chinese contractor the M. C. Building amount due him as long as any money remained in the hands of the Treasurer. Mr. Johnson said that the Chinese Contractor if not paid had recourse thro' his own Consul.

⑥ Mr. Johnson read a letter from Mr. Heard dated May 8 stating that the President of the F. O. had written the Jenchuan Kamni to pay at once to the M. C. all money now due to them & hereafter to pay moneys received from taxpayers immediately on receipt of same, less amount due to Korean Govt. Mr. Stripling proposed, sec. by Mr. Krien. With regard to Mr. Heard's despatch of May 8 the Kamni not having paid over to the M. C. any of the rent collected for 1892, & as the Hon. Sec. states that the funds in hand amount to $1,500 only, whereas the liabilities due on June 1 amount to $1,710 that another letter be addressed by the Hon. Sec. to the For. Reps. urging them to press the claim for immediate payment of rent collected and due to the M. C. Discussion followed & Mr. Johnson offered to see Kamni the same day & press for payment.

1893년 6월 26일 회의록

번역문

① 1893년 6월 26일 신동공사 회의를 개최하였다. 크린 씨(의장), 류자충 씨, 스트리플링 씨, 존슨 씨, 타운젠드 씨가 참석하였다.[41] 지난 번 회의록을 낭독하고 승인하였다. 지난 번 회의 이후 도착한 편지들을 낭독하였다.

② 타운젠드 씨는 신동공사 회관 건축을 맡은 중국인 건설업자에게 수중에 있던 모든 돈을 주었으나, 5월 30일자 사바친 씨의 편지에 따라 200달러는 지불하지 않았다고 진술하였다. 그는 사바친 씨가 건축 과정에서 변동 사항이 있었음을 밝혔고 건물 지붕과 관련된 9월 1일 잔액도 정확한 것으로 판명되었으니 건설업자에게 100달러를 지불하자고 발의하였다. 통과되었다.

③ 타운젠드 씨가 발의하였다. "신동공사 회관이 정리되었으니 락스데일 씨에게 6월 30일에 이사하라고 합시다. 또한 경찰관들에게도 지시하여 같은 날 신동공사 회관으로 숙소를 옮기게 합시다." 스트리플링 씨가 다음과 같은 수정안을 발의하였다. "신동공사 회관은 주민들이 사는 곳에서 너무 멀어 경찰관 숙소로 적합하지 않습니다. 그러니 신동공사 회관과 부지를 경매에 붙여 최고입찰자에게 팝시다." 재청하는 사람이 없었으므로 타운젠드 씨의 제안이 통과되었다. 타운젠드 씨는 1892

---

41) 주한미국공사 허드, 제물포주재일본부영사 노세, 인천항 경찰관 우경선, 선출직 위원 니시와키는 불참하였다. 허드는 이 회의가 열린 다음날 공사직에서 물러났다.

년 6월 7일 회의에서 만장일치로 건축 계약을 체결하였으므로 이제 와서 신동공사 회관의 타당성을 논하면 안 되고, 건물이 완공되었으니 최대한 잘 활용해야 한다고 발언하였다.[42] 스트리플링 씨는 자신이 그 회의에 있었으나 투표하지 않았으므로 만장일치가 아니라고 강조하였다.

④ 타운젠드 씨는 일본인 경찰관 1명이 아파서 보름째 쉬고 있고 중국인 경찰관 1명은 고국에 다녀온다며 두 달간 휴가를 신청하였다고 보고하였다. 후자는 스스로 대체 인력을 구하겠다고 제의하였다는데, 류자충 씨는 그 대체 인력이 어떤 사람인지 조사해 보겠다고 이야기하였다. 집행위원회는 제물포주재일본부영사 노세 씨에게 병가 중인 일본인 경찰관의 대체 인력을 알아봐 달라고 부탁하기로 했다.

⑤ 일본 조계와 부두를 잇는 도로에 대하여 의논하였다. 타운젠드 씨가 발의하고 스트리플링 씨가 재청하였다. "서기께 요청합니다. 각국 외교 대표들께 편지를 써 주십시오. 선박과 수레가 통행할 수 있도록 갯벌과 제방을 항상 비워 두겠다는 명확한 합의가 없다면, 신동공사는 해관 창고를 따라 도로를 건설하는 데 반대하고 차라리 제방을 따라 너비 15미터의 도로를 건설할 것을 재차 요청합니다." 존슨 씨는 타운젠드 씨가 발의한 내용 중 "선박과 수레가 통행할 수 있도록 갯벌과 제방을 항상 비워 두겠다는 명확한 합의가 없다면"을 그대로 두고, 해관 창고 옆에 도로를 건설하되 도로 바깥쪽에 울타리를 두르지 못하도록 각국 외교 대표들의 도움을 청하자는 수정안을 제의하였다. 재청하는 사람이 없었으므로 타운젠드 씨의 발의가 통과되었다.

---

42) 1892년 6월 7일은 신동공사 회관 건축 입찰 공고를 낸 날이다. 이 날의 회의록은 남아 있지 않다. 1892년 8월 25일 회의록을 참고할 것.

⑥ 서기는 감리가 보내 온 편지를 제출하였다. 세금 2,000달러를 신동공사에 전달하면서 아직 들어오지 않은 세금은 들어온 후 보내겠으나 이번 일이 전례가 되어서는 안 된다는 내용이었다. 하루빨리 돈을 받기 위하여 긴급 조치를 취해야 했다. 크린 씨는 각국 조계 장정 제3조 제5항 "A 부지 등의 세금은 신동공사 기금이다"를 거론하였다. 그는 감리가 신동공사 기금을 받았으면 즉시 신동공사에 전달하는 것이 마땅하고 현재 감리의 태도는 도저히 납득할 수 없다고 발언하였다. 스트리플링 씨가 발의하였다. "감리는 회장인 허드 씨의 5월 8일자 지시를 무시하였습니다. 그는 신동공사에 2,000달러만 보냈으며 이 일이 전례가 되어서는 안 된다고 이야기하였습니다. 각국 외교 대표들께 다시 한 번 편지를 보내 감리가 세금 전액을 내놓도록 독촉해 달라고 합시다." 존슨 씨가 재청하였으며 통과되었다.

⑦ 타운젠드 씨는 기무라 씨가 그의 땅(D62 구역)과 가까운 공용 도로에 우물을 파려 한다고 밝혔다. 기무라 씨는 자비를 들여 우물을 파되 모두가 사용할 수 있도록 항상 열어 놓을 것이며, 신동공사가 요청하면 언제든 우물물을 채워 놓을 것이라고 한다. 스트리플링 씨는 신동공사가 이 일을 허락할 경우 기무라 씨에게 제물포주재일본부영사의 직인이 찍힌 서류를 요구해야 하고, 해당 서류에는 신동공사가 허락한 방식대로 모두가 편리하게 쓸 수 있는 우물을 만들겠다는 내용이 있어야 한다고 생각하였다. 신동공사는 원칙상 기무라 씨의 요청을 허락하였으나 집행위원회는 이 일의 실행 과정에서 제약을 가할 권한이 있다.

⑧ 타운젠드 씨는 다음 회의 때 신동공사 회관에 놓을 가구를 구입할 비용 250달러를 신청하겠다고 예고하였다. 스트리플링 씨도 최종 도면

에 명시된 도로의 평탄화 작업을 위하여 1,000달러를 신청하겠다고 공지하였다.

⑨ 오전 11시쯤 회의를 시작하고 오후 1시 30분에 휴회하였다. 3시 15분에 속개하여 4시 30분에 회의를 마쳤다.

·· – **원문** – ··

① Meeting of June 26, 1893. Present: Messrs. Krien (in chair), Liu, Stripling, Johnson & Townsend. Minutes of last meeting read & confirmed. Correspondence since last meeting read.

② Mr. Townsend stated that he had paid the Chinese contractor for Municipal Buildings all monies due to him in his contract with the exception of two hundred dollars held back by him in conformance with Mr. Sabatin's letter of May 30. He suggested that contractor should be paid $100.00 in making alterations as suggested by Mr. Sabatin & the balance on Sept. 1 of roof is found to be right. Suggestion adopted.

③ Proposed by Mr. Townsend, sec. by Mr. Johnson: "That Mr. Ragsdale be ordered to move into the Municipal Building on June 30th the building being now in order. Also that the constables be ordered to move into their quarters on the same date." Amendment by Mr. Stripling "that as the M. C. building is too far from the residents to be suitable for police purposes, the house & lot be advertised for sale of let to the highest bidder" not seconded. Mr. Townsend's proposition as above carried. Mr. Townsend stated during discussion on the subject that the question of the advisability of the Municipal Building being built could not now be discussed as the contract had been agreed to unanimously by the

M. C. meeting June 7' 92 & that the building being now finished we must put it to its best use. Mr. Stripling stated emphatically that the vote was not unanimous as he having been present at the meeting did not vote for it.

④ Mr. Townsend referring to the Police force said that two men were now off duty — one Japanese — sick (had been so for half a month) & one Chinese — wanted leave for two months to go home. The latter offered to provide a substitute. Mr. Liu said that he would inquire into the character of the Chinese substitute. The Exce. Com. were asked to apply to the Jap. Consul Mr. Nossé for character of Jap. substitute.

⑤ Discussion with regard to road between Jap. settlement & Jetty. Proposed by Mr. Townsend & sec. by Mr. Stripling "That the Sec. be requested to write to the For. Reps. that the M. C. object to accepting a road along the Customs Godowns without a definite agreement that the foreshore & sea-wall be always kept open to boats & traffic, & without such agreement they must again request that the 15 metre road be laid out along the sea-wall. Amendment by Mr. Johnson, That the part of Mr. Townsend's proposition as above be adopted down to the words "boats & traffic" but that the road next the Customs Godowns should be pressed for & the help of the For. Reps. be called for to prevent any inclosure outside this being made. — not amended. Mr. Townsend's prop. as above carried.

⑥ The Hon. Sec. put forward a letter from the Kamni stating that altho' he handed over $2,000 on account of money that he had received as land rents, there were some amounts still not paid and he did not consider himself found to pay any until they were all paid. This payment was not to be taken as a precedent. Discussion on this letter: it was considered that urgent steps should be taken to obtain the receipt of the amount of rents due to the Council from the Korean Govt. as soon as any payment on this account was made to the

Korean Govt. Mr. Krien referred to Art. 5 Para. 3 of the agreement saying that the "yearly rental of A lots etc. shall belong to the Municipal Fund." He said that the money being the property of the M. C. has to be refunded by the Kamni as soon as he receives it, & that the position at present assumed by the Kamni is utterly untenable. Proposed by Mr. Stripling, sec. by Mr. Johnson, "That referring to Mr. Heard's letter of May 8 as the Kamni has ignored the President's instructions & paid the M. C. only $2,000 which the Kamni says is not to be regarded as a precedent, that another letter be addressed to the For. Reps. urging them to insist upon the immediate payment of the total amount due," carried.

⑦ Mr. Townsend said that Mr. Kimura (Lot. D. 62) wants to make a well in public road close by his lot. He proposes to make the well at his own expense, to be always open to public use & promises to fill it up at any time when so requested by the M. C. Mr. Stripling thinks that if the M. C. agree to allow the well to be built the M. C., the M. C. should get from Mr. Kimura a document in writing to be stamped by the Jap. Consul to the effect that Mr. Kimura will build the well in a way approved by the M. C. & in such a way as not to be inconvenient to the public. Approved in principle by the M. C. the Exce. Com. however to have power to put such restrictions on the carrying out of the work as they may think necessary.

⑧ Mr. Townsend stated that he should propose an appropriation of $250 for furniture for the Municipal Building at next meeting. Mr. Stripling gave notice that at the next meeting he would make application for the appropriation of $1000 for grading all the roads laid down in the approval plan of the settlement.

⑨ The meeting commenced at about 11 a. m. adjourned about 1.30 p. m. met again at 3:15 p. m. & closed at about 4.30 p. m.

1893년 7월 24일 회의록

·· – **번역문** – ··

① 7월 24일 오전 11시 제물포주재영국부영사관에서 신동공사 회의를 개회하였다. 존슨 씨(부회장)가 의장석에 앉았다. 헤롯 씨, 노세 씨, 타운젠드 씨, 스트리플링 씨가 참석하였다.[43] 지난 번 회의록을 낭독하고 승인하였다.

② 서기가 지난 번 회의 이후 도착한 편지들을 낭독하고 위원들에게 돌렸다. 첫 번째 편지는 해관장이 신동공사 경찰 조직과 관련하여 정보를 요청하는 내용이었다. 두 번째 편지는 각국외교대표단장 드미트레프스키 씨가 쓴 것으로, 각국 조계에 도로를 건설하는 일과 관련하여 외아문 독판이 만든 제안서(9개 조항)의 사본을 전달하기 위한 것이었다.[44] 세 번째 편지는 감리가 쓴 것이었다. 1892년도 세금의 잔액인 2,541.93달러짜리 수표를 전달하기 위한 것이었다.

③ 첫 번째 편지와 관련하여 스트리플링 씨는 해관장의 요청에 응하는 것을 강력하게 반대하였다. 신동공사가 각국 조계 주민들의 불만에 관심을 기울여야 하는 것은 맞지만, 경찰관들에 대한 정보를 외부인에게 제공할 의무는 없다는 이유였다. 존슨 씨는 그의 뜻에 동의하면서

---

43) 주일미국공사관 서기관 헤롯이 미국 대표로 참석하였다. 그는 1893년 6월 27일부터 8월 31일까지 주한미국대리공사로 복무하였다. 서울주재독일총영사 크린, 제물포주재 중국부영사 류자충, 인천항 경찰관 우경선, 선출직 위원 니시와키는 참석하지 않았다.

44) 드미트레프스키는 1891~1893년 주한러시아대리공사로 복무하면서 1893년 각국외교대표단장을 역임하였다.

해관장에게 보낼 답장의 초안을 제시하였는데, 이는 논의 후 헤롯 씨가 내놓은 다음 초안으로 대체되었다. "귀하의 편지와 관련하여 알립니다. 신동공사는 각국 조계의 경찰 제도를 개관해 달라는 귀하의 요청에 응하는 것이 우리의 정책에 맞지 않는다는 결론을 내렸습니다. 그러나 특수한 경우 즉, 경찰관 1명 이상이 근무 태만이나 무능력을 보일 때에는 토지소유주들이 제기하는 불만을 기꺼이 들을 것입니다."

④ 두 번째 편지와 관련하여 서울의 총세무사에게서 나왔음이 분명한 제안서를 낭독하고 도면에 명시된 장소들을 알아보았다.[45] 신동공사는 도로를 건설하되 어떤 선박도 도로에 가로질러 밧줄을 치면 안 되고 반대로 도로가 선박을 방해해도 안 된다고 판단하였다.

⑤ 세 번째 편지와 관련하여 타운젠드 씨는 감리가 보내 온 수표를 바꾸기 위하여 일본 은행에 다녀왔다. 그는 감리의 잔액이 503달러 정도였다고 밝혔다. 노세 씨가 발의하였다. "서기께 요청합니다. 감리에게 전보를 보내 그의 수표가 부도 수표인 것을 알리고, 이틀 안에 돈을 보내지 않으면 이 문제를 각국 외교 대표들께 제출하겠다고 전해 주십시오." 타운젠드 씨가 재청하였으며 통과되었다.

⑥ 타운젠드 씨가 발의하였다. "신동공사 회관에 놓을 가구를 구입하기 위하여 집행위원회의 감독 아래 250달러를 지출합시다." 그는 이 돈이 공용 사무실을 꾸미는 데만 쓰일 것이며 경찰관 숙소에는 쓰이지 않을 것이라고 설명하였다. 스트리플링 씨가 재청하였으며 통과되었다.

⑦ 스트리플링 씨가 발의하였다. "각국 조계의 도로 정비와 배수 처

---

45) 당시 총세무사는 1892년 6월 1일 인천해관장으로 부임하였다가 11월 총세무사대리로 임명되어 약 1년간 복무한 영국인 모건이었다.

리를 위하여 1,000달러를 지출합시다. 집행위원회는 이 일을 하루빨리 진행해 주십시오." 타운젠드 씨가 재청하였다.

⑧ 스트리플링 씨는 일부 도로의 상태가 매우 좋지 않으나 한국 정부가 전혀 움직이지 않는다면서 볼터 씨의 땅으로 이어지는 도로를 예로 들었다. 타운젠드 씨는 주거 지역과 가까운 도로부터 차례대로 정비하자고 제안하였다. 스트리플링 씨의 발의는 통과되었다.

⑨ 스트리플링 씨가 발의하였다. "감리가 1892년도 세금 2,541.93달러를 주지 않고 있으니, 토지소유주들의 위원회를 구성하여 토지 규칙 및 조례의 개정안 초안을 작성하게 합시다. 신동공사는 초안을 승인한 후 각국 외교 대표들께 그것을 제출하여 심의와 승인을 받고, 서기는 토지소유주들께 회람을 돌려 사실을 알려야 합니다." 타운젠드 씨가 재청하였다. 스트리플링 씨가 또 발언하였다. "신동공사가 납세자들의 목소리를 충분히 반영하지 않는다는 불평이 많습니다." 존슨 씨는 스트리플링 씨가 발의한 내용 중 "토지소유주들의 위원회" 앞에 "7명 이하의" 라는 구절을 넣자고 제의하였다. 스트리플링 씨가 그의 제의를 받아들여 통과되었다.

⑩ 노세 씨는 사바친 씨가 만든 각국 조계 도면이 신동공사의 승인을 받았는지, 만일 그렇다면 신동공사가 앞으로 어떤 단계를 밟아야 하는지 질문하였다. 그는 신동공사가 사바친 씨의 도면을 조건부로 승인하였으나 아직 각국 외교 대표들에게 제출하지는 않았다는 답변을 들었다. 도면을 일부 수정하는 문제는 다음 회의 때 의논하기로 했다.

⑪ 스트리플링 씨가 발의하였다. "서기께 요청합니다. 서울의 각국 외교 대표들께 편지를 써서 외아문 독판에게 다음을 부탁해 달라고 하십

시오. 외아문 독판은 감리에게 각국 조계 토지소유주들의 이름과 토지 면적, 해당 토지에 부과된 세액의 완벽한 목록을 신동공사에 전달하라고 지시해야 합니다. 우리가 유사한 내용을 여러 번 요청하였으나 감리는 관심을 기울이지 않습니다." 타운젠드 씨가 재청하였으며 통과되었다.

⑫ 스트리플링 씨가 발의하였다. "임기 동안 신동공사를 기꺼이 지원한 주한미국공사 겸 직전 각국외교대표단장 허드 씨께 공식적인 감사 인사를 전합시다. 서기는 이 일과 관련하여 그에게 편지를 써 주십시오." 타운젠드 씨가 재청하였으며 통과되었다.

⑬ 존슨 씨가 부회장직과 서기직에서 물러날 뜻을 밝혔다. 타운젠드 씨가 발의하였다. "유감이지만 존슨 씨의 사임을 수락하고 폭스 씨를 서기로 선출합시다." 노세 씨가 재청하였으며 통과되었다. 타운젠드 씨는 노세 씨를 부회장으로 선출하자고 발의하였다. 존슨 씨가 재청하였으며 만장일치로 통과되었다. 존슨 씨에게 공식적인 감사 인사를 전하자는 발의도 만장일치로 통과되었다.[46]

회장 크린 (서명)

서기 폭스 (서명)

46) 이 날은 1893년도 신동공사 부회장 겸 서기 존슨이 제물포주재영국대리부영사로 일하는 마지막 날이었다. 그가 물러나면서 부회장직은 노세에게, 서기직은 그의 후임 폭스에게 돌아갔다. 폭스는 1893년 7월 25일부터 이듬해 2월 5일까지 제물포주재영국대리부영사로 복무하였다.

·· – 원문 – ··

① Meeting at H. B. M's Vice Consulate on July 24th Commencing at 11 a. m. Present: Mr. Johnson (Vice President) in chair; Messrs. Herod, Nosse, Townsend & Stripling. The minutes of the last meeting were read and confirmed.

② The Hon. Secretary read out & afterwards handed round the following correspondence, received since the last meeting:- (1) Letter from the Commissioner of Customs asking for information concerning the organisation of the Municipal Police. (2) Letter from Mr. Dmitresky, Doyen of the Foreign Representatives, forwarding copy of nine proposals by the President of the Foreign Office for the construction of roads in the Foreign Settlement. (3) Letter from the Kamni enclosing cheque for the balance of 1892 rents ($2541.93) not yet handed over to the Council.

③ Discussion on No (1) — Mr. Stripling was strongly opposed to the Commissioner of Customs request being acceded to, maintaining that the Council were not obliged to furnish outsiders with information regarding their police arrangements, although every attention should of course be given to definite complaints laid before them. Mr. Johnson was of the same opinion and submitted a draft answer to that effect, for which after some discussion, the following draft by Mr. Herod, in the same sense, was substituted. "Referring to yours:- I beg to inform you that the Municipal Council has concluded that it is not consistent with their policy to furnish upon your application a general outline of the system of policing the Foreign Settlement. The Council is willing, however to hear any complaint which many be made by a landholder relative to the negligence or inefficiency of one or more of its officers in particular cases."

④ Discussion on (2) — The proposals which, it was explained, really emanated from the Chief Commissioner of Customs in Seoul were read out and the places referred to identified on the plan. The sense of the Council was that the road in question should be made, with the understanding that no vessels should be allowed to stretch ropes across it otherwise obstruct it.

⑤ Discussion on (3) — Mr. Townsend, who had gone to the Japanese Bank to cash the Kamni's cheque, returned and informed the Council that the balance in the Kamni's name was $503 odd. Mr. Nosse then proposed that the Hon. Secretary should be instructed to write to the Kamni informing him that his cheque had been dishonoured, and giving him two days within which to pay the sum in question, after which time, if it still remained unpaid, the matter would be laid before the Foreign Representatives. Seconded by Mr. Townsend & carried.

⑥ Proposed by Mr. Townsend "that the sum of two hundred and fifty dollars be appropriated for the purpose of buying furniture for Municipal buildings, to be expended under direction of the Executive Committee." Seconded by Mr. Stripling. Mr. Townsend explained that only the public offices would be furnished out of this sum, and not the constables quarters. Carried.

⑦ Proposed by Mr. Stripling "that a sum of one thousand dollars be appropriated for the purpose of grading roads and making drains in the General Foreign Settlement and that the Executive members be requested to proceed with the work without delay." Seconded by Mr. Townsend.

⑧ Mr. Stripling explained that the Corean Government refused to move a finger in the matter and that some of the roads, as for instance, the one leading up to Mr. Wolter's lot were in a very bad condition and urgently needed repair. Mr. Townsend suggested that the roads running past inhabited lots should first be repaired and afterwards those farther away from the houses. Mr. Stripling's proposal was carried.

⑨ Proposed by Mr. Stripling "that in view of the fact that the Kamni has withheld the sum of $2541.93, taxes due to the Council for 1892, that the

Council invite a Committee of landowners to draft a revised set of Land Regulations and By-Laws to be submitted to the Council for their consideration, and, if approved, to be forwarded by the Council to the Representatives for their favorable consideration and approval, and that the Secretary be invited to inform the landrenters of the fact by circular." Seconded by Mr. Townsend. Mr. Stripling said that many landrenters were complaining of not having a sufficient voice in the expenditure of their money and that it was only fair that they should be given some opportunity of expressing their views. Mr. Johnson suggested the words "not less than seven" should be inserted after a Committee of landowners. Mr. Stripling accepted this suggestion and the proposal was carried.

⑩ Mr. Nosse asked whether the Council had given their approval to the plan of the Foreign Settlement drawn up for them by Mr. Sabatin and, if so, what steps would be taken with regard to it. He was informed that it had been conditionally approved of by the Council, but had not yet been submitted to the Foreign Representatives. The consideration of some proposed alterations in the plan was deferred to the next meeting.

⑪ Proposed by Mr. Stripling "that the Hon. Secretary be requested to write to the Representatives in Seoul asking them to be good enough to request the President of the Foreign Office to instruct the Kamni to furnish the Council with a full and complete list of the landowners of the General Foreign Settlement, with size of lots and amounts of taxes on each lot no attention having been paid to previous requests of a similar nature." Seconded by Mr. Townsend and carried.

⑫ Proposed by Mr. Stripling "that a very cordial vote of thanks be given to the Hon. Augustine Heard, U. S. Minister and late Doyen of the Foreign Representatives in Seoul for the kind support and assistance be rendered the

Council during his term of office and that the Hon. Secretary be requested to write to him to that effect." Seconded by Mr. Townsend; carried.

⑬ Mr. Johnson begged to tender his resignation as vice President & Hon. Secretary. Proposed by Mr. Townsend "that Mr. Johnson's resignation be accepted with regret and that Mr. Fox be elected Secretary of the Municipal Council. Seconded by Mr. Nosse; carried." Mr. Townsend proposed that Mr. Nosse be elected vice President. Seconded by Mr. Johnson and carried unanimously. A cordial vote of thanks to Mr. Johnson was proposed and carried unanimously.

(signed) F. Krien, President.
(signed) H. H. Fox, Hon. Secretary.

1893년 9월 2일 회의록

·· - 번역문 - ··

① 1893년 9월 2일 오전 11시 제물포주재영국부영사관에서 신동공사 회의를 개최하였다. 크린 씨(의장), 노세 씨(부회장), 타운젠드 씨, 스트리플링 씨, 우경선 씨, 폭스 씨(서기)가 참석하였다.[47)]

② 감리 대행이 표면적으로는 크린 씨의 요청에 따라, 실제로는 외아문 독판의 지시를 받아 동석하였다. 크린 씨는 자신이 와아문 독판에게 감리가 아닌 신동공사 당연직 위원 우경선 씨의 참석을 부탁하였으나 실수로 이름을 잘못 말한 것 같다고 설명하고, 신동공사와 감리 사이에 한두 가지 조율할 문제가 있으니 감리 대행이 회의장에 남아 회의 진행을 듣게 하자고 제안하였다. 스트리플링 씨는 우경선 씨가 이미 한국 정부의 대표로서 와 있는데다 신동공사가 위원이 아닌 사람의 동석을 거부한 전례가 있다며 반대하였다. 표결에 부친 결과 크린 씨의 제안이 통과되었다. 감리 대행은 회의장에 남아 신동공사의 질문에 기꺼이 답변하기로 했다. 지난 번 회의록을 낭독하고 승인하였다.

③ 서기는 감리가 보내 온 편지를 낭독하였다. 신동공사가 현재 평탄화 작업을 진행하고 있는 도로에 대한 정보를 요청하는 내용이었다. 스트리플링 씨는 도면을 보고 이미 공사를 완료한 도로와 집행위원회가

---

47) 주한미국대리공사 알렌, 제물포주재영국부영사 류자충, 선출직 위원 니시와키는 불참하였다. 주한미국공사관 서기관 알렌은 1893년 8월 31일부터 7개월간 주한미국대리공사로 복무하였다.

현재 공사를 진행 중인 도로를 가리켰다. 우경선 씨는 신동공사가 무슨 권한으로 B1~B2 구역 앞의 땅을 메우는지 질문하고 한국 당국과 상의한 후 공사에 착수할 것을 제의하였다. 신동공사는 이 토지가 만조선 너머에 있으므로 각국 조계의 땅이며, 밀물 때문에 도로를 건설할 수 없으므로 먼저 제방을 쌓는 것이라고 설명하였다. 또한 제방을 쌓는 비용은 신동공사가 부담할 것이라고 했다. 스트리플링 씨는 도로를 평탄화하는 과정에서 발생하는 흙을 옮길 장소로서 그곳이 최선의 장소이자 거의 유일한 장소라고 지적하였다. 우경선 씨는 신동공사가 그곳을 메우는 것을 계속 반대하고 다른 위원들이 이 일을 승인하는 데 항의하였다.

④ 폭스 씨는 제물포주재영국부영사관에서 해관을 지나 제방에 이르는 도로의 상태에 주목하고, 이 도로는 현재 공사를 진행 중인 도로 일부보다 훨씬 중요하니 즉시 보수하자고 제안하였다.

⑤ 감리에게 보낼 답장과 관련하여 크린 씨는 각국 조계의 도로를 평탄화하는 일은 한국 정부의 의무라고 단언하였다. 스트리플링 씨는 허드 씨가 신동공사에 보내 온 편지를 거론하면서 각국 외교 대표들이 감리에게 즉시 평탄화 작업을 시작하라고 지시한 사실을 밝혔다. 크린 씨가 발의하였다. "현재 평탄화 작업을 진행 중인 몇몇 도로를 제외하고 공식 도면에 표시된 모든 도로에 평탄화 작업을 시작해 달라고 감리에게 요청합시다. 또한 작업이 완료되기 전에는 비용을 지불하지 맙시다." 노세 씨가 재청하였으며 통과되었다.

⑥ 크린 씨는 묘지 문제로 외아문 독판에게 편지를 보낸 사실을 알렸다. 한국 당국이 한국인들의 무덤을 옮기겠다는 약속을 지키지 않았기 때문에 외국인 묘지의 외관이 좋지 않다는 내용이었다. 외아문 독판은

즉시 한국인들의 무덤을 옮기겠다고 답변하였다고 한다. 한편 감리는 이 일과 관련하여 지시를 받았으며 그대로 시행할 것이지만, 무덤 주인들이 멀리 살고 있고 그들과 상의해야 하므로 당장은 어렵다고 이야기하였다. 폭스 씨는 전임 감리가 이 일을 약속한 것이 4년 전인데 지금도 무덤이 그대로 있다고 지적하였다. 크린 씨가 발의하였다. "서기는 감리에게 앞으로 8일 안에 무덤을 옮겨 달라고 요청하십시오. 그렇지 않으면 신동공사가 직접 옮길 것입니다." 폭스 씨가 재청하였으며 만장일치로 통과되었다. 우경선 씨는 감리가 한국인들의 무덤을 즉시 옮기되 공원에 있는 무덤도 같이 옮겨야 한다고 발언하였다.[48)]

⑦ 타운젠드 씨는 묘지 둘레에 옹벽을 쌓기 위하여 500달러를 책정하겠다고 공지하였다. 신동공사는 이 공사에 즉시 착수하기로 결정하였다.

⑧ 타운젠드 씨는 간단한 식사를 위하여 휴회하였다가 오후 2시 30분에 속개하자고 발의하였다. 폭스 씨가 재청하였으며 통과되었다. 감리대행은 회의장을 떠났다. 크린 씨는 회의장에 동석해 준 그에게 신동공사를 대표하여 감사의 뜻을 밝혔다.

⑨ 오후 2시 45분에 회의를 속개하였다. 참석자는 오전과 같았다.

⑩ 신동공사 회관에 놓을 가구에 대하여 의논하였다. 타운젠드 씨는 가구를 구입하였으므로 다음 회의를 신동공사 회관에서 개최할 수도 있다고 이야기하였다.

⑪ 치안에 대하여 의논하였다. 서기는 총세무사가 신동공사 회장에

---

48) 한국인들의 무덤을 옮기는 일은 1889년 3월 27일 선출직 위원 타운젠드가 발의하고 제물포주재일본부영사 하야시가 재청하여 통과된 사안이었다. 『제물포 각국 조계지 회의록 1』 77~78쪽을 참고할 것.

게 보내 온 편지를 낭독하였다. 경찰의 보호가 충분치 않다며 불평하는 내용이었다. 논의 후 총세무사에게 보낼 답장의 초안을 다음과 같이 마련하였다. (1) 신동공사는 각국 조계의 재산을 보호하고 거리를 순찰하기 위하여 할 수 있는 모든 일을 할 것입니다. 그러나 해관의 보호를 위하여 경비원을 고용하는 것은 해관 당국의 의무라고 생각합니다. (2) 신동공사는 총세무사가 계속해서 손실을 입고 있는 점을 유감스럽게 생각합니다. 그러나 각국 조계에서 발생하는 모든 좀도둑질을 막는 것까지는 우리가 할 수 없습니다. (3) 사건이 신동공사 경찰국에 즉시 알려지지 않은 것을 유감스럽게 생각합니다. 만일 그랬다면 신동공사는 해당 미국 군함의 함장과 의사소통할 수 있었을 것입니다. 군함의 선원들을 상대할 때 유일하게 믿을 수 있는 사람은 함장입니다. (4) 해당 인물은 이미 처벌을 받았습니다. 신동공사는 이러한 종류의 사건들에 대처하는 경찰국장 1명과 경찰관 6명을 두고 있습니다.[49)]

⑫ 스트리플링 씨가 발의하였다. "신동공사가 보내는 모든 편지의 초안을 신동공사 회의 때 만듭시다." 재청하는 사람이 없었다. 그는 제안을 철회해 달라는 요청을 거절하였다.

⑬ 선박을 등록하는 일에 대하여 의논하였다. 서기는 총세무사가 보내 온 편지를 낭독하였다. 신동공사 소유의 선박 몇 척이 등록되어 있지 않다는 내용이었다. 각국 외교 대표들이 잠정적으로 승인한 부두 규정의 합법성과 관련하여, 크린 씨와 노세 씨는 그들이 각기 자국민만을

49) 총세무사가 신동공사 경찰력에 대하여 불만을 제기한 이 사건은 1893년 7월 24일 인천해관장대리가 신동공사 경찰 조직에 대한 정보를 요청한 일의 연장선상에 있는 것으로 보인다. 1893년 7월 24일 회의록을 참고할 것.

대상으로 규정을 만들고 있다고 언급하였다. 우경선 씨는 이 선박들이 싣고 있던 돌이 어디에서 온 것인지 질문하고 중국인 도급업자가 공급한 것이라는 답변을 들었다. 스트리플링 씨는 이 선박들이 돌을 나르는 데에만 사용되었다고 설명하였다. 타운젠드 씨는 돌을 버리는 것을 통제하는 일이 해관 당국의 권리라고 인정하면서도 편지에 드러난 총세무사의 어조에는 반대하였다. 크린 씨, 노세 씨, 폭스 씨도 같은 의견이었다. 스트리플링 씨는 신동공사 선박들이 다른 선박에 손상을 입히지 않을 곳에만 돌을 버렸다고 이야기하였으나, 노세 씨는 이 선박들이 부둣가에 버린 돌 때문에 어떤 선박들이 손상을 입었다고 발언하였다. 우경선 씨는 돌을 버릴 장소를 한 군데 정하자고 제안하였다. 논의 후 크린 씨가 다음과 같이 발의하였다. "해관 당국에 공식적으로 알립시다. 신동공사는 신동공사 소유의 선박들에 '신동공사 1호'와 '신동공사 2호'라고 표시하고 앞으로 돌을 버릴 때마다 해관에 공지할 것입니다." 스트리플링 씨가 반대하였으나 통과되었다. 크린 씨는 신동공사의 선박들을 등록하는 일이 불필요하다고 생각하였으나 다른 위원들은 우려하였다. 신동공사는 총세무사에게 보내는 답장에 다음 내용을 넣기로 했다. "신동공사는 우리의 선박들을 포위하고 구금한 해관의 조치에 반대합니다. 또한 해관이 이 문제에서 신동공사를 적절히 배려하지 않았다고 생각합니다." 우경선 씨는 이 선박들이 포위되었을 당시 그것들이 신동공사의 소유라는 사실이 알려지지 않았다고 설명하였다. 스트리플링 씨는 다음 회의 때 신동공사가 선박 허가의 주체가 되어야 한다는 내용을 제안하겠다고 예고하였다.

⑭ 노세 씨가 발의하였다. "제물포 일본인 소방대가 각국 조계 14개

장소의 도로변 지하에 목조 물탱크를 설치하는 것을 허가합시다. 이는 사계절 내내 물을 비축하여 화재에 대비하기 위한 것으로, 그밖에는 물을 구할 수 있는 다른 좋은 방법이 없습니다." 물탱크는 높이가 6.5피트, 윗부분의 폭이 6피트, 아랫부분의 폭이 5.5피트, 입구의 폭이 약 2.5피트였다(그림 첨부). 노세 씨는 일본 조계에도 이와 비슷한 것들이 있고 비용은 일본인 소방대가 부담할 것이며, 토지소유주들에게 허락을 받은 후 설치를 진행할 것이라고 설명하였다. 타운젠드 씨가 재청하였다. 노세 씨에게 감사의 뜻을 밝히면서 만장일치로 통과되었다.

⑮ 스트리플링 씨가 발의하였다. "선거가 다가옵니다. 지난 선거 때 해관장대리와 제물포주재영국대리부영사와 복음전도협회 대리인이 투표하였는데, 그들 중 누구도 등록된 토지소유주가 아니었고 위임 투표는 애초에 금지되어 있습니다.[50] 각국 외교 대표들께 편지를 써서 그들의 투표가 합법적인지 아닌지 문의합시다." 재청하는 사람이 없었다. 우경선 씨는 중요한 업무가 있다며 회의장을 떠났다.

⑯ 스트리플링 씨가 발의하였다. "신동공사는 지난 1월 1일 이후 열린 모든 회의록의 요약문과 회의석상에 제출된 공식 편지들을 현지 신문과 기타 신문에 싣거나 모든 토지소유주들께 사본을 제공해야 합니다." 재청하는 사람이 없었다. 그가 다시 발의하였다. "앞으로는 날짜와 요일을 기입한 회의소집장을 인쇄하여 모든 위원들께 보냅시다." 타운젠드

50) 스트리플링은 1892년 12월 7일 제물포주재영국대리부영사 존슨과 영국국교회 한국선교부 책임자 코프가 투표권을 행사한 데 불만을 제기하였다. 그는 이전 선출직 위원 선거 때도 등록된 토지소유주가 아닌 사람이 투표권을 갖는 데 항의한 바 있다. 인천해관장대리의 투표권 문제는 『제물포 각국 조계지 회의록 1』, 24~29쪽과 103~104쪽을 참고할 것.

씨가 재청하였으며 통과되었다.

⑰ 가로수에 대하여 의논하였다. 타운젠드 씨는 2년 전 얼마간의 돈을 들여 가로수를 심었으나 대부분이 절도나 훼손으로 사라졌다고 이야기하였다. 그는 각국 조계에 심을 가로수를 구입하기 위하여 100달러를 책정하는 문제를 발의하겠다고 공지하였다.

⑱ 오후 5시 30분에 회의를 마쳤다. 다음 회의는 10월 첫째 주에 개최하기로 했다.

·· – **원문** – ··

① Meeting held at H. B. M.'s vice Consulate on September 2nd 1893, at 11 a. m. Present: Mr. Krien (in chair), Mr. Nosse (vice Pres.), Messrs. Townsend, Stripling, Wu and Fox (Hon. Sec.)

② The acting Kamni was present under instructions from the President of the Foreign Office, ostensibly at the request of Mr. Krien. Mr. Krien explained that he had asked the President to instruct Mr. Wu, the Corean official member of the Council, to attend, and not the Kamni, a mistake evidently having been made in the names. As, however, there were one or two matters which the Council wished to settle with the Kamni, he suggested that the Kamni should be invited to remain and listen to the proceedings. Mr. Stripling objected on the ground that the Corean Government were already represented by Mr. Wu, and that on a previous occasion the Council had refused to allow a non-member to be present. The question was then put to the vote and Mr. Krien's proposal carried. The Kamni kindly consented so remain and answer any questions the Council wished to pus to him. The minutes of the previous meeting were then read and confirmed.

③ The Hon. Secretary read out a letter from the Kamni, requesting information about the roads at present being graded by the Council. Mr. Stripling pointed out on the plan of the Settlement the roads that had already been graded and the ones the Executive Committee had in hand at present. Mr. Wu wished to know what authority the Council had for filling in the ground in front of lots B1 and 2 and suggested that the Corean authorities ought to have been consulted before undertaking the work. It was explained that the ground in question was beyond high water mark and therefore belonged to the General Foreign Settlement. Also that the road marked in the plan could not be made unless an embankment were first built to support it and prevent the sea washing it away. The expense of the wall at present being constructed for that purpose would be borne by the Council. Mr. Stripling pointed out that the earth taken from the roads being graded must be thrown somewhere, and that this was the best and almost only, place available. Mr. Wu still objected to this place being filled in at present, and as the other members approved of the work, begged to lodge a protest against its being confirmed.

④ Mr. Fox drew attention to the state of the road leaching from the British vice Consulate to the Bund, past the Custom House, and suggested that it should be required at once, it being of much greater importance than some of the roads at present being graded by the Executive Committee.

⑤ Answer to Kamni's letter. Mr. Krien said it was the duty of the Corean government to grade roads in the Settlement and Mr. Stripling referred to a letter from Mr. Heard to the Council, in which they were informed that the Kamni had been instructed to proceed with the grading at once. Mr. Krien proposed that the Kamni should be informed that it was intended to grade all the roads marked in the official plan, but at present certain roads (to be specified) were being graded, and until they were finished their length, and expense could not be given. Seconded by Mr. Nosse, & carried.

⑥ Cemetery. Mr. Krien said that he had written to the President of the Foreign Office pointing out, the disgraceful state of the Foreign Cemetery owing to the Corean Authorities having neglected to remove some Corean graves, as they had after promised, and that the President had replied that they should be removed at once. The Kamni was informed of this and said he would have the graves removed, but that it could not be done at once, as the owners lived far away and would have to be consulted. Mr. Fox pointed out that the Kamni's predecessor had said the same thing four years ago and on several subsequent occasions, yet the graves still remained. Mr. Krien proposed that the Hon. Secty request the Kamni to have the graves removed within eight days, after which period, if not done, the Council would do it themselves. Seconded by Mr. Fox and carried unanimously. Mr. Wu said the Kamni would have the graves removed at once, together with some in the Public Garden.

⑦ Mr. Townsend gave notice of an appropriation of $500, for the purpose of building a wall round the cemetery. It was decided that the work should be taken in hand at once.

⑧ Mr. Townsend proposed that the meeting be adjourned for tiffin, till 2.30. Seconded by Mr. Fox & carried. The Kamni took his leave at this point being thanked by Mr. Krien on behalf of the Council for his kindness in attending.

⑨ Meeting confirmed at 2.45 p. m. Members present as before.

⑩ Furniture for Municipal Buildings. Mr. Townsend said that the furniture was being bought and that the next meeting could probably be held in the Municipal Building.

⑪ Policing of Settlement. The Hon. Secretary read out a letter from the Commissioner of Customs to the President of the Municipal Council, complaining of insufficient Police protection. After some discussion, the following answers to the Commissioner's complaints were drafted by the Council. (1) that the Council will do all they can to protect property and patrol the streets in the General Foreign Settlement, but they are of opinion that it is the duty of the Customs authorities to hire watchmen for their own protection, as is done elsewhere. (2) The Council regrets the losses the Commissioner has sustained, but cannot undertake to prevent every petty larceny that occurs in the Settlement. (3) The Council regrets that notice was not given at once to the Municipal police authorities, so that the Captain of the American man of war could have been communicated with; this being the only recourse when dealing with sailors from man of war. (4) The man has been punished already. The Council employs a Police constable and six policemen who should be applied to in cases of this kind.

⑫ Mr. Stripling proposed "that all official letters emanating from the Council be drafted at the meeting of the Council." Not seconded. Mr. Stripling was asked to withdraw his proposal, but refused.

⑬ Registration of Boats. The Hon. Secretary read out a letter from the Commissioner of Customs drawing attention to the fact that some boats belonging to the Council were not registered. As regards the legality of the Harbour Regulations which had only been approved provisionally by the Foreign Representatives. Mr. Krien and Mr. Nosse said they were building so far as their nationals were concerned. Mr. Wu asked where the stones carried in the Municipal boats had come from. He was informed that they were supplied by a Chinese contractor. Mr. Stripling explained that the boats were only used for carrying stones. Mr. Townsend admitted the right of the Customs authorities to control the "dumping" of stones, but objected to the tone of the Commissioner's letter. Messrs. Krien, Nosse, and Fox concurred in this opinion. Mr. Stripling said that the stones thrown from Municipal boats were always put in places where they could not obstruct or damage other craft. Mr. Nosse remarked that boats had been damaged by stone thrown with the Harbour. Mr. Wu suggested that a place should be fixed for the "dumping" of stones. After some further discussion, Mr. Krien proposed, seconded by Mr. Fox "that the Customs authorities be officially informed that the boats owned by the Municipal Council had been marked "M. C. Nos. 1 and 2" and that notice would be given whenever stones were to be landed." Mr. Stripling objected. Mr. Krien proposal carried. With regard to the Municipal boats being registered, Mr. Krien thought this was not necessary, other members concerning. The Council agreed that the following clause be added to the letter "that the Council object to the action of the Customs authorities in seizing and detaining there boats and are of opinion that a proper regard for the Municipal Council has not been shown in the matter." Mr. Wu explained that when the boats were seized, it was not known that they belonged to the Council. Mr. Stripling gave notice of a proposal for the licensing of boats by the Municipal Council, at the next meeting.

⑭ Mr. Nosse proposed "that the Council give permission to the Chemulpo Japanese Fire Brigade to sink underneath the roadside wooden tubs at fourteen different places in the General Foreign Settlement to keep water all the seasons, to be always ready in time of fire, there being no other reliable way to get the water." Height of tub 6½ ft. Breadth 6 ft. at top. Breadth 5½ ft. at bottom. Wooden mouth to be about 2½ ft. broad (Diagram appended). Mr. Nosse explained that similar wells were being placed in the Japanese Settlement and that the cost of the ones in question would be defrayed by the fire Brigade. The holders of that lots in front of which these tubs were to be lowered would of course first be asked and obtained for their permission. Seconded by Mr. Townsend. Proposal carried unanimously with thanks to Mr. Nosse.

⑮ Mr. Stripling proposed "that in view of the coming election and the fact that at previous elections votes had been cast by the Acting Commissioner of Customs, the Acting British Vice Consul and the local agent for the Society for the Propagation of the Gospel. Neither of whom are personally registered landholders, and, as voting by proxy is not allowed that the Council address a letter to the Representatives asking them to kindly favour the Council with their opinion as to whether the votes in question were, or were not, legal." Not seconded. Mr. Wu withdrew at this point having important business to attend to.

⑯ Mr. Stripling proposed "that for the benefit of the landholders a precis of the Minutes of all meetings held since the 1st of January last, and of all meeting thereafter, together with the official correspondence laid upon the table, be published in the local and other papers, or that a copy be supplied to each of the landholders." Not seconded. Mr. Stripling proposed "that in future the summons convening the Municipal meetings be on a printed form in which only the day and dates require to be filled in and that a copy of the summons be sent to each member of the Council." Seconded by Mr. Townsend & carried.

⑰ Trees in Foreign Settlement. Mr. Townsend said that a sum of money had been voted two years ago for trees, most of which had been stolen or destroyed. He now gave notice of an appropriation of $100 to purchase trees to be planted in the Settlement.

⑱ The meeting closed at 5.30 p. m. Next meeting was fixed for the first week in October.

1893년 10월 10일 회의록

·· – **번역문** – ··

① 10월 10일 오전 10시 30분 제물포주재영국부영사관에서 신동공사 회의를 개회하였다. 크린 씨(의장), 노세 씨, 타운젠드 씨, 스트리플링 씨, 폭스 씨가 참석하였다.[51] 류자충 씨가 보내 온 편지를 낭독하였다. 긴급한 업무 때문에 회의에 불참한다며 양해를 구하는 내용이었다. 지난 번 회의록을 낭독하였다. 각국 조계에 소화전을 설치하는 일과 관련하여 노세 씨가 제안한 내용에 "허락을 받은 후"라는 구절을 넣고 승인하였다.

② 감리에게 편지를 써서 도로평탄화 작업 비용 2,100달러의 지불을 독촉하기로 결의하였다. 각국 영사들과 현지 한국인 관계자들은 신동공사가 이 금액을 정당하게 청구할 수 있다는 데 동의하였다. 노세 씨는 합의서의 사본을 영사들에게 돌렸다고 언급하였다. 신동공사도 사본 1부를 얻기로 결정하였다.[52]

③ 묘지와 가로수에 대하여 의논하였다. 타운젠드 씨는 지난 번 회의 때 자신이 제안한 것과 관련하여 묘지 둘레에 옹벽을 쌓는 비용 500달러와 가로수를 심는 비용 100달러의 지출을 확정하자고 발의하였다. 스트리플링 씨가 재청하였으며 만장일치로 통과되었다.

---

51) 주한미국대리공사 알렌, 제물포주재중국부영사 류자충, 인천항 경찰관 우경선, 선출직 위원 니시와키는 불참하였다.

52) 이렇게 하여 신동공사는 (각국 조계 토지소유주들이 납부한) 1892년도 세금 2,541.93달러와 도로평탄화 작업 비용 2,100달러를 합하여 4,641.93달러를 감리에게 청구하기 시작하였다.

④ 도로 정비에 대하여 의논하였다. 폭스 씨는 각국 조계의 동쪽 경계를 이루는 도로의 평탄화 작업과 배수 공사가 부분적으로만 되어 있다고 발언하였다. 도로 윗부분은 빗물에 의하여 서서히 유실되어 회복불가능한 상태가 되었다는 것이다. 그는 이 도로에 당장 평탄화 작업을 시작할 수 없으나 곧 정비를 시작할 것이라는 답변을 들었다.

⑤ 크린 씨는 외아문 독판이 제방을 따라 너비 15미터의 도로를 건설하는 데 동의하였다는 사실을 신동공사에 알렸다. 다음과 같이 결의하였다. "각국 외교 대표들이 도로의 위치를 결정할 가능성은 없어 보이지만, 도로 건설은 긴급한 사안인 만큼 그들께 편지를 써서 이 사실을 알립시다. 또한 한국 정부에 제방 축조를 요청해 달라고 부탁합시다. 그렇지 않으면 도로를 완공할 수 없습니다."

⑥ 경찰력에 대하여 의논하였다. 폭스 씨가 발의하고 노세 씨가 재청하였다. "각국 조계의 순찰, 특히 야간 순찰을 위하여 고용한 현재의 경찰력이 적절하지 않으니 경찰관의 수를 6명에서 12명으로 늘립시다." 폭스 씨는 주간에는 1명이 각국 조계 전역을 담당하지만 야간에는 1명이 조계 동쪽 끝, 1명이 일본 및 중국 조계의 북쪽을 순찰하며, 제방과 부두, 조계 서쪽 끝은 완전히 비보호 상태라고 설명하였다. 일본 조계는 각국 조계의 4분의 1 규모이지만 매일 밤 4명이 근무한다고 한다. 타운젠드 씨와 스트리플링 씨는 비용이 많이 든다는 이유로 반대하였으나 현재의 경찰력이 매우 불충분하다는 점에는 동의하였다. 폭스 씨는 주민들이 경찰의 보호가 불충분하다며 불평한다고 언급하였다. 타운젠드 씨는 월급을 3달러 인상하고 근무 시간을 하루 12시간으로 늘리되 경찰관의 수는 6명을 유지하자는 수정안을 발의하였다. 스트리플링 씨가 재청하였다. 폭스 씨는

타운젠드 씨의 방법이 효과를 거둘 수 없을 것이라고 주장하면서도 시도해 보는 데 찬성하였다. 통과되었다.

⑦ 해관장대리가 보내 온 편지 두 통을 낭독하였다. 하나는 경찰, 하나는 선박 등록에 대한 내용이었다.

⑧ 오후 2시까지 휴회하였다. 2시 15분에 위원들이 모였다.

⑨ 폭스 씨는 아이와 개, 기타 요소가 테니스장을 망치지 않도록 테니스장 둘레에 작은 울타리를 둘러도 되는지 문의하였다. 반대하는 사람이 없었다.

⑩ 노세 씨는 제물포의용소방대가 강력 펌프(펌프구입비 400달러, 운송비 30달러, 도합 430달러)를 구입할 수 있도록 300달러를 기부하자고 발의하였다. 그는 소방대가 각국 조계에 훌륭한 소방서를 세워 잘 관리하는 것은 물론 화재가 일어날 경우 주민들의 재산을 보호할 것이라고 설명하였다. 또한 요코하마에 중고 소방차 한 대를 살 수 있는 기회가 있다고 언급하였다. 타운젠드 씨는 신동공사가 일정 비용을 부담하여 소방차의 소유권을 갖자고 발의하였다. 논의 후 노세 씨는 소방차 구입을 위하여 최대 300달러를 책정하는 문제를 발의하겠다고 공지하였다.

⑪ 스트리플링 씨가 발의하였다. "각국 조계 부두에 정기적으로 드나드는 임대 선박은 신동공사의 허가와 규제를 받아야 합니다." 그는 금액 변경이 가능하게끔 요금표를 만들었다며 그것을 모든 선박에 적용하자고 이야기하였다. 폭스 씨는 현재 신동공사의 권한으로는 그러한 규정을 집행하는 것이 불가능하다고 지적하였다. 논의가 이루어졌으나 재청하는 사람이 없었다.

⑫ 스트리플링 씨는 제물포주재영국부영사(대리), 코프 주교, 해관장

(대리)의 투표권이 적법한가 하는 질문을 또 다시 제기하였다. 그는 각국 외교 대표들로부터 이 문제에 관한 답변 듣기를 고대하였다. 규정상 위임 투표는 허용되지 않는다. 폭스 씨는 승인된 대리인 또는 법인 대표가 투표할 경우 위임 투표가 아니며, 그들의 투표가 불허된다면 각국 조계의 매우 넓은 지역이 대표성을 갖지 못하게 된다고 발언하였다. 논의 후 이 문제에 대하여 더 이상 언급하지 않기로 결정하였으나, 스트리플링 씨는 다음 선거 때 이의를 제기하겠다고 밝혔다.

⑬ 노세 씨는 최근 세금 납부와 관련하여 어떤 일이 이루어졌는지 문의한 후, 앞으로는 감리에게 세금을 내지 말고 다이이치은행에 내자고 제안하였다. 스트리플링 씨가 발의하였다. "연말 잔고는 1,500달러 정도로 추산됩니다. 한국 정부로부터 도로평탄화 작업 비용 2,100달러(합의서 동봉)를 받을 것이니 세금을 50% 감면해도 무방합니다. 각국 외교 대표들께 편지를 써서 금년도 세금을 반액만 낼 수 있도록 한국 정부와 조율해 달라고 합시다." 타운젠드 씨가 재청하였으며 통과되었다.

⑭ 다음 회의는 11월 둘째 주에 개최하기로 했다. 오후 4시에 회의를 마쳤다.

–원문–

① Meeting held at H. B. M.'s Vice Consulate on October 10th at 10. 30 a. m. Present: Mr. Krien (in Chair), Messrs. Nosse, Townsend, Stripling and Fox. A letter was read from Mr. Liu excusing himself on account of urgent business. The minutes of the last meeting were read and confirmed, after the words "and obtained" had been added to Mr. Nosse's proposal with regard to the sinking of fire-wells in the Settlement.

② Grading roads. Resolved that a letter be addressed to the Kamni pressing for payment of the $2,100, the sum agreed upon at the meeting of the Foreign Consuls & Corean local authorities as a just Settlement of the Council's claim for grading roads. Mr. Nosse mentioned that copies of the agreement had been sent round to the Consuls. It was decided to obtain one for the Municipal Council.

③ Cemetery and trees. Mr. Townsend moved that the appropriation recommended at the last meeting of $500 for building a wall round the Cemetery and $100 for trees to be planted in the Settlement, be now confirmed. Seconded by Mr. Stripling — carried unanimously.

④ Repairs to road. Mr. Fox drew attention to the state of the road forming the Eastern boundary of the Settlement, part of which only had been graded and drained. The upper part was being gradually washed away and rendered impossible by the rain. He was informed that the road would be repaired immediately but could not be graded at present.

⑤ Bundroad. Mr. Krien informed the Council that the President of the Foreign Office agreed to a 15 metre road being made along the sea-wall. Resolved, that as there seemed no likelihood of the F. F. R. R.'s deciding where the road should be, and as its construction was of urgent necessity, a letter be addressed to the F. F. R. R.'s informing them that the Council have decided to proceed with the construction of a 15 metre broad road along the sea-wall, at once, and requesting them to ask the Corean Government to build up the sea-wall, otherwise the road could not be completed.

⑥ Police. Mr. Fox proposed, seconded by Mr. Nosse "that in view of the inadequacy of the present force of Police employed by the Council to patrol the Settlement especially during the night time, its number be increased from six to twelve constables." Mr. Fox explained that in the day time only one man was on duty, at a time for the whole Settlement, and during the night only two, one of whom remained at the Eastern end while the other patrolled the street running along the North of the Japanese & Chinese Settlement. The Bund, jetty & Western end of the Settlement were left totally unprotected. The Japanese Settlement, about ¼ the size of the Foreign Settlement, had four men on duty every night. Messrs. Townsend & Stripling opposed the proposal on the ground of the extra expense on increase of the force would curtail, and also because they, were of opinion that the present force was quite sufficient. Mr. Fox mentioned that frequent complaints had been made by residents of insufficient police protection. Mr. Townsend proposed an amendment to the effect that the wages of the Municipal Police should be raised $3 each per month and that the hours of duty be raised to twelve hours per day and the number be restricted to six at present. Seconded by Mr. Stripling. Mr. Fox maintained that this would not have the desired effect, but agreed to the proposal being given a trial. The amendment was then carried.

⑦ Two letters from the Commissioner of Customs referring to Police and Registration were then read.

⑧ Meeting adjourned to 2 p. m. Members reassembled at 2. 15 p. m.

⑨ Tennis Court. Mr. Fox asked if the Council had any objection to a small fence being put round the lawn tennis court in the Public Garden, so as to present children, dogs and other nuisances spoiling the Court. The Council had no objection.

⑩ Fire Brigade. Mr. Nosse proposed that an appropriation of a sum of $300 be made towards the subscription to the Chemulpo Volunteer Fire Brigade for the purchase of one powerful pump (the cost of it being $400, and freight

$30=$430) in consideration of the great amount of work undertaken by the Brigade for the protection of property against fires in the General Foreign Settlement, where one fire station, everything complete is to be established and kept always in good order. Mr. Nosse mentioned that an opportunity presented itself for purchasing a seconded hand fire engine in Yokohama. Mr. Townsend suggested that the M. C. should take a share in the purchase and ownership of the engine. After some discussion, Mr. Nosse gave notice of an appropriation of not more than $300 for the part purchase by the Council of a fire engine.

⑪ Proposed by Mr. Stripling "that the boats plying for hire at the jetties within the Foreign Settlement be licensed and regulated by the Municipal Council." Mr. Stripling said he had drawn up a table of changes, subject to alterations, which would be applied in every licensed boat. Mr. Fox pointed out that with the present Municipal Police force, it would be impossible to enforce such a regulation. After some further discussion, the proposal was not seconded.

⑫ Mr. Stripling again referred to the question of the legality of the votes of the Act. British Vice Consul, Bishop Corfe and the Commissioner of Customs. He desired that the F. F. R. R.'s should be asked for their opinion on the subject; Voting by proxy was not allowed by the Regulations. Mr. Fox begged to state that the vote of an accredited agent or representative of a Corporate body was not a vote by proxy within the meaning of the regulation, and that if these votes were disallowed, a very considerable portion of the land in the Foreign Settlement would be unrepresented. After some further discussion the matter was allowed to drop, Mr. Stripling announcing his intention of challenging the votes in question at the next election.

⑬ Taxes. Mr. Nosse asked if anything had been done with regard to the payment of taxes for the present years. It was suggested that the money should be paid into the First National Bank instead of to the Kamni. Mr. Stripling proposed, seconded by Mr. Townsend "that as the estimated balance at the end of the year will be about $1,500 with a additional amount of $2,100 due (by the enclosed agreement) from the Corean Government for the grading of roads, that half rents only will be necessary, and that the Representatives be asked to kindly arrange with the Corean Government that half taxes only be collected for the current year." Carried.

⑭ The next meeting was fixed for the second week in November. The meeting closed at 4 p. m.

1893년 11월 16일 회의록

·· - 번역문 - ··

① 11월 16일 오전 10시 30분 신동공사 회관에서 신동공사 회의를 개회하였다. 크린 씨(의장), 노세 씨, 류자충 씨, 타운젠드 씨, 알렌 씨, 스트리플링 씨, 폭스 씨(서기)가 참석하였다.[53)]

② 크린 씨는 신동공사의 전용 공간에서 첫 번째 회의를 열게 된 것을 축하하는 짧은 연설을 하고, 한 해 동안 신동공사 회의 때마다 공간을 빌려 준 제물포주재영국부영사에게 감사의 뜻을 전하였다.[54)]

③ 타운젠드 씨는 일본인 경찰관 1명이 사망한 사실을 보고하였다. 신동공사는 그의 장례식을 위하여 30달러를 지급하기로 했다.

④ 신동공사는 사바친 씨에게 집행위원회와 협력하여 각국 조계 도면을 완성해 달라고 요청하되, 각국 외교 대표들이 다음 회의를 열기 전까지 도면을 완성할 수 있는지도 문의하기로 했다.

⑤ 지난 번 회의 때 소방차를 구입하기 위하여 300달러를 책정하자는 이야기가 있었다. 노세 씨는 일본인 소방대의 자금 사정이 넉넉하지 않아 소방차 구입을 위하여 돈을 낼 수도 소방차 유지비를 댈 수도 없다

---

53) 인천항 경찰관 우경선과 선출직 위원 니시와키는 불참하였다.

54) 신동공사는 1891년 5월 7일 D44 구역(3,780㎡)을 매입하고 10월 22일 부동산 권리증을 받았다. 1892년 봄부터 신동공사 회관 건축을 계획하여 5월 10일 설계도를 제시하였으며, 6월 7일 입찰 공고를 내고 8월 25일 중국인 건축업자를 선정하였다. 완공된 건물의 일부는 1893년 6월 30일부터 신동공사 경찰국장 및 경찰관들의 숙소로 사용되었다. 신동공사 회관 설계도는 『제물포 각국 조계지 회의록 1』 251쪽을 참고할 것.

고 발언하였다. 소방대는 현재로서는 이 문제를 보류하기를 희망하였다. 따라서 소방차 구입 자금은 확정되지 않았다.

⑥ 타운젠드 씨는 신동공사의 금년 지출 내역, 가용 잔고의 추정치, 내년 지출 내역의 추정치를 담은 성명서를 제출하였다. 세금을 50% 감면하는 문제에 관하여 의논하였다. 10월 24일자 편지에서 각국 외교 대표들이 요청한 대로, 서기는 이 성명서를 각국 외교 대표들에게 전달하라는 지시를 받았다.

⑦ 서기는 감리에게 토지소유주들의 명단 최신판을 요청하라는 지시를 받았다.

⑧ 스트리플링 씨의 임기가 끝났으므로 그의 후임을 뽑는 선거를 12월 6일 오전 10시부터 오후 1시까지 실시하기로 결정하였다.[55)]

⑨ 다음 회의는 12월 7일에 개최하기로 했다.

·· – **원문** – ··

① Meeting held at the Municipal Buildings on November 16th at 10. 30 a. m. Present: Mr. Krien (in chair), Messrs. Nosse, Liu, Townsend, Allen, Stripling, Fox (Hon. Sec.)

② Mr. Krien in a short speech congratulate the Council on meeting for the first time in their own board room, and thanked the British Acting Vice Consul for the loan of a room at the Consulate during the present year.

③ Police. Mr. Townsend reported that one of the Council's Japanese police

55) 스트리플링은 1891년 12월 2일 선거에서 10표를 얻어 1892~1893년 선출직 위원으로 복무하였다. 같은 날 니시와키는 12표를 얻어 임기 3년의 선출직 위원이 되었다.

constables had just died. The Council voted a sum of $30 to defray his funeral expenses.

④ Plan of the Settlement. It was decided that Mr. Sabatin, in conjunction with the Executive Committee, should be requested to complete the plan of the General Foreign Settlement, if possible before the next meeting of the Foreign Representatives.

⑤ Fire Engine. On a proposal to confirm the appropriation of a sum of $30 for the part purchase of Fire Engine, made at last meeting. Mr. Nosse said that the Japanese Fire Brigade had not at present sufficient funds at their disposal to take part in the purchase, and afterwards maintain this fire engine. They desired that the matters should be allowed to remain over for the present. The appropriation was accordingly not confirmed.

⑥ Municipal Council's Budget. Mr. Townsend presented a statement showing the expenses incurred by Council during the present year, the estimated balance in hand, and estimated expenditure for next year. After some discussion on the subject of half taxes, the secretary was requested to forward this statement to the Foreign Representatives for their perusal in accordance with their request in a letter to the Secretary, dated Oct. 24th.

⑦ List of land-holders. The Secretary was instructed to ask the Kamni for a list of land-holders compiled up to date.

⑧ Election. The election of a member of the Council to fill the vacancy caused by the retirement of Mr. Stripling, was fixed for December 6th next between of 10 a. m. and 1 p. m.

⑨ Next meeting to be held on the 7th of December.

1893년 12월 6일 선거록

·· – **번역문** – ··

① 1893년 12월 6일 오전 10시부터 오후 1시까지 신동공사 선출직 위원 1명을 뽑기 위한 선거를 실시하였다. 노세 씨, 류자충 씨, 우경선 씨, 폭스 씨(당연직 위원)가 참석하였다. 크린 씨와 알렌 씨는 서울에서 업무가 있어 참석하지 못했다.

② 뫼르젤 씨가 보내 온 편지(편지 1)를 낭독하였다. 당연직 위원들은 선거에 소요되는 세 시간이 충분하지 않고 선거 공지가 좀더 일찍 이루어졌어야 한다는 점에 동의하였다. 그러나 바람직하지 않은 사정—뫼르젤 씨의 증기선은 제물포로 들어오고 있었으나 꽤 멀리 있었다—을 고려하여, 부득이하게 일찍 오지 못한 사람들도 투표할 수 있도록 오후 3시에 투표함을 다시 열기로 결정하였다. (이후 뫼르젤 씨는 자신의 편지를 철회하였다.)

③ 코프 주교가 복음전도협회의 대표 자격으로, 제물포주재영국부영사 폭스 씨가 영국 정부의 대표 자격으로 투표한 후, 유권자 여러 명의 서명을 담은 항의서 두 통(편지 2와 편지 3)이 도착하였다. 두 사람에게 투표권을 주는 데 반대한다는 내용이었다. 이 문제에 대하여 의논한 결과 코프 주교의 투표권은 만장일치로 통과되었다. 폭스 씨의 투표권은 노세 씨, 류자충 씨, 우경선 씨의 찬성으로 통과되었다.

④ 오후 1시에 투표함을 완전히 닫았다가 3시에 다시 열었다. 오전에 모였던 당연직 위원들이 다시 모였다. 3시 15분에 개표를 시작하여 결

과를 알렸다. 우리탕 씨가 12표, 스트리플링 씨가 7표를 얻었으므로 우리탕 씨가 선출되었음을 선언하였다.[56)]

⑤ 1893년 12월 6일 선출직 위원 1명의 선거

순서	성명	토지
1	뤼어스	B1, B2
부재	로저스	B3
11	스트리플링	B4, D2, D4
부재	마이어(A)	C1, C2, C3, C4, D25, D26, D27, D28, D37
7	볼터	C5, C6, C7, C8, D1, D19, D33
부재	리윈눈	C9
〃	마이어(B)	C10, C11, D42
14	리키타케	C12
부재	쿠리가와	C13
〃	구마모토	C14
15	신도	C15, C16
19	뫼르젤	C17, C20, C29, C30, C31, D13
13	호리	C18, C26, C27
16	히구치	C19
17	스에나가	C21
9	우리탕	C23, C24, C28, C32, D16, D17, D30
5	니시와키	C25
8	고르샬키	D3

56) 스트리플링의 후임을 뽑는 선거에서 중국인 우리탕이 스트리플링을 이기고 선출직 위원이 되었다. 우리탕은 1889년 3월 23일 독일인 쉐니크와 볼터에 이어 초대 선출직 위원으로 뽑혔으나 두 사람과 마찬가지로 복무를 거절한 바 있다. 『제물포 각국 조계지 회의록 1』 48~53쪽과 93~94쪽을 참고할 것.

10	브링크마이어	D7, D8, D9
4	홉킨스	D10, D12[57)
부재	허치슨	D11, D12
〃	도미타	D14
18	홀링스워스	D15
3	보리오니	D18
부재	타운젠드	D21, D22, D23, D34, D35, D36
〃	알마허	D31, D32
6	영국 정부	D38
2	복음전도협회	D43
12	기무라	D50

⑥ 사본 — 편지 1[58)]

1893년 12월 5일 제물포

제물포 선거위원회 신사 여러분께,

저는 토지소유주들에게 선거일을 공지하는 회람을 보지 못하였으나, 이번 달 6일에 선거가 실시되는 것과 투표함이 오전 10시부터 오후 1시까지만 열리는 것을 알고 있습니다. 예전에는 투표함을 3시나 4시까지 열었습니다. 저는 오후 1시까지는 갈 수 없으나 이후에는 갈 수 있습니다. 저는 이 문제에 일정한 이해 관계가 있는 사람으로서 투표 시간이 짧은 데 이의를 제기하고, 예전처럼 3시나 4시까지 투표함을 열어 주실

57) 기록 과정에서 착오가 있었던 것으로 생각된다. 홉킨스는 D10 구역만 소유하였다.

58) 편지 1은 독일인 토지소유주 뫼르젤이 신동공사에 보낸 것으로 자신이 투표할 수 있도록 오후에도 투표함을 열어 달라는 내용이다. "뫼르젤 (서명)" 이하의 세 문장은 서기 폭스가 뫼르젤의 요청이 합당하지 않은 이유를 기록한 부분이다.

것을 요청합니다. 그럼 이만.

뫼르젤 (서명)

회람을 두 차례 돌린 후 신동공사 회관에 붙였다.

지난 번 회의 때 오전 10시부터 오후 1시까지 투표함을 열기로 결정하였다.

12월 18일에는 투표함을 오후 3시부터 5시까지 두 시간밖에 열지 않았다.

폭스 (서명)

⑦ 사본 — 편지 2[59)]

제물포 각국 조계의 등록된 토지소유주인 우리는 등록된 토지소유주가 아닌 제물포주재영국대리부영사 폭스 씨가 선출직 위원 선거에서 투표권을 갖는 것에 항의합니다.

1893년 12월 6일 제물포

볼터, 스트리플링, 고르샬키, 뫼르젤, 뤼어스 (서명)

⑧ 코프 주교의 투표권에 대해서도 유사한 항의가 접수되었다. 작성자는 볼터 씨였지만 볼터 씨도 뤼어스 씨도 서명하지 않았다.

---

59) 편지 2는 스트리플링을 포함한 토지소유주 5명이 신동공사에 보낸 것으로 폭스의 투표권 행사에 반대하는 내용이다. 스트리플링은 제물포주재영국(대리)부영사와 복음전도협회 대리인에게 투표권을 주면 안 된다고 계속 주장해 왔다. 흥미로운 것은 그가 영국인이었고 볼터, 고르샬키, 뫼르젤, 뤼어스는 독일인이었다는 사실이다. 무슨 이유인지는 확실치 않지만 그는 자국민인 폭스와 코프보다 독일인들과 이해 관계를 같이한 것 같다.

·· ― 원문 ― ··

① Record of the Election of one non official member of the Council on Dec. 6, 1893 from 10 a. m. to 1 p. m. Present: Messrs. Nossé, Liu, Wu, and Fox (official members), Messrs. Krien & Allen were prevented from attending by business in Seoul.

② A letter (No. 1) from Mr. Mörsel was read. The official members were of opinion that three hours were sufficient for the election, and also, that the application should have been made earlier. However, in view of the exceptionable circumstances (Mr. Mörsel's steamer having been seen in the distance approaching Chemulpo) it was decided to reopen the ballot box at 3 p. m. for a quarter of an hours, so as to give those who were unavoidably prevented from attending earlier, a chance to vote. (Mr. Mörsel afterwards withdrew his letter.)

③ After Bishop Corfe had recorded his vote (as representative of the Society for the Propagation of the Gospel), and Mr. Fox, H. M.'s Acting Vice Consul (as representative of H. M.'s Government) had voted, two protests (No. 2 & 3) were presented to the meeting, signed by several voters, against the above mentioned votes being received. As on former occasions, the question was shortly discussed by the meeting, and the vote recorded by Bishop Corfe was allowed unanimously and that of Mr. Fox, by Messrs. Nossé, Liu, and Wu.

④ The Ballot box was sealed up at 1 p. m. and reopened at 3 p. m. official members present as before. At 3. 15 the votes were counted the result announced, as follows:- Mr. Woolitang 12. Mr. Stripling 7. Mr. Woolitang was therefore declared elected by a majority.

⑤ Election of one non official member, Dec. 6, 1893.

Order of Voting	Name	Lots
1	C. Lührs	B1 & 2
absent	E. Rogers	B3
11	A. B. Stripling	B4, D2, 4
absent	H. E. Meyer	C1, 2, 3, 4, D25, 26, 27, 28, 37
7	C. Wolter	C5, 6, 7, 8, D1, 19, 33
absent	Li Yün Noon	C9
〃	Capt. F. Meyer	C10 & 11, D42
14	H. Rikitaki	C12
absent	Kurikawa	C13
〃	Kumamoto	C14
15	S. Shinto	C15, C16
19	F. H. Mörsel	C17, 20, 29, 30, 31, D13
13	Hori Kintaro	C18, 26, 27
16	S. Higuchi	C19
17	T. Suyenaga	C21
9	Woolitang	C23, 24, 28, 32, D16, 17, 30
5	C. Nishiwaki	C25
8	A. Gorschalki	D3
10	R. Brinckmeier	D7, 8, 9
4	L. A. Hopkins	D10 & 12
absent	W. Hutchison	D11 & 12
〃	S. Tomita	D14
18	T. Hollingsworth	D15
3	R. Borioni	D18
absent	W. D. Townsend	D21, 22, 23, 34, 35, 36
〃	F. Allmacher	D31 & 32
6	H. B. M's Government	D38
2	Society for the Propagation of the Gospel	D43
12	Kimura	D50

⑥ Copy — No. 1

Chemulpo, 5 December 1893

The Election Committee, Chemulpo

Gentlemen,

Although having seen no circular notifying the Land owners the date of election, I been giving to understand the same to take place the 6th Instant, and that the Poll Box is to be only open from 10 a. m. till 1 p. m, as in pervious years the Poll Box just to be open until 3 & 4 p. m. and I for one not able to attend during the above state time, but able to be present later on, and as I have some interest in the matter I protest against the shortness of time and request that the time as in previous years be extended to 3 or 4 o'clock.

I beg to remain etc.

(Sg.) F. H. Mörsel

Circular sent round the Settlement twice & then posted up at the Municipal Buildings. 10 a. m. to 1 p. m. decided at last meeting of Council. Dec. 18 Ballot box open from 3 to 5, two hours only.

(Sd) H. H. F.

⑦ Copy — No. 2

We the undersigned registered landholders in the General Foreign Settlement of Chemulpo protest against Mr. H. H. Fox, H. B. M.'s Acting Vice Consul, who is not a registered landholder in the General Foreign Settlement, being allowed to cast his vote at this meeting for the election of a registered landholder in the Council.

Chemulpo, 6th December, 1893.

(Sig.) C. Wolter, A. B. Stripling, A. Gorschalki, F. H. Mörsel, C. Lührs

⑧ A similar protest was entered against Bishop Corfe, written by Mr. Wolter, but not signed by him or Mr. Lührs.

1893년 12월 15일 회의록

·· – **번역문** – ··

① 12월 15일 오전 10시 30분 신동공사 회관. 7일에 휴회하였던 신동공사 회의를 속개하였다. 노세 씨(의장), 라인스도르프 씨, 타운젠드 씨, 우경선 씨, 니시와키 씨, 스트리플링 씨, 폭스 씨(서기)가 참석하였다. 크린 씨가 보내 온 편지를 낭독하였다. 자신은 회의에 참석하지 못하게 되었으므로 라인스도르프 씨가 참석할 것을 재가한다는 내용이었다.[60] 지난 번 회의록을 낭독하고 승인하였다.

② 스트리플링 씨는 얼마 전 선거 때 제물포주재영국대리부영사와 코프 주교가 투표권을 행사한 것이 부당하다면서, 내년도 임원 선거와 기금 책정과 관련하여 아무 것도 하지 않겠다고 밝혔다.

③ 1894년도 임원 선거를 실시하였다. 타운젠드 씨는 크린 씨를 회장으로 재선하자고 발의하였다. 폭스 씨가 재청하였으며 만장일치로 통과되었다. 폭스 씨는 노세 씨를 부회장으로 재선하자고 발의하였다. 타운젠드 씨가 재청하였으며 만장일치로 통과되었다. 타운젠드 씨는 자신이 회계로 재선되는 것을 사양하고 니시와키 씨를 추천하였다. 만장일치로 통과되었다. 타운젠드 씨는 폭스 씨를 서기로 재선하자고 발의하였다. 우경선 씨가 재청하였으며 만장일치로 통과되었다. 짧은 논의 후 만장일치로 노세 씨, 타운젠드 씨, 폭스 씨를 집행위원회로 선출하였다.

---

60) 서울주재독일총영사 크린 대신 부영사 라인스도르프가 참석하였다. 주한미국대리공사 알렌과 제물포주재중국부영사 류자충은 불참하였다.

④ 1894년도 신동공사 기금을 책정하였다. 경찰국장 봉급으로 900달러를 책정하였다. 경찰관 6명의 봉급 960달러와 관련하여 폭스 씨가 발의하고 니시와키 씨가 재청하였다. "경찰관의 수를 6명에서 8명으로 늘리고 금액을 960달러에서 1,272달러로 늘립시다." 논의 후 투표하여 다수결로 통과되었으므로(노세 씨, 우경선 씨, 니시와키 씨, 폭스 씨가 찬성하고 라인스도르프 씨와 타운젠드 씨는 반대하였다.) 경찰관 8명의 봉급으로 1,272달러를 책정하였다.[61] 노세 씨는 경찰관 제복 구입에 300달러—경찰국장 제복 50달러를 포함하여—를 지출하자고 발의하였다. 만장일치로 통과되었으므로 제복 구입에 300달러를 책정하였다. 청소부 봉급으로 240달러를 책정하였다. 니시와키 씨가 발의하고 폭스 씨가 재청하였다. "집행위원회가 지정하는 곳에 가로등 15개를 설치합시다." 논의 후 만장일치로 통과되었으므로 가로등 26개 구입비로 200달러를 책정하였다. 도로 정비에 500달러, 예비비 450달러—경찰관 숙소에 설치할 스토브 2개의 비용을 포함하여—를 책정하여 경상 지출 총액은 3,862달러가 되었다. 도로평탄화 작업에 500달러, 배수 처리와 옹벽 건설에 500달러, 신동공사 회관 가구에 100달러, 가로수에 100달러, 묘지 배치에 100달러를 책정하여 1,300달러를 임시 지출 총액으로 잡았다. 1894년도 기금 책정 총액 5,162달러에 모두 동의하였다.

⑤ 노세 씨는 우경선 씨에게 도로평탄화 작업 비용 2,100달러를 감리로부터 받아 줄 수 있는지 문의하였다. 우경선 씨는 그렇게 하겠다고 약속하였다.

---

61) 폭스는 약 2개월 전인 1893년 10월 10일 경찰력의 규모를 늘리자고 제안하였으나 비용이 많이 든다는 이유로 타운젠드와 스트리플링의 반대에 부딪힌 바 있다.

⑥ 타운젠드 씨는 토지 대부분이 이미 구역 획정된 상태인데다 크린 씨가 도면을 가지고 있기 때문에, 현재로서는 각국 조계 전역에 구역을 획정하기가 불가능하다고 밝혔다. 폭스 씨는 감리의 공문을 언급하면서 다음과 같이 발언하였다. "감리에게 부탁하여 도면을 서울에 보내는 것이 적절한 절차입니다. 감리가 외아문 독판에게 도면을 보내면 그가 각국 외교 대표들께 그것을 보낼 것입니다." 스트리플링 씨는 도면은 신동공사가 비용을 부담하였으니 신동공사의 소유이고, 신동공사가 각국 외교 대표들에게 직접 도면을 보내야 한다는 의견을 제시하였다. 또한 그는 만일 감리가 도면을 원하면 돈을 지불해야 한다고 했다. 논의 후 대다수의 위원들은 감리를 통하여 도면을 보내는 데 동의하였다. 그러나 도면이 서울에 있는 상황을 고려하고 시간도 절약하기 위하여, 크린 씨가 외아문 독판에게 도면을 보내고 감리에게 이 일을 설명하도록 서기에게 부탁하였다. 또한 서기는 크린 씨에게 편지를 써서 신동공사가 각국 조계 북서쪽 끝 해변에 도로를 놓고자 한다는 것을 각국 외교 대표들에게 알려 달라고 부탁하기로 했다. 보류 중인 현재 도면에는 이 도로를 표시하지 않았다.

⑦ 회계는 스트리플링 씨의 제안에 따라 1892~1893년도 회계 내역을 인쇄 및 출판해 달라는 요청을 받았다.

⑧ 오후 4시 30분에 회의를 마쳤다. 다음 회의 날짜는 현지 위원들이 결정하기로 했다.

-- 원문 --

① Adjourned meeting of Dec. 7 held at the Municipal Buildings on Dec. 15 at 10.30 a. m. Present:- Mr. Nossé (in Chair), Messrs. Reinsdorf, Townsend, Wu, Nishiwaki, Stripling and Fox (Hon. Sec.) A letter was read from Mr. Krien informing the Council of his inability to attend the meeting and authorising Mr. Reinsdorf to take his place. The minutes of the last meeting were then read and confirmed.

② Mr. Stripling declined to take any part in the election of officers and appropriation of funds for the ensuing year in the grounds that the votes cast at the recent election by H. B. M's Acting Vice Consul and Bishop Corfe, were irregular.

③ Election of officials for 1894:- Mr. Townsend proposed, seconded by Mr. Fox "that Mr. Krien be re-elected President for the ensuing year." Carried unanimously. Mr. Fox proposed, seconded by Mr. Townsend "the Mr. Nossé be re-elected Vice President." Carried unanimously. Mr. Townsend having refused to serve again Treasurer, he proposed Mr. Nishiwaki who was elected unanimously. Mr. Townsend proposed, seconded by Mr. Wu "that Mr. Fox be re-elected Secretary," carried unanimously. After a short discussion, the Executive Committee were unanimously elected as follows:- Messrs. Nossé, Townsend & Fox.

④ Appropriations for 1894:- Chief Constable's salary $900. On the motion to appropriation $960, wages for six police, Mr. Fox moved, seconded by Mr. Nishiwaki "that the number of police be increased from 6 to 8 and that the appropriation be increased from $960 to $1272." After some discussion the motion was put to the vote and carried by a majority. (Messrs. Nossé, Wu, Nishiwaki & Fox for; Messrs. Reinsdorf & Townsend against.) Wages of Eight police — $1272. Mr. Nossé proposed that a sum of $300 be appropriated for police uniforms (including $50 for Chief Constables). Carried unanimously. Police uniforms — $300. Scavengers — 240. Mr. Nishiwaki proposed, seconded by Mr. Fox that 15 new lamps be set up in the Settlement at places to be fixed by the Executive Committee. Carried unanimously after a discussion. Lamps (26) $200, Appropriation (cont.), Repairs to Roads $500, Contingent Expenses $450 (To include 2 stoves for Constable's quarters.), Total ordinary expenditure $3,862. Grading nub roads 500, Making drains & walls 500, Furniture for Municipal Building 100, Trees 100, Laying out cemetery 100, Total Extraordinary expenditure $1,300. Total appropriations of funds for 1894 5,162. Agreed to unanimously.

⑤ Grading accounts: Mr. Nossé asked Mr. Wu to speak to the Kamni, and if possible obtain from him, the sum of $2,100 due the Council for grading roads in the Settlement. Mr. Wu promised to do so.

⑥ Plan of Settlement: Mr. Townsend said that it would be impossible to mark out the whole Settlement at present, a good many lots had been marked out and the Plan was now in Seoul with Mr. Krien. Mr. Fox referring to the Kamni's despatch, said the proper course would be to send up the Plan to Seoul through the Kamni, who would forward it to the Foreign Office, who in their turn would lay it before the Foreign Representatives for approval & signature. Mr. Stripling was of opinion that the Plan belonged to the Council, as they had paid for it, that the Council should send the plan to the Foreign Representatives and that if the Kamni wished for a plan he should pay for it. After some discussion, the Majority of Members agreed that the proper course was to send the plan through the Kamni, but that under the circumstances (the plan being in Seoul), and with a view to save time, the Hon. Sec. should ask Mr. Krien to send the plan to the Foreign Office, and reply to the Kamni explaining the matter to him. It was further decided that the Hon. Sec. in his letter to Mr. Krien, should ask him to inform the Representatives that it is the desire of the Council to make a road at some future date along the shore on the North West side of the Settlement, and although not marked now on the Plan that permission be reserved to do so.

⑦ The Hon. Treasurer was asked, at the suggestion of Mr. Stripling, to have the account for 1892 & 1893. Printed & published.

⑧ The meeting closed at 4.30 p. m. Next meeting to be arranged by local members.

1894년 3월 5일 회의록

·· – **번역문** – ··

① 1894년 3월 5일 신동공사 임시 회의를 개최하였다. 크린 씨(회장), 노세 씨, 타운젠드 씨, 니시와키 씨, 우리탕 씨, 초우 씨, 윌킨슨 씨가 참석하였다.[62] 초우 씨는 제물포주재중국부영사 류자충 씨의 편지를 제출하였는데 자기 대신 회의에 참석하여 표결하라고 지시하는 내용이었다. 크린 씨는 초우 씨가 표결권을 가지는지에 대하여 위원들의 의견을 물었다. 라인스도르프 씨가 크린 씨를 대신하여 표결한 선례를 두고 비공식적인 논의가 이루어졌다. 크린 씨는 라인스도르프 씨가 한국 전역을 총괄하는 부영사직을 맡고 있으며 자신이 부재중일 때 본인에게 주어진 권한 안에서만 행동하였다고 설명하였다. 초우 씨에게는 이번만 표결권을 주기로 했다. 윌킨슨 씨에게 임시로 서기직을 맡아 달라고 부탁하였다. 지난 번 회의(12월 15일)의 회의록을 낭독하고 승인하였다.

② 크린 씨는 폭스 씨가 보내 온 편지를 낭독하였다. 서기와 집행위원회에서 물러난다는 내용이었다. 크린 씨는 윌킨슨 씨에게 서기직을 맡기자고 발의하였다. 만장일치로 통과되었다. 윌킨슨 씨는 폭스 씨를 대신하여 집행위원회로도 선출되었다.[63]

---

62) 서울주재독일총영사 크린, 제물포주재일본부영사 노세, 폭스의 뒤를 이어 제물포주재영국대리부영사로 부임한 윌킨슨, 선출직 위원 겸 회계 니시와키, 선출직 위원 겸 집행위원 타운젠드, 선출직 위원 우리탕이 참석하였다. 초우(Chou)는 류자충을 대신하여 참석한 제물포주재중국부영사관 서기관의 성이다. 주한미국대리공사 알렌과 인천항 경찰관 우경선은 참석하지 않았다.

③ 크린 씨는 토지소유주 3명(볼터 씨, 타운젠드 씨, 스트리플링 씨)이 보내 온 1893년 11월 28일자 편지를 제출하였다. 한국 정부가 제의한 부두 확장과 관련하여 대안을 제시하는 내용이었다. 크린 씨는 위원들의 질문을 받고 각국 외교 대표 중 4명이 한국 정부의 제의를 받아들였으나 2명은 받아들이지 않았다고 대답하였다. 타운젠드 씨는 하루빨리 기존 부두를 보수하고 진입로에 쇄석을 까는 것이 중요하다고 지적하였다. 크린 씨는 예전 협정으로 돌아가 너비 8미터의 도로를 건설하는 것이 최선이라는 의견을 피력하였다. 타운젠드 씨가 발의하였다. "서기께 요청합니다. 해관 창고 앞에 포장 도로를 건설해야 하는 긴급한 필요성을 고려하여, 각국외교대표단장께 편지를 써서 한국 정부와 다음을 합의해 달라고 하십시오. 신동공사는 지금 당장 우리의 기금을 가지고 제방도로의 한 지점—일본우선회사 건물 중 제방과 가까운 쪽 모퉁이의 맞은편—부터 기존 부두를 잇는 너비 15미터의 도로에 쇄석을 깔고 배수공사를 시작할 것입니다. 이 도로는 각국 외교 대표들과 한국 정부가 합의하였을지도 모르는 갯벌 매립이나 부두 확장 계획을 침해하지 않을 것입니다." 만장일치로 통과되었다.

④ 노세 씨는 각국 조계에 가로수를 심는 것에 관한 질문을 받고 자신이 이 일을 위하여 일본에 편지를 보냈다고 대답하였다. 신동공사는 아카시아나무처럼 저렴한 나무가 가장 적합하다는 의견을 밝혔다.

⑤ 크린 씨는 각국 조계 도면 중 A 부지의 구역 획정이 완료되지 않은 것을 보고 담당자에게 이 일을 부탁하였으며, 구역 획정이 완료된 후

63) 이렇게 하여 1894년도 신동공사 임원은 회장 크린, 부회장 노세, 회계 니시와키, 서기 윌킨슨, 집행위원회 노세, 타운젠드, 윌킨슨으로 구성되었다.

외아문 독판에게 도면을 보냈다고 설명하였다. 또한 구역 획정되지 않은 토지는 지금까지의 관행에 따라 매각할 수 있다고 진술하였다.

⑥ 니시와키 씨는 지난 번 회의에서 결의한 대로 1892~1893년 회계 내역의 사본을 제출하였다. 그는 자신이 잠시 제물포에 없을 것이라고 밝혔다. 그가 없는 동안 서기가 회계 업무를 대행하기로 했다.

⑦ 노세 씨가 발의하였다. “각국 외교 대표들께 요청하여 한국 정부로부터 2,100달러를 받아 달라고 합시다. 이는 감리와 제물포 주재 영사들이 합의한 것으로 각국 조계가 도로평탄화 작업을 위하여 1893년 1월 1일까지 지출한 액수입니다.” 타운젠드 씨가 재청하였으며 만장일치로 통과되었다.

⑧ 크린 씨는 독일인 토지소유주들이 자신에게 선출직 위원 재선거를 요구하는 진정서를 제출하였다고 밝혔다. 그들은 1893년 12월 5일 선거가 불법이었다는 의견을 고수하고 있었다. 당시 투표권을 행사한 제물포주재영국부영사 폭스 씨가 등록된 토지소유주가 아니기 때문에 당연직 위원이라고 하더라도 선출직 위원을 뽑을 수 없다는 것이었다. 크린 씨는 자신도 그들의 의견을 지지한다면서 앞으로는 제물포주재영국부영사가 투표권을 갖는 데 반대한다고 덧붙였다.

⑨ 집행위원회는 묘지를 위한 규칙의 초안을 작성하여 다음 정기 회의 때 제출하기로 했다.

⑩ 우리탕 씨는 자신의 토지와 인접한 도로에 평탄화 작업이 이루어지기를 희망하였다. 타운젠드 씨는 옹벽 건설에 들어가는 비용 때문에 공사를 시행하기 어렵다고 설명하고 1891년 11월 6일과 20일에 논의한 내용을 언급하였다.

⑪ 다음 정기 회의는 현지 위원들이 정하는 날짜에 열기로 결정하였다.

- 원문 -

① Extraordinary meeting held March 5th 1894. Present: Mr. Krien (President), Mr. Nosse, Mr. Townsend, Mr. Nishiwaki, Mr. Woolitang, Mr. Chou, Mr. Wilkinson. Mr. Chou handed in a letter from Mr. Liu, Chinese Consul, instructing him to act and vote for him at the meeting. Mr. Krien suggested that the views of the members should be taken as to Mr. Chou's qualification to vote. An informal discussion followed in the course of which the precedent of Mr. Reinsdorf being referred to Mr. Krien explained that that gentleman held a commission as Vice Consul for the whole of Corea, but could only act in that Capacity in his, Mr. Krien's absence. The question whether Mr. Chou should be admitted to vote on this one occasion being put, it was carried. Mr. Wilkinson was asked to act temporarily as Secretary. The minutes of the last meeting (Dec. 15th) were read and approved.

② A letter from Mr. Fox tendering his resignation as Secretary and member of the Executive Committee was read by the President. Mr. Wilkinson was proposed by Mr. Krien as Secretary and elected unanimously; He was also elected in place of Mr. Fox as a member of the Executive Committee.

③ Mr. Krien handed in a letter (Dated Nov. 28, 1893) from 3 landholders (Messrs. Wolter, Townsend and Stripling) suggesting an alternative scheme to the proposal of the Corean Government for an enlarged jetty. In answer to questions by members Mr. Krien stated that the Corean Government's proposal had been accepted by four of the Foreign Representatives, but not by two others. Mr. Townsend pointed out the importance of doing something at once to repair and metal the approach to the existing jetty. Mr. Krien was of opinion that it would be best to go back to the old agreement and construct a road 8 metres wide. Mr. Townsend moved that "In view of the urgent necessity for a metalled road in front of the Customs Godowns as far as the jetty, the Secretary be requested to write to the Doyen of the Foreign Representatives to arrange with the Corean Government that the Municipal Council carry out at once, and at their, the Council's own expense, the metalling and draining of a road 15 metres wide from a point on the Bund opposite the Nippon Yusen Kaisha's corner along the sea-wall, to the existing jetty, such road to be made without prejudice to any plan for filling in the foreshore or the enlargement of the jetty that may be agreed upon between the Foreign Representatives and the Corean Government." Carried unanimously.

④ In answer to a question respecting trees for the Settlement, Mr. Nosse replied that he had written to Japan for them. The Council were of opinion that inexpensive trees such as accacia are the most suitable.

⑤ On the subject of the Settlement Plan, Mr. Krien explained that he found that the A lots had not been marked. He therefore asked the Surveyor to fill in those lots. This had been done and the plan sent in to the President of the Foreign Office. Mr. Krien stated that land within the limits of the Foreign Settlement not marked out in the Plan would continue to be saleable according to the Practice hitherto observed.

⑥ Mr. Nishiwaki, Hon. Treasurer, handed in copies of the accounts for 1892) 3 printed in accordance with the resolution of last meeting. Mr. Nishiwaki giving notice that he would be absent from Chemulpo for a short period, it was agreed that the Hon. Secretary should be authorised, to act also as Treasurer during his absence.

⑦ Mr. Nossé proposed "That the Foreign Representatives be requested to obtain from the Corean Government repayment of the sum of $2,100, agreed upon between the Kamni of Inchön and the Consular body at Chemulpo as the amount expended in grading roads in the General Foreign Settlement up to January 1st 1893." Seconded by Mr. Townsend. Carried unanimously.

⑧ Mr. Krien stated that the German land renters had addressed a representation to him asking for a new election of a non official member, maintaining that the election of the 5th Dec, 1893 was illegal on the ground that Mr. Fox, H. B. M. Vice Consul, who voted on that occasion was not entitled to do so because he was not a registered land holder and because he was not himself eligible for election as a non official member being an official. Mr. Krien added that he himself endorsed this opinion, and that he would oppose any voting by the British Vice-Consul in future.

⑨ It was arranged that the Executive Committee should draw up rules for the Cemetery and lay them before the next ordinary meeting.

⑩ Mr. Woolitang expressed a wish that the road adjoining his lot should be graded. Mr. Townsend explained that the difficulty was connected with the incidence of cost of the necessary retaining walls, and referred to a discussion on the 6th and 20th Nov: 1891.

⑪ The next ordinary meeting will take place at a date to be fixed by the local members.

1894년 4월 23일 회의록

·· – **번역문** – ··

① 1차 정기 회의를 개회하였다. 크린 씨(회장), 알렌 씨, 류자충 씨, 노세 씨, 윌킨슨 씨, 타운젠드 씨, 우리탕 씨가 참석하였다.[64] 지난 번 회의록을 낭독하고 승인하였다.

② 지난 번 회의 때 논의된 우리탕 씨의 토지와 인접한 도로에 평탄화 작업을 시행하는 문제와 관련하여, 타운젠드 씨는 마이어상사의 대표 뤼어스 씨와 상담한 내용을 설명하였다. 마이어상사는 이 도로와 인접한 1개 구역을 소유하고 있다. 뤼어스 씨는 해관이 1891년 신동공사가 D39 구역 둘레에 세운 옹벽의 비용을 지불하지 않는 이상 자신은 마이어상사의 토지 둘레에 옹벽을 건설할 수 없고 비용을 부담할 수도 없다고 단언하였다.[65] 크린 씨는 해관이 이 비용을 내지 않는 한 자신은 자국민들에게 돈을 내라고 말하지 않겠다고 이야기하였다. 타운젠드 씨는 1891년 10월 6일 회의록을 언급하였다. 그에 따르면 D39 구역 둘레에 옹벽을 세우기로 결의하고 비용 문제를 10월 20일 회의로 넘겼으며, 10월 20일 회의에서는 관련 토지소유주들이 비용을 부담하기로 결정하였다는 것이다.[66] 윌킨슨 씨는 해관이 1891년 신동공사가 세운 옹벽의 비용을

64) 인천항 경찰관 우경선과 선출직 위원 겸 회계 니시와키는 불참하였다. 니시와키는 한동안 제물포에 없을 것이라고 1894년 3월 5일 회의 때 밝혔다.

65) D39 구역은 1884년 10월 23일 미국인 쿠퍼가 샀다가 그가 사망한 후 인천해관의 소유가 되었다. 동쪽에는 공원, 남쪽에는 제물포주재중국부영사관이 있었다.

66) 『제물포 각국 조계지 회의록 1』 190~193쪽과 198~201쪽을 참고할 것.

내는 것은 별개의 문제이지만, 토지소유주들은 1891년 10월 20일 결의에 따라 그들의 땅 둘레에 이미 세웠거나 앞으로 세울 옹벽의 비용을 지불할 의무가 있다는 의견을 피력하였다.

③ 문제가 되고 있는 도로—D39~D40 구역을 통과하는—와 관련하여, 제물포주재중국부영사 류자충 씨는 1891년 신동공사가 제물포주재중국부영사관에 공지하지 않은 채 이 도로를 팠다고 발언하였다. 또한 그는 중국 조계에 접한 부분을 각국 조계에 접한 부분만큼 깎은 것은 제물포주재중국부영사관을 위험에 빠뜨린 일이라며, 신동공사가 옹벽을 세울 비용을 지불하거나 각국 조계에 접한 부분을 일부 메워야 한다고 이야기하였다. 크린 씨는 회의 후 이 도로를 살펴보러 가자고 제의하였다.

④ 서기가 지난 번 회의 이후 오고간 편지들(받은 편지는 1-4, 보낸 편지는 1-5)을 낭독하였다. 크린 씨는 제방 도로와 관련하여 각국 외교 대표들의 회의가 소집되었다가 연기된 사실을 알렸다. 감리는 4월 21일자 공문을 통하여 도로평탄화 작업 비용이라는 명목으로 1,000달러를 전달하였는데, 이와 관련하여 신동공사는 1894년도 세금은 이 문제와 아무 관계가 없다는 의견을 밝힌 바 있다. 알렌 박사가 발의하고 크린 씨가 재청하였다. "서기께 요청합니다. '잔액 1,100달러는 1894년도 세금 납부 당시 약속된 것입니다. 신동공사는 세금 납부에 따라 이 잔액을 상환하겠다는 귀하의 뜻을 납득할 수 없습니다. 해당 세금은 1,100달러보다 액수가 적은데다 도로평탄화 작업 비용과는 무관하기 때문입니다. 그러므로 신동공사는 귀하가 조속한 시일 내에 1,100달러를 줄 것을 다시 한 번 요청합니다'라는 답장을 감리에게 보내 주십시오." 통과되었다.[67)]

⑤ 집행위원회가 묘지 규칙의 초안을 제출하였다. 다음 회의 때 그것을 하나하나 논의하기로 결정하였다.

⑥ 알렌 박사가 발의하였다. "서기께 요청합니다. 서울묘지위원회가 주문한 것과 유사한 매장지 명부 두 권을 워털루앤선즈상사를 통하여 구입해 주십시오." 타운젠드 씨가 재청하였으며 만장일치로 통과되었다.

⑦ 서기는 회계를 대신하여 4월 23일 현재 신동공사 기금 잔액이 5,845.16달러라고 보고하였다. 크린 씨는 신동공사 부지와 공원에 울타리를 두르기 위하여 200달러를 책정하자고 제안하였다. 모두 승인하였다. 신동공사는 이 울타리를 가시철사로 만들어야 한다는 의견이었다.

⑧ 제물포주재영국부영사관의 한국인 서기 방경희에게 10달러의 사례비를 지급하는 문제를 표결에 부쳤다. 지난 1년간 그가 신동공사 서기의 사무를 보조하였기 때문이다.

⑨ 타운젠드 씨는 집행위원회를 대표하여 집행위원회가 채택한 반(半)금속화 시스템에 관하여 설명하였다. 반금속화 시스템은 도서 지역에서 가져온 자갈을 도로의 가운데에 펴고 그 위에 화강암 부스러기를 올린 후, 일본 조계가 빌려 준 롤러를 사용하여 도로 전체에 압력을 가하는 것인데 매우 성공적인 방법임이 입증되었다고 한다. 그는 해관 앞 도로, 특히 검사관보(영자수) 사무실과 부두 사이의 도로 상태에 주목하였다. 이 도로는 수레가 다니기 불가능하여 짐꾼들의 삯이 비싸고 거래가 어려우며, 배수 처리가 되어 있지 않아서 쌀가마니를 쌓아 둘 경우 맨 밑의 가마니는 피해가 심각하다. 또한 공간이 협소하여 쌀과 기타 품목을

---

67) 1893년 9~10월 감리는 신동공사가 시행한 도로평탄화 작업에 대하여 2,100달러를 지불하기로 합의한 바 있다. 1893년 10월 10일 회의록을 참고할 것.

쌓아 놓으면 사람이 지나다니기 힘들 정도라는 것이었다.

⑩ 서기는 오늘 아침 제물포주재일본부영사 노세 씨가 보내 온 편지를 낭독하였다. 일본인 토지소유주들로부터 도로 정비를 요구하는 청원서를 받았다는 내용이었다. 타운젠드 씨는 각국 외교 대표들에게 이 청원서의 사본을 보내자고 발의하였다. 우리탕 씨가 재청하였으며 통과되었다.

⑪ 다음 정기 회의는 현지 위원들이 정하는 날짜에 열기로 결정하였다. 우리탕 씨의 토지와 인접한 도로를 살펴보러 나갔다. 신동공사 위원들은 이 도로 중 교차로가 있는 지점을 깎지 않는 데 동의하였다. D39~D40 구역을 통과하는 도로도 조사하였다. 그들은 중국 조계에 접한 부분을 평탄화하기 위해서는 류자충 씨가 그곳의 중국인 주민과 상담해야 할 것이라고 판단하였다.

-- **원문** --

① First Ordinary Meeting. Present: Messrs. Krien (President), Allen, Liu, Nosse, Wilkinson, Townsend, Woolitang. The minutes of last meeting were read & approved.

② With reference to the grading of the road adjoining Mr. Woolitang's lot, which had formed a subject of discussion at the last meeting, Mr. Townsend explained that he had consulted Mr. Lührs, the representative of Messrs. Meyer & Co, owners of one of the lots abutting on the road, and that Mr. Lührs had stated that he could not construct, or pay for the construction of a wall along Messrs. Meyer's lot, unless and until the Corean Customs paid for the retaining wall built by the Council in 1891 off D39. Mr. Krien said that as long as this latter reimbursement was not made by the Customs he would not advise his countrymen to pay. Mr. Townsend referred to the minutes of October 6, 1891, which showed that the wall off D39 had been constructed in consequence of a resolution, one condition of which was that the question of liability for the cost be left to the meeting of the 20th October; and that at the latter meeting (Oct. 20th) it was resolved that any walling required should be paid for by the lotholders affected; Mr. Wilkinson was of opinion that, apart from any question of the liability of the Customs for the wall erected in 1891, lotholders are liable for the erection of any retaining walls erected, or to be erected, since the date of the resolution of Oct. 20th of that year, off their respective lots.

③ With regard to the road in question (past lots D39, 40), Mr. Liu, the Chinese Consul, observed that it was dug in 1891 without special official notification to the Chinese Consulate, and that to cut down the Chinese half of the road to the level of the Municipal portion would endanger the walls of that Consulate. He suggested that the Municipal Council should either pay for the necessary retaining wall, or should partially fill up their own portion of the road. Mr. Krien proposed that the Council should proceed at the close of the meeting to examined the road.

④ The Hon. Secretary read the correspondence that had taken place since the date of the last meeting [Nos. 1-4 received Nos. 1-5 sent]. With reference to the Bund, Mr. Krien stated the a meeting of the Foreign Representatives had been summoned, but had been postponed. With regard to the Kamni's despatch of April 21st, forwarding $1,000 on account of the cost of grading roads, the Council were of opinion that the now payment of the rents for 1894 had nothing to do with the question. Dr. Allen proposed, and Mr. Krien seconded a resolution that "The Secretary be directed to reply to the Kamni that as regards the balance of $1,100, which is promised when the 1894 rents are paid, the Municipal Council cannot allow that repayment to be conditioned upon payment of rents, as the amount from the latter source will be insufficient, and moreover has nothing to do with the grading of roads. The Council therefore again request payment of this $1,100 at an early date." The resolution was carried.

⑤ The Executive Committee submitted the draft of the Cemetery Regulations which it was agreed should be discussed seriatim at the next meeting.

⑥ Dr. Allen moved that the Secretary be requested to procure from Messrs. Waterlow and Sons two burial registers similar to those ordered for the Söul Cemetery Committee. Seconded by Mr. Townsend. Carried unanimously.

⑦ The Secretary in his capacity of Acting Treasurer stated that the balance of funds in the Municipal Chest on April 23 was $5,845.16. Mr. Krien gave notice of an appropriation of $200 for the fencing in of the Municipal Lot and the Public Garden. This was unanimously approved. The Council were of opinion that the fencing should be by means of barbed wire.

⑧ A gratuity of $10 to Pang Kyenghi, Corean writer at H. B. M. Vice Consulate was voted for the clerical assistance given by him to the Hon. Secretary during the past year.

⑨ Mr. Townsend, on behalf of the Executive Committee, explained the system of half metalling adopted. Gravel was obtained from the islands, and was spread over the centre of the roads. On the top was placed disintegrated granite, and the whole was pressed by the stone roller kindly lent by the Japanese Settlement. The system had proved very successful. He drew attention to the condition of the road in front of the Customs, particularly from the Tidewaiter's office to the jetty. Owing to the impossibility of employing carts, the carrying coolies had put up rates and trade suffered. Moreover the space on which cargo was stored required to be drained; the lowermost tier of the rice begs had suffered seriously on this account. Space too was insufficient, the heaps of rice and other articles having in some cases left barely ten feet of passage way.

⑩ The Secretary read a letter received that morning from Mr. Nossé, H. I. J. M. Consul, covering a petition from the Japanese lotholders asking that the roadway in question might be put into repair. Mr. Townsend proposed that a copy of the petition be sent to the Foreign Representatives for their consideration. This was seconded by Mr. Woolitang, and carried.

⑪ It was agreed that the next ordinary meeting should take place on a date to be fixed by the local members. The Council then proceeded to inspect the road adjoining Mr. Woolitang's premises. They were of opinion that the road should not be cut down at its junction with the crossroad ("Ladder Lane"). They also examined the road by D39, 40, and it was understood that Mr. Liu should consult with the Chinese Resident with a view to the due grading of the Chinese half of this road.

1894년 6월 25일 회의록

·· – 번역문 – ··

① 1894년 6월 25일 2차 정기 회의를 개회하였다. 참석 인원이 4명(크린 씨를 대신하여 라인스도르프 씨, 타운젠드 씨, 우리탕 씨, 윌킨슨 씨)밖에 되지 않았으므로 26일 화요일 오전 10시에 속개하기로 하고 휴회하였다.

·· – 원문 – ··

① Second Ordinary Meeting. June 25, 1894. As only 4 members (Messrs. Reinsdorf for Mr. Krien; Townsend; Woolitang & Wilkinson) attended, the meeting was adjourned till 10 a. m. on Tuesday, June 25.

1894년 6월 26일 회의록

·· – 번역문 – ··

① 1894년 6월 26일 신동공사 회의를 속개하였다. 노세 씨(부회장), 크린 씨를 대신하여 라인스도르프 씨, 류자충 씨(통역관 초우 씨를 대동하고), 윌킨슨 씨, 타운젠드 씨, 우리탕 씨가 참석하였다.[68] 크린 씨가 불참하였으므로 노세 씨가 의장직을 맡았다. 지난 번 회의록을 낭독하고 승인하였다. 서기는 지난 번 회의 이후 오고간 편지들(받은 편지는 6–10, 보낸 편지는 7–12)을 낭독하였다.

② 신동공사가 1892년 12월 31일 이후 시행한 도로평탄화 작업 비용을 한국 정부에 청구한 일과 관련하여, 윌킨슨 씨는 자신과 타운젠드 씨가 집행위원회를 대표하여 감리와 비공식 회담을 가졌다고 보고하였다. 그 결과 신동공사는 감리로부터 550달러—아직 받지 못한 1,100달러에 더하여—를 받는 대신 도로 두 곳의 평탄화 작업을 완료하기로 합의하였다. 하나는 신동공사 토지와 영국국교회 한국선교부 토지의 북쪽으로 향하는 도로이고, 다른 하나는 감리아문과 각국 조계를 잇는 도로이다. 회담 당사자들은 이 합의에 만족하였다고 한다.

③ 묘지 규칙의 초안을 다시 한 번 제출하였다. 타운젠드 씨는 네 번째 조항의 "너비 5피트, 길이 10피트"를 "최소 너비 4피트, 길이 8피트"로 바꾸자면서, 다른 조항은 그대로 두고 이것만 수정하여 통과시키

---

68) 1894년 4월 30일 주한미국공사로 부임한 실, 인천항 경찰관 우경선, 선출직 위원 겸 회계 니시와키는 불참하였다.

자고 발의하였다. 윌킨슨 씨가 재청하였으며 만장일치로 통과되었다.

④ 뫼르젤 씨의 편지를 낭독하였다. 자신이 세놓은 집들에서 일본군 병력이 철수한 것에 대하여 불평하면서, 이 일 때문에 혹시 세입자들이 떠난다면 세금을 내지 않겠다는 내용이었다. 답장을 보낼 필요가 없다고 판단하였다.

⑤ 윌킨슨 씨가 발의하였다. "신동공사는 더 많은 무장 세력—질서 유지를 위하여 가끔씩은 절대적으로 필요하지만—이 제물포항과 인근에 주둔하는 것을 강력히 반대합니다. 가까운 이웃에 대규모 병력이 존재하는 것은 각국 조계의 평화와 번영에 매우 해로우며 주민들의 생명과 재산에 상당한 위험 요인이 된다고 생각합니다." 라인스도르프 씨가 재청하였으며 만장일치로 통과되었다. 서기에게는 이 결의안의 사본을 각국외교대표단장에게 보내고 그가 각국 외교 대표들에게 이 일을 알리게 해 달라고 요청하였다.

⑥ 6월 23일자 기무라 씨의 편지를 낭독하였다. D67~D68 구역의 북쪽을 동서 방향으로 통과하는 도로에 우물을 만들어도 되는지 문의하는 내용이었다. 만장일치로 승인하였다. 조건은 각국 조계의 모든 토지 소유주들과 세입자들이 우물을 자유롭게 사용하는 것, 그리고 우물물은 기무라가 자비로 채우는 것이었다.

⑦ 서기는 신동공사가 최근의 토지 매각을 통하여 무려 3,095달러를 받았으나 경매업자에게는 최저경매가의 2.5퍼센트인 2.27달러밖에 주지 않은 사실을 환기시켰다. 타운젠드 씨는 이 땅(D62, D63, D65, D67, D68 구역)을 팔기 위하여 힘써 준 경매업자 와이어스 씨에게 15달러를 지급하자고 발의하였다. 만장일치로 통과되었다.[69]

⑧ 라인스도르프 씨는 공원과 신동공사 부지에 울타리를 두르기 위하여 200달러를 책정하자고 발의하였다. 만장일치로 통과되었다.

⑨ 타운젠드 씨가 발의하였다. "곧 여름인데다 중국 남방에 전염병이 돌고 있으니 신동공사는 클로르석회 최소 5헌드레드웨이트를 즉시 확보해야 합니다."[70] 윌킨슨 씨가 재청하였다. 그는 주민들의 부주의 때문에 특히 각국 조계 동쪽의 배수 시설이 자주 멈춘다고 이야기하였다. 타운젠드 씨의 결의안은 만장일치로 통과되었다.

⑩ 윌킨슨 씨가 발의하였다. "신동공사는 아직 팔리지 않은 D46 구역의 동쪽 모퉁이를 매입하고 그곳에 공용 우물을 만들어야 합니다." 타운젠드 씨가 재청하였으며 만장일치로 통과되었다.

⑪ 다음 정기 회의는 9월 첫째 주에 열기로 결정하였다.

의장 대행 타운젠드 (서명)

서기 윌킨슨 (서명)

·· – 원문 – ··

① Adjourned Meeting, June 26, 1894. Present: Mr. Nossé (Vice President), Mr. Reinsdorf [representing Mr. Krien], Mr. Liu [accompanied by Mr. Chow as interpreter], Messrs. Wilkinson, Townsend and Woolitang. In the absence

---

69) 각국 조계 북서쪽에 위치한 D62(1,100m^2), D63(1,200m^2), D65(1,800m^2), D67(880m^2), D68(1,500m^2) 구역에 대한 경매는 1894년 5월 12일 항무장(이선청) 사무실에서 열렸다.

70) 클로르석회는 표백 및 살균 작용을 가진 물질이다. 1헌드레드웨이트는 영국에서는 112파운드(50.802kg), 미국에서는 100파운드(45.359kg)이다.

of Mr. Krien, Mr. Nossé took the chair. The minutes of the last meeting were read and confirmed. The correspondence that had taken place since the date of the last meeting was read by the Hon. Secretary [No. 6-10 received, 7-12 sent].

② With reference to the further claim against the Corean Government for grading undertaken subsequent to the 31st Dec. 1892, Mr. Wilkinson explained that he and Mr. Townsend, on behalf of the Executive Committee, had entered into pourparlers with the Kamni, and that, it was probable that the Claim of the Council might be settled for a payment of $550 [in addition to the $1,100 yet unpaid] the Council agreeing to complete the grading of the two roads (a) to the North of the Municipal & E. C. Mission lots (b) between the Kamni's Yamûn and the Settlement. The opinion of the meeting was that a Settlement on the above basis would be satisfactory.

③ The draft of the cemetery Regulations was again submitted, and Mr. Townsend moved that: The words "five feet by 10 feet" be substituted for the words "at last four feet by eight feet" in Regulation 4, and that the Regulations with this one amendment be passed as they stand. Seconded by Mr. Wilkinson and carried unanimously.

④ A letter from Mr. F. H. Mörsel complaining of the withdrawal of the Japanese troops from the houses occupied by his tenants, and declaring tho if those tenants left in consequence, he should object to pay ground rent, was read. It was decided that it was not necessary to answer it.

⑤ Mr. Wilkinson moved and Mr. Reinsdorf seconded, a resolution that; "The Council deprecate the stationing upon any of the Settlement's comprised in the port area of Chemulpo, or their vicinity, of more armed men that may from time to time be absolutely necessary to maintain order, believing that the presence of any large member of troops in the near neighborhood is in a high degree prejudicial to the peace and prosperity of the General Foreign Settlement, and a very possible source of danger to the lives and property of the residents." The resolution was carried unanimously, and the Secretary was directed to forward a copy of it to the Doyen of the Diplomatic Body, requesting him to be good enough to bring it to the notice of the Foreign Representatives.

⑥ A letter from Mr. Kimura (dated June 23) was read, in which permission was asked to construct a second well in the projected road running east and west past the north of Lots D67, 68. It was unanimously decided to grant the permission requested, on the conditions that all land renters in the General Foreign Settlement and their tenants shall have free access at any time to the well, and that should the Council hereafter decide that the well must be filled up it shall be filled up at Mr. Kimura's expense.

⑦ The Secretary having drawn attention to the fact that although by the recent sale of land the Council received no less a sum than $3095, the auctioneer, had been paid only $2.27, or 2½% on the upset price, Mr. Townsend moved that a present of $15 be made to Mr. Wyers, the auctioneer, for his services in connection with the sale of the five lots in question (D62, 63, 65, 67, 68), carried unanimously.

⑧ Mr. Reinsdorf moved the appropriation of $200 for fencing in the public garden and Municipal grounds. Carried unanimously.

⑨ Mr. Townsend proposed that, in view of the approach of summer and the prevalence in the South of China of a form of plague, the Council should at once procure not less than 5 cwt of Chloride of lime. Mr. Wilkinson seconded the resolution, taking the opportunity to draw attention to the frequent stoppage of drains, especially in the east of the Settlement, by the carelessness of residents. The resolution was carried unanimously.

⑩ Mr. Wilkinson proposed and Mr. Townsend seconded; That a suitable portion of ground in the South east corner of Lot D46 (which lot has not yet been sold) should be acquired by the Council, and that upon it a public well should be sunk. Carried unanimously.

⑪ It was arranged that the next ordinary meeting should take place the first week in September.

(signed) W. D. Townsend, Acting Chairman.
(signed) W. H. Wilkinson, Hon. Sec.

1894년 11월 9일 회의록

-- 번역문 --

① 1894년 11월 9일 제물포에서 3차 정기 회의를 개최하였다. 감리 박세환(통역사 신씨를 대동하고), 제물포주재일본대리부영사 에이타키 씨(통역관 고니시 씨를 대동하고), 타운젠드 씨, 우리탕 씨, 윌킨슨 씨(서기)가 참석하였다.[71] 윌킨슨 씨는 타운젠드 씨에게 의장을 맡아 달라고 요청한 후 10월 20일자 감리의 편지 내용을 설명하였다. 그에 따르면 감리는 우경선 씨의 뒤를 이어 한국 대표로 참석하라는 외아문의 지시를 받았다고 한다. 또한 윌킨슨 씨는 제물포주재일본부영사 노세 씨가 전속되고 제물포주재일본대리부영사 에이타키 씨가 일본 측 당연직 위원이 되었다고 이야기하였다. 감리와 에이타키 씨가 자리에 앉았다. 지난 번 회의록을 낭독하고 승인하였으며 지난 번 회의 이후 오고간 편지들(보낸 편지는 13-21, 받은 편지는 13-17)을 낭독하였다.

② 타운젠드 씨가 집행위원회를 대표하여 진술하였다. 신동공사가 고용한 경찰력 8명이 한때 1명으로 줄어들었으며, 현재는 4명이지만 적합한 사람이 구해지면 최소 6명까지 늘리겠다는 내용이었다.

③ 클로르석회와 울타리로 쓸 가시철사를 확보하여 현재 신동공사 토지에 보관 중이다.

---

71) 서울주재독일총영사 크린, 주한미국공사 실, 제물포주재중국부영사 류자충, 선출직 위원 겸 회계 니시와키는 불참하였다. 1894년 8월 감리로 부임한 박세환(朴世煥)이 우경선의 뒤를 이어 한국 대표로 참석하였다. 한편 1894년 10월 1일 제물포주재일본대리부영사로 부임한 에이타키가 노세의 뒤를 이어 일본 대표로서 참석하였다.

④ 에이타키 씨가 노세 씨를 대신하여 집행위원회에 선출되었다.

⑤ 신동공사 토지와 공원에 울타리를 두르는 일을 당분간 연기하기로 결정하였다.

⑥ 우리탕 씨는 각국 조계 서쪽 경계에 인접한 서울행 도로 길목의 상태를 언급하였다. 서기는 감리에게 편지를 써서 그곳에 있는 장애물을 제거해 달라고 부탁하라는 요청을 받았다.

⑦ 에이타키 씨는 경찰관들을 위한 지침서가 필요하다는 점을 지적하였다. 타운젠드 씨는 경찰력이 잘 갖춰져 있던 지난 봄 노세 씨가 초안을 만들었으나, 경찰관 8명을 상정하고 만든 것이기 때문에 현재로서는 쓸 수 없다고 설명하였다. 에이타키 씨는 경찰관 4명을 위한 초안을 만들어 달라는 요청을 받고 곧 착수하였다.

⑧ 다음 회의 날짜는 현지 위원들이 결정하기로 했다.

회장 크린 (서명)

서기 윌킨슨 (서명)

·· – **원문** – ··

① Third Ordinary Meeting Chemulpo 9th Nov; 1894. Present;- Pak Syei Hoan, the Kamni (Mr. Shin interpreting), Mr. Eitake, Japanese Vice Consul (Mr. Konishi interpreting), Mr. Townsend, Mr. Woolitang, Mr. Wilkinson (Hon. Sec.). Mr. Townsend having been requested to take the Chair, Mr. Wilkinson explained that by a communication under date October 20th last the Kamni had stated that he was instructed by the Corean Foreign Office to himself fill the place as Corean Delegate on the Council lately held by Wu Kyöng Sön, and that Mr. Nossé, the late Japanese Consul having been transferred else, Mr. Eitaki, the vice Consul and present Acting Consul, would succeed him as the Japanese official member. The Kamni and Mr. Eitaki then took their seats. The minutes of the previous meeting were read and confirmed, and the correspondence since the date of that meeting was read (sent Nos. 13-21; Received Nos. 13-17).

② On behalf of the Executive Committee Mr. Townsend stated that the member of Police in the employ of the Council had at one time dwindled down from 8 to 1; that there were now 4, but that it was intended to raise the number to 6 at least, as soon as suitable men could be obtained.

③ The Chloride of lime and wire for fencing had been procured and were now in store on the Municipal Premises.

④ Mr. Eitaki was elected a member of the Executive Committee in the place of Mr. Nossé.

⑤ It was decided to postpone the fencing in of the Municipal Lot and of the Public Garden for the present.

⑥ Mr. WooLitang having drawn attention to the condition of the entrance to the Söul road abutting on the Western border of the Settlement, the Secretary was requested to write to the Kamni to ask that the obstruction existing there should be removed, and the ground kept open.

⑦ Mr. Eitaki having pointed out the need for deficit instructions to the Police, Mr. Townsend explained that last spring when the force was more complete, Mr. Nossé had been good enough to draw upon a scheme. That scheme, however, as it presupposed 8 men to be in the force would not now be applicable. Mr. Eitaki was requested to suggest a scheme for 4, with an alternative for 6 men; which he undertook to do.

⑧ The date of the next meeting will be fixed by the local members.

(signed) F. Krien, President.
(signed) W. H. Wilkinson, Hon. Sec.

1894년 11월 24일 회의록

-- 번역문 --

① 1894년 11월 24일 제물포에서 4차 정기 회의를 개최하였다. 크린 씨(회장), 실 씨, 감리, 에이타키 씨, 타운젠드 씨, 우리탕 씨, 윌킨슨 씨(서기)가 참석하였다.[72] 에이타키 씨와 감리는 통역관을 대동하였다. 회장은 미국 측 당연직 위원으로 참석한 실 씨를 환영하였다. 11월 9일 회의록을 낭독하고 승인하였다. 이후 오고간 편지들(보낸 편지는 22, 받은 편지는 18~19)을 낭독하였다.

② 서울행 도로 길목에 있는 한국인 판자촌의 무단점유자들이 돌아오는 봄까지 그곳에 살도록 허락을 받았다는 감리의 이야기(받은 편지 18)와 관련하여, 감리는 한국 달력으로 음력 3월 말까지 이 도로의 모든 장애물을 제거하기로 했다.[73]

③ 오스본 씨가 제기한 불만(받은 편지 19)과 관련하여 즉시 도로를 정비하기로 결의하였다. 감리는 규칙에 따라 교통국에 벌금을 낼 책임이 있음을 경고하기로 했다. 에이타키 씨도 일본인 노동자들이 공원과 그 인근에서 벌이는 유사한 소동을 줄이겠다고 약속하였다.[74]

④ 크린 씨는 뤼어스 씨의 불만 사항을 전달하였다. 라포르트 씨의

---

72) 제물포주재중국부영사 류자충과 선출직 위원 겸 회계 니시와키는 불참하였다.

73) 1894년 11월 9일 회의 말미에 우리탕이 서울행 도로 길목의 상태에 대해서 문제를 제기한 바 있다.

74) 오스본이 신동공사에 보낸 편지가 남아 있지 않아 정확한 내용은 알 수 없지만, 해관장 자택과 공원 사이의 도로를 정비해 달라는 요청인 것 같다.

집 근처 교차로를 가로지르는 배수로에 다리가 놓여 있지 않다는 내용이었다. 락스데일 씨에게 지시하여 그곳을 살펴보기로 결의하였다.[75]

⑤ 타운젠드 씨는 집행위원회를 대표하여 경찰관들을 위한 새 외투가 필요하다고 진술하였다. 에이타키 씨는 일본을 통하여 옷감을 구하는 일에 착수하였다.

⑥ 에이타키 씨는 경찰관들을 위한 지침서 초안을 만들었으나 영어로 번역할 시간이 없었다고 이야기하였다.

⑦ 크린 씨는 신동공사의 바람에 따라 외무대신에게 조계 도면을 보냈다고 밝혔다. 그에 따르면 11월 5일자 편지에서 외무대신은 하루빨리 각국 외교 대표들과 만나 이 일을 검토하기로 약속하였다고 한다.

⑧ 우리탕 씨는 C27 구역의 일본인 노동자들이 자신과 다른 중국인들에게 습관적으로 욕을 하고 돌을 던진다는 불만을 제기하였다. 에이타키 씨는 그들의 무례한 관행이 계속되고 있는지 알아보기로 했다.[76]

⑨ 니시와키 씨가 선출직 위원에서 물러날 차례가 되었으므로 12월 5일 화요일 오전 10시부터 오후 1시 사이에 선거를 실시하기로 했다.

⑩ 다음 회의는 12월 6일에 열기로 결정하였다.

서기 윌킨슨 (서명)

---

75) 프랑스인 라포르트는 D24, D29, D48 구역의 토지소유주였다. 문제가 되고 있는 장소는 마이어상사의 토지인 D27, D28 구역과 라포르트의 토지인 D29 구역 사이에 있는 교차로로 추정된다.

76) C27 구역은 다이부츠 호텔 운영자 호리의 땅이었다.

·· – 원문 – ··

① Fourth Ordinary Meeting Chemulpo 24th Nov; 1894. Present;- Mr. Krien (President); Mr. Sill; the Kamni; Mr. Eitaki; Mr. Townsend; Mr. WooLitang; Mr. Wilkinson (Hon. Sec.) Mr. Eitaki & the Kamni were accompanied by their interpreters. The President welcomed Mr. Sill on taking his seat as U. S. official member. The minutes of the meeting of Nov; 9th were read and confirmed, and the correspondence was read (sent No. 22, Received Nos. 18-19).

② With reference to the Corean shanties at the entrance of the Seoul road and to the Kamni's suggestion (v. No 18 Received) that the squatters be permitted to remain till the spring, the Kamni undertook that the road should be clear of all obstructions by the close of the third moon of next year, Corean Calendar.

③ With regard to Mr. Osborne's complaint (v. No. 19 Received), it was resolved to proceed at once to put the road in order, and the Kamni undertook to warn the Transport Office of their liability to be fined under the bylaws. Mr. Eitaki also promised to cause similar nuisances by Japanese coolies on the public garden and its neighborhood to be abated.

④ Mr. Krien said that a complaint had been made by Mr. Lührs of the absence of a bridge over a drain crossing the Ladder Lane near Mr. Laporte's entrance. Resolved to direct Ragsdale to examine.

⑤ On behalf of the Executive Committee Mr. Townsend stated that new overcoats being required for the Police, Mr. Eitaki had undertaken to procure the necessary cloth from Japan.

⑥ Mr. Eitaki stated that he had prepared a scheme of duties for the Police, but that there had not yet been time to translate it into English.

⑦ New plan of the Settlement, Mr. Krien stated that he had, in accordance with the wishes of the Council, communicated the plan to the President of the

Corean Foreign Office. The President in a letter dated the 5th instant, had promised to convene a meeting of the Foreign Representative at an early date for its consideration.

⑧ Mr. WooLitang complained that Japanese coolies on Lot C27 were in the habit of insulting him and other Chinese, and of throwing stones. Mr. Eitaki undertook to see that the objection able practice was discontinued.

⑨ It was decided to hold the Election for an Elective Member in the place of Mr. Nishiwaki (retiring on rotation) on Wednesday the 5th December, between the hours of 10 a. m. and 1 p. m.

⑩ The next meeting was fixed for the 6th December.

(signed) W. H. Wilkinson, Hon. Sec.

1894년 12월 6일 회의록

·· – **번역문** – ··

① 1894년 12월 6일 5차 정기 회의를 개최하였다. 실 씨, 감리, 에이타키 씨, 타운젠드 씨, 우리탕 씨, 윌킨슨 씨가 참석하였다.[77] 감리와 에이타키 씨는 통역관을 대동하였다. 회장이 불참하였으므로 실 씨에게 의장직을 부탁하였다. 지난 번 회의록을 낭독하고 승인하였다. 12월 5일에 실시한 선거 결과를 알렸다(니시와키 씨 12표, 뤼어스 씨 8표).[78]

② 에이타키 씨는 지난 번 회의 때 제기된 불만과 관련하여 일본인 노동자들이 소동을 피우지 못하도록 조치를 취하였다고 진술하였다. 그는 경찰관들을 위한 지침서 초안을 아직 영어로 번역하지 못하였으나 경찰관 외투를 만들 옷감을 일본에 주문하였다.

③ 니시와키 씨는 교통국과 오스본 씨 자택 사이의 도로가 정비되고 있으며 배수로에도 작은 다리가 놓였다고 이야기하였다.[79]

④ 타운젠드 씨가 해관 창고 남쪽의 매립지를 통과하는 도로의 정비와 쇄석 공사의 필요성을 언급하였다. 그에 따르면 이 도로는 비나 눈이 오면 거의 이용할 수 없어 거래에 막대한 영향을 끼치는데다가, 배수

---

77) 서울주재독일총영사 크린, 제물포주재중국부영사 류자충, 선출직 위원 겸 회계 니시와키는 불참하였다.

78) 1894년 12월 5일 선거에서 니시와키가 뤼어스를 누르고 선출직 위원이 되었다. 이렇게 하여 그는 1892~1894년 선출직 위원으로 복무한 데 이어 또 다시 선출직 위원으로 일하게 되었다.

79) 기록에 착오가 있었던 것 같다. 이 날 니시와키는 참석하지 않았다.

처리가 잘 되어 있지 않기 때문에 화물을 쌓을 경우 맨 밑에 깔린 것은 침수 피해를 입는다. 이는 수년간 불만거리였지만 한국 정부는 아무 일도 하지 않았다고 한다. 윌킨슨 씨는 한국 정부가 지난 봄 부두 보수 및 확장을 시작하였으며, 이 계획에는 제방을 따라 해관 창고 앞에 도로를 건설하는 것도 포함된다고 지적하였다. 또한 이 유익한 공사가 안타깝게도 정치적 문제 때문에 진행되지 못하고 있다고 했다. 타운젠드 씨는 해관이 신동공사 회장과 토지소유주들의 항의에도 불구하고 이 공사에 착수하였다고 발언하였다. 윌킨슨 씨는 그의 오해를 바로잡기 위하여 1893년 가을 2명을 제외한 각국 외교 대표들이 부두와 제방 도로의 신속한 확장을 포함하는 계획을 승인하였다고 이야기하였다. 2명 중 한 명은 한국을 떠났고 한 명은 추후 그 계획에 찬성하였다고 한다. 그러자 타운젠드 씨가 다음을 제안하고 윌킨슨 씨가 재청하였다. "서기께 요청합니다. 각국 외교 대표들께 편지를 써서 제방 끝(일본우선회사 옆)에서부터 부두에 이르는 구간에 너비 15미터의 도로를 건설하는 문제를 한국 정부와 조율해 달라고 하십시오. 신동공사가 빠르면 1895년 3월 그곳에 도로평탄화 작업과 쇄석 처리를 할 수 있도록 말입니다." 에이타키 씨는 이 도로에 보관되고 있는 화물을 어떻게 처리하면 좋을지 질문하였다. 그는 모든 화물과 석재는 개인의 재산이든 정부의 재산이든 다른 곳으로 옮겨야 하고, 그곳을 쇄석 처리한 후에는 철저하게 통행료를 징수해야 한다는 답변을 들었다. 타운젠드 씨의 제안은 통과되었다. 윌킨슨 씨가 또 제안하였다. "쇄석 공사와 배수 처리를 시작할 수 있도록, 각국 외교 대표들은 이 도로와 해관 창고 앞 사이에 있는 모든 화물 창고에 대하여 최대한 빨리 한국 정부와 합의해야 합니다."

감리는 화물 창고를 소유하고 운영하는 사람들이 이 결의안에 의문을 제기하지 않을지 질문하였고, 쇄석 공사와 적절한 배수 처리는 모두에게 이로운 것이므로 문제가 되지 않는다는 대답을 들었다. 타운젠드 씨가 재청하였으며 만장일치로 통과되었다.

⑤ 고르샬키 씨가 보내 온 편지를 낭독하였다. B1~B2 구역 앞의 토지와 우물 2개를 임대해 달라는 내용이었다. 타운젠드 씨는 이 토지가 도로라는 점을 지적하였고, 신동공사는 도로를 임대하는 것은 불가능하다는 데 동의하였다. 윌킨슨 씨는 다이부츠 호텔의 호리 씨가 그곳에 배관을 설치하고 우물물을 끌어다가 선박들에 판매하고 있으며, 그곳에는 상당한 양의 상품이 쌓여 있다고도 이야기하였다. 실 씨는 공용 우물물을 주민이 아닌 사람에게 판매하거나 공용 도로에 상품을 쌓아 두면 안 된다는 의견을 밝혔다. 상품을 쌓아 둔 사람에게는 그것을 치워 달라고 요청하고, 호리 씨에게는 각국 조계에서 나온 물을 판매하는 특권이 기무라 씨에게만 있음을 알리기로 결의하였다.

⑥ 집행위원회는 묘지를 위하여 매장지 명부 두 권을 마련한 사실을 보고하였다.[80]

⑦ 한국 정부로부터 받아야 할 도로평탄화 작업 비용과 관련하여, 신동공사는 1893년에 합의된 금액 2,100달러의 잔액인 1,100달러를 받아야 한다. 또한 1893년 1월 1일부터 1894년 12월 31일까지 시행한 도로평탄화 작업에 대해서는 550달러를 추가로 받아야 한다는 데 의견을 같이하였다. 이는 올해 2차 정기 회의의 회의록에 기록되어 있다.[81]

---

80) 이는 1894년 4월 23일 알렌의 요청에 따른 것이었다.

81) 1894년 6월 26일 회의록을 참고할 것.

⑧ 다음과 같이 기금을 책정하였다. 경찰국장 봉급으로 900달러(월 75달러), 경찰관 6명(필요에 따라 충원할 예정)의 봉급으로 1,080달러(월 15달러), 제복 구입에 300달러, 청소부 4명의 봉급으로 432달러(월 9달러), 가로등 구입에 200달러, 도로 정비에 500달러, 예비비 450달러를 책정하여 경상 지출 총액은 3,862달러가 되었다. 도로평탄화 작업과 배수공사, 도로 건설을 위한 임시 지출에 500달러를 책정하여 총 4,362달러를 내년도 기금 총액으로 결정하였다. 만장일치로 통과되었다.

⑨ 1895년도 회장에 실 씨, 부회장에 크린 씨, 서기에 윌킨슨 씨, 회계에 니시와키 씨, 집행 위원에 에이타키 씨, 타운젠드 씨, 윌킨슨 씨가 만장일치로 선출되었다.

⑩ 다음 회의는 2월 중에 현지 위원들이 정하는 날짜에 열기로 결정하였다.

서기 윌킨슨 (서명)

·· – **원문** – ··

① Fifth Ordinary Meeting, Chemulpo Dec. 6th 1894. Present; Mr. Sill; the Kamni; Mr. Eitaki; Mr. Townsend; Mr. WooLitang and Mr. Wilkinson. The Kamni and Mr. Eitaki were accompanied by their interpreters. In the absence of the President, Mr. Sill was invited to take the chair. The minutes of the previous meeting were read and confirmed, and the result of the election held on the 5th December was announced. [Mr. Nishiwaki 12 votes, Mr. Lührs 8 votes.]

② Mr. Eitaki stated that he had taken measures to prevent the recurrence of the acts of nuisance on the part of Japanese coolies concerning which complaints had been made at the last meeting. He had not yet had time to have the scheme of police duties translated into English, but the order for the cloth for police uniforms had gone to Japan.

③ Mr. Nishiwaki stated that the road leading past the Transport Office and Mr. Osborne's house was in process of repair; and that a small bridge had been thrown over the drain in Ladder Lane.

④ Road in front of Customs Godowns. Mr. Townsend drew the attention of the Council to the necessity for keeping open, and properly metalling, a road through the reclaimed land south of the Customs Godowns. In rain or snow the track was scarcely possible, and a heavy loss was inflicted on the trade of the port not only by this circumstance, but also by the damage accruing, through insufficient drainage, to the lower tiers of merchandize piled on the ground. It had been a subject of complaint for some years, but the Corean Government had done nothing. Mr. Wilkinson pointed out that last spring the Corean Government had commenced to repair and enlarge the jetty, and that in the scheme was to have been included the making of a road in front of the Godowns along the bund. This useful work had been unfortunately interrupted by political complications. Mr. Townsend observed that the work in question had been undertaken by the Customs without authority and against the protests of the President of the Council and of the landholders. Mr. Wilkinson ventured to correct that he left to be a misapprehension. The scheme which embraced at once an extended jetty and the bund-road had been approved in the Autumn of 1893 by all the Foreign Representatives with the exception of two. Of those two, one had left Corea and the other had since given in his adhesion to the scheme. Mr. Townsend then moved, and Mr. Wilkinson seconded a resolution. That the Secretary be requested to write to the Foreign Representatives requesting that they will, in concert with the Corean government, have a road laid out from the end of the bund next to the Nippon Yusen Kaisha along the bund to the jetty, 15 metres wide, so that the Municipal Council can grade and metal this road early in March 1895. Mr. Eitaki asked what would be done with the cargo on the 15 metre strip. It was replied that all such cargo and stones, whether private of the property of any government, must be removed elsewhere, as the strip when metalled would be kept open as a thorough fare. The resolution was then carried. Mr. Wilkinson moved, as a corollary to the last resolution. That the Foreign Representatives should be requested to confer with the Corean government with a view the metalling and draining, as soon as possible, of all the cargo space between the 15 metre road referred to in the resolution just carried, and in front of the Custom's Godowns. In answer to a question from the Kamni, it was explained that the resolution raised no question as to the persons in whom the ownership and control of the cargo space are vested. The macadamizing of this ground and its proper drainage, would be of the greatest benefit to every one. Mr. Townsend seconded the resolution, which was carried unanimously.

⑤ A letter from Mr. Gorschalki was read requesting that the ground in front of the lots B1 and B2, with the two wells upon it, might be leased to him. Mr. Townsend point out that the ground in question was a roadway. The Council were of opinion that it was impossible to lease ground of such a character. Mr. Wilkinson observed that Mr. Hori of Daibutsu's Hotel had laid down pipes along this land, and was selling water from the two public wells to to the shipping; he also drew attention to the fact that a quantity of merchandize had been piled on the ground. The Council, agreeing with the opinion of Mr. Sill, held that it was improper for anyone landholder to sell to non residents water from a public well, and that merchandize could not be stacked on a public road. The owners of the merchandize should be required to remove it, and Mr. Hori should be informed that the privilege of selling water from the General Foreign Settlement could only be granted on the terms given earlier to Mr. Kimura.

⑥ The Executive Committee reported of two register book for the Cemetery.

⑦ With regard to the amount still due from the Corean Government on account of the grading of roads the Council were of opinion that the Kamni should be asked to pay as soon as possible the $1,100, balance of the $2,100 agreed upon in 1893, & in addition the sum of $550 for grading carried out between Jan 1st 1893 & Dec 31st 1894, on the conditions recorded in the Minutes of the second Ordinary Meeting of this year.

⑧ The following appropriations were unanimously passed: Chief of the Police, Salary @ $75 $900. Policemen; 6 (to be added to in case of need) @ $15 1,080. Uniforms 300. Scavengers; 4 @ $9 432. Lamps 200. Repairs to roads 500. Contingent expenses 450. 3,862. Extra Expenditure; Grading and draining new roads 500. 4,362.

⑨ The following officers were unanimously elected for 1895. President: Mr. Sill. vice President: Mr. Krien. Secretary: Mr. Wilkinson. Treasurer: Mr. Nishiwaki. Executive Committee: Messrs. Eitaki, Townsend & Wilkinson.

⑩ The next meeting will take place in February, on a day to be fixed by the local members.

(signed) W. H. Wilkinson, Hon. Sec.

1895년 3월 7일 회의록

·· – **번역문** – ··

① 1895년 3월 7일 제물포에서 1차 정기 회의를 개최하였다. 감리, 진다 씨, 타운젠드 씨, 윌킨슨 씨, 우리탕 씨가 참석하였다.[82] 회장과 부회장 모두 참석하지 않았으므로 타운젠드 씨에게 의장직을 맡아 달라고 부탁하였다. 진다 씨는 지난 번 회의 이후 제물포주재일본부영사로 임명되어 에이타키 씨를 대신하였다. 지난 번 회의록과 이후 오고간 편지들을 낭독하였다.

② 실 씨가 각국외교대표단장직 때문에 신동공사 회장직을 맡지 않기로 결정한 것은 유감이다. 회장은 엄밀하게 말해서 회의를 주재하는 사람으로 신동공사 회관 밖에서는 신동공사의 대표자로 불리지 않는다. 그는 한국 정부와 직접적인 관계가 있는 직책을 가져야 하고, 그렇지 않을 경우에는 신동공사의 이름으로 의사소통하기 위하여 특별 허가를 받아야 한다. 이러한 점을 생각해 볼 때 실 씨는 회장직을 수행하기 위하여 시간을 많이 할애하지 않아도 되며, 그가 회장이 되었더라면 신동공사에 도움이 되었을 것이다. 타운젠드 씨는 실 씨의 결정을 되돌릴 수 없을 것이라고 장담하였다. 크린 씨가 만장일치로 회장에 선출되었다. 진다 씨는 부회장이 되었고 집행위원회로도 선출되었다.[83]

---

82) 주한미국공사 실, 서울주재독일총영사 크린, 제물포주재중국부영사 류자충, 선출직 위원 겸 회계 니시와키는 참석하지 않았다. 진다는 1895년 1월 20일부터 5월 25일까지 약 4개월간 제물포주재일본부영사로 복무하였다.

83) 이렇게 하여 1895년도 신동공사 회장과 부회장은 실과 크린에서 크린과 진다로 바뀌었

③ 해관이 석조 부두의 보수 및 확장을 위하여 어떤 일본인과 계약을 체결하였고 4개월 안에 공사를 완료할 것이라고 한다. 신동공사는 해관 창고 앞에 너비 15미터의 도로를 건설하는 문제를 최대한 빨리 진행하기로 했다. 진다 씨는 도로에 쌓여 있는 상품을 치우기 위하여 일본인 소유주에게 공지하고, 집행위원회는 적합한 쇄석 공급을 확보하는 데 필요한 조치를 취하기로 결의하였다.[84]

④ 진다 씨는 천연두처럼 심한 전염병에 걸린 환자들을 위하여 격리 병원이 필요하다고 발언하였다. 서기는 랜디스 박사와 코지마 박사에게 편지를 써서 격리 병원을 공동 설립하는 건을 요청하기로 했다.

⑤ 1894년도 회계 내역의 대차대조표는 다음과 같다.

날짜	항목	금액
1월	1893년도 이월금	$1,420.26
4월 11일	1893년도 세금	4,457.84
〃	도로평탄화 작업 비용의 1차 불입금	1,000.00
5월 12일	토지 매각(경매업자에게 준 돈을 뺀 나머지 금액)	3,080.90
12월 31일	장례비	35.00
〃	면허	170.00
〃	예금 이자	141.86
		10,305.86

다. 그러나 진다가 5월 25일 전속되었으므로 이후 부회장직은 그의 후임에게 돌아갔거나 공석으로 남았을 것이다. 1895년 제물포주재일본부영사관 책임자는 진다 이후 세 번 더 교체되었다.

84) 1894년 12월 6일 회의록을 참고할 것.

12월 31일	경찰	봉급(벌금을 뺀 나머지 금액)	1870.74	$1,870.74
		제복 등		163.59
〃	도로	청소부	278.13	
		가로등 등	204.94	483.07
		건설과 보수	694.92	
		가로수	19.03	713.95
〃	인쇄와 문구			14.73
〃	신동공사 회관	세금	75.60	
		보험	28.13	
		석탄	100.10	
		잡화	7.85	211.68
〃	묘지	명부	32.25	
		분묘	6.00	38.25
〃	공원	철사 등		172.00
〃	사무	한국인 서기에게 봉사료 지급		10.00
12월 31일	잔액			6,627.85
				10,305.86

⑥ 진다 씨는 월킨슨 씨와의 공동 조사 후 자신이 제안한 변경 사항을 표시한 도면의 투사본을 보여 주었다. 각국 조계의 최북단 지역은 경인 철도의 노선이 아직 결정되지 않았기 때문에 토지 편성이 어렵다는 지적이 나왔다.

⑦ 우리탕 씨는 지난 달에 내린 눈을 치우지 않은 결과 도로를 사용할 수 없게 되었다고 발언하였다. 주민들은 조례에 따라 자기가 살고 있는 곳에 인접한 보도의 눈을 치워야 하지만, 도로에 쌓인 눈은 신동공사가 고용한 청소부들이 치워야 한다는 주장이 제기되었다.

⑧ 도로평탄화 작업 비용의 잔액과 관련하여, 감리는 외무아문의 간섭을 제한 후 서기의 편지에 회신하겠다고 진술하였다.

⑨ 다음 회의는 4월 첫째 주 현지 위원들이 정하는 날짜에 열기로 결정하였다.

·· – **원문** – ··

① First ordinary meeting, Chemulpo, March 7th 1895. Present; The Kamni, Messrs. Chinda, Townsend, Wilkinson & Woolitang. In the absence of both the President and the vice President, Mr. Townsend was invited to take the Chair. Mr. Chinda, who since the date of last meeting had been appointed H. I. J. M's Consul at Chemulpo, took his seat vice Mr. Eitaki. The Minutes of the previous meeting were read and confirmed and the correspondence was read.

② The meeting learnt with regret of Mr. Sill's determination not to accept the post of President for which his doyennage in the Consular Body more particularly indicated him. It was pointed out that the functions of the President were, strictly speaking, confined to presiding at the meetings of the Council, and that he was not called upon to represent the Council outside the walls of the Municipal Buildings. It was, at the same time, convenient that he should be one who in some other capacity was in direct relations with the Corean Government at Seoul, although he could not, unless authorized ad hos by the Council communicate with that Govt in the name of the Council. Mr. Sill's time would not therefore be greatly infringed upon, while his acceptance of the post would be a convenience to the Council. Mr. Townsend having assured the members that Mr. Sill's decision was irrevocable, Mr. Krien was unanimously elected President for the current year in his stead, with Mr. Chinda as Vice

President. Mr. Chinda was also elected a member of the Executive Committee in the room of Mr. Eitaki.

③ Bundroad in front of Customs Godown. It is understood that the Royal Corean Customs have entered into a contract with a Japanese for the repair and extension of the stone jetty, the work to be completed in four months. The Council propose to proceed as soon as possible, meanwhile, with the 15 metre road, and it was arranged that Mr. Chinda, as Japanese Consul, should give notice to any Japanese owner of goods in sites to prepare to remove them, which the Executive Committee took steps to procure a supply of suitable metalling.

④ Mr. Chinda drew attention to the need for a pesthouse, to which victims of infectious diseases of the more serious kind, such as smallpox, could be removed. It was agreed that the Secretary should write to Drs. Landis & Kojima requesting them to be good enough to favor the pesthouse when established should be under the joint conduct of the Settlements.

⑤ Accounts for 1894. A balance sheet was shown as follows;-

Date		
1894 Jan	Balance from 1893	$1,420.26
Apl. 11	Rents for 1893	4,457.84
Apl. 11	Grading account, first instalment from Corean Govt.	1,000.00
May 12	Sale of land (less auctioneer's fees)	3,080.90
Dec. 31	Burial fees	35.00
〃	License	170.00
〃	Interest on Current account	141.86
		10,305.86

Dec. 31	Police	Wages (less fines)	1870.74	$1,870.74
		Clothing etc.		163.59
〃	Roads	Scavengers	278.13	
		Lamps etc.	204.94	483.07
		Construction & repair	694.92	
		Trees	19.03	713.95
〃	Printing & Stationary			14.73
〃	Municipal Building	Rent	75.60	
		Insurance	28.13	
		Coal	100.10	
		Miscellaneous	7.85	211.68
〃	Cemetery	Registers	32.25	
		graves	6.00	38.25
〃	Public Garden	Wire etc.		172.00
〃	Clerical	gratuity, Corean writer		10.00
Dec. 31	Balance			6,627.85
				10,305.86

⑥ New Plan of Settlement. Mr. Chinda showed a tracing of the plan on which certain alteration were marked proposed by him after consultation with Mr. Wilkinson and joint inspection of the ground. With regard to the more Northern part of the Settlement, it was pointed out that it was difficult to lay it out into lots pending a decision as to the course of the projected Chemulpo-Seoul railway.

⑦ Mr. WooLitang drew attention to the circumstance that the snows that had fallen last month was allowed to remain in the streets instead of being promptly removed, with the consequence that it rendered the roads impossible.

It was held that the Byelaws require each occupant to remove the snow from the foot walk abutting on his premises, but that the roads ought to be cleared by the Council's Scavengers.

⑧ Balance of grading account. The Kamni stated that he would reply to the Secretary's letter on this subject after obtaining obstructions from the Foreign Office.

⑨ The next meeting will be held in the first week in April on a day to be fixed by the local members.[85)]

85) 「제물포 각국 조계 회의록 제2권」은 여기에서 끝난다.

1898년 9월 21일 회의록

- 번역문 -

① 1898년 9월 21일 4차 정기 회의를 개최하였다. 이시이 씨, 라인스도르프 씨, 샌즈 씨, 오트월 씨, 감리, 볼터 씨, 스즈키 씨, 타운젠드 씨(서기)가 참석하였다. 회장과 부회장 모두 공석인 관계로 이시이 씨에게 의장직을 부탁하였다.[86] 3차 정기 회의의 회의록을 낭독하고 승인하였다. 이후 오고간 편지들을 낭독하였다.

② 1898년 9월 1일자로 경찰관들의 월급을 올리기로 결정하였다. 에클런드 80달러, 시마자키 30달러, 키츠키 24달러, 키지야마 20달러. 간수, 점등원, 청소부의 월급은 충분하다고 여겨 그대로 두었다.

③ 인접한 찻집에서 소음이 심하다는 몬디니 씨의 불만 편지를 낭독하였다. 이시이 씨는 자신이 찻집 주인에게 경고하였으며 그에게 신동공사 규정을 준수하겠다는 약속을 받았다고 이야기하였다.

④ 마다는 B1 구역 앞의 제방에 목재 등을 보관하는 대신 세금을 내겠다며 신동공사의 허가를 요청하였다. 허가하지 않았다.

⑤ 후지와라는 C4~C5 구역의 도로 밑에 철제 수도관을 놓고 싶다며 신동공사의 허가를 요청하였다. 수도관을 놓은 후 도로 상태가 좋아야 하고 신동공사가 요청하면 언제든지 수도관을 철거해야 한다는 것을

86) 서울주재독일부영사 라인스도르프, 제물포주재일본부영사 이시이, 제물포주재영국대리부영사로 부임한 오트월, 감리, 선출직 위원 겸 서기 타운젠드, 선출직 위원 볼터와 스즈키가 참석하였다. 주한미국공사관 서기관 샌즈는 9월 17일 신동공사 회장직을 내놓은 주한미국공사 알렌을 대신하여 미국 대표로 참석하였다.

조건으로 걸고 허가하였다.

⑥ 경찰국장은 제방에 대나무 등이 장기간 쌓여 있어 통행에 방해가 된다고 보고하였다. 집행위원회는 규정이 준수되고 있는지 조사해 보라는 요청을 받았다.

⑦ 공원과 관련하여 볼터 씨가 발의하고 타운젠드 씨가 재청하였다. "집행위원회가 제출한 정원사와의 계약을 완료하기 위하여 추가로 100엔을 책정합시다." 만장일치로 통과되었다. 오트윌 씨가 발의하고 스즈키 씨가 재청하였다. "공원 정원사와 문지기의 사택을 위하여 최대 800엔을 지출할 수 있도록 집행위원회에 권한을 줍시다." 만장일치로 통과되었다.

⑧ 샌즈 씨는 죄수를 수감하기 위하여 신동공사 교도소를 빌려 달라고 요청하였다. 그는 모든 비용을 자신이 부담하고 중국인 경찰관을 경비원으로 쓰겠다고 했다.

⑨ 중국 조계의 경계선과 관련하여 오트윌 씨가 발의하고 이시이 씨가 재청하였다. "각국 조계와 중국 조계 사이의 경계선을 명확하게 해 달라고 집행위원회에 요청합시다." 만장일치로 통과되었다. 집행위원회는 묘지 지점 북쪽의 해변을 따라 놓여 있는 너비 15미터의 도로를 경계선으로 확정해 달라는 요청을 받았다.

⑩ 신동공사 회장과 관련하여 타운젠드 씨가 발의하고 볼터 씨가 재청하였다. "1898년 12월 31일까지 복무할 제물포 신동공사 회장으로 이시이 씨를 선출합시다." 만장일치로 통과되었다. 이 선거는 1898년 9월 17일자 편지를 통하여 사임한 알렌 씨의 자리를 채우기 위하여 실시되었다.

⑪ 신동공사 부회장과 관련하여 라인스도르프 씨가 발의하고 타운젠

드 씨가 재청하였다. "1898년 12월 31일까지 복무할 제물포 신동공사 부회장으로 오트윌 씨를 선출합시다." 만장일치로 통과되었다. 이 선거는 최근에 세상을 떠난 전 제물포주재영국부영사 졸리 씨의 자리를 채우기 위하여 실시되었다.[87]

⑫ 현지 위원들이 정하는 날짜에 회의를 속개하기로 하고 휴회하였다.

·· ─ **원문** ─ ··

① FOURTH ORDINARY MEETING, Sept. 21st. 1898. Messrs. Ishii, Reinsdorf, Sands, Ottewill, the Kamni, Wolter, Suzuki and Townsend, Hon. Secy. In the absence of the President, Mr. Ishii was invited to take the chair. The minutes of the Third Ordinary Meeting were read and confirmed. The correspondence was read by the Hon. Secy.

② POLICE.- The meeting decided to increase wages of Police to following amounts, to begin September 1st, 1898. Eklundh Yen 80.00 per month, Shimazaki Yen 30.00 per month, Kitsuki Yen 24.00 per month, Kijiyama Yen 20.00 per month. Wages of Jail bay, lamplighter and scarvengers [scavengers] to remain as before, being deemed sufficient.

③ COMPLAINT read from Mr. Mondini regarding noise from adjoining tea house. Mr. Ishii said he had warned the proprietor of tea-house, who had promised to observe the Municipal Regulations.

④ MADA.- Application received from Mada, requesting permission to store

87) 이렇게 하여 1898년도 신동공사 회장과 부회장은 알렌과 졸리에서 이시이와 오트윌로 바뀌었다. 1897년 9월 9일 제물포주재영국부영사로 부임한 졸리는 이듬해 6월 23일 사망하였다.

wood, etc. on Bund front of Lot B#1 on payment of rent for ground used. NOT GRANTED.

⑤ FUJIWARA.- Application received from Fujiwara to lay down an iron water pipe under road between Lots C#4 & 5. Permission granted on condition that road be put in good order after laying pipe, which must also be removed at any time when requested by the Municipal Council.

⑥ BAMBOOS, ETC. STORED ON BUND.- Chief of police reports obstruction of Bund by Bomboos [Bamboos], etc. stred [stored] there for long periods. The Ex. Committee were asked to see that the Regulations be observed.

⑦ PUBLIC GARDEN.- Moved by Mr. Wolter seocnded [seconded] by Mr. Townsend that a further sum of yen 100.00 be appropriated for the completion of Gardener's contract, which was laid before the meeting by the Ex. Committee. Carried U. Moved by Mr. Ottewill. Seconded by Mr. Suzuki. That the Ex. Committee be empowered to spend a sum not exceeding yen 800.00 for a Gardener's and Gate Keepers house in the Public Garden. Carried U.

⑧ MR. SANDS requested loan of Municipal Jail, all expenses to be paid by him for prisoner and be to provide Chinese Police as watchman.

⑨ BOUNDARY OF CIINESE [CHINESE] SETTLEMENT.- Moved by Mr. Ottewill. Seconded by Mr. Ishii. That the Ex. Committee be requested to define boundary line between the General Foreign Settlement and the Chinese Settlement. Carried U. The Ex. Committee were also requested to fix boundary line of 15 metre road along the north shore to the Cemetery point.

⑩ PRESIDENT OF MUNICIPAL COUNCIL. Moved by Mr. Townsend. Seconded by Mr. Wolter. That Mr. Ishii be elected President of the Chemulpo Municipal Council for the term ending Dec. 31st, 1898. Carried U. The above election was held to fill the vacancy caused by the resignation of the Hon. H. N. Allen, received in his letter dated Sept. 17th 1898.

⑪ VICE PRESIDENT OF MUNICIPAL COUNCIL. Moved by Mr. Reinsdorf. Seconded by Mr. Townsend. That Mr. Ottewill be elected Vice President of the Chemulpo Municipal Council for the term ending Dec. 31st, 1898. Carried U. The above election was held to fill the vacancy caused by the death of H. Bencraft Joly, Esq. late H. B. M.'s Vice-Consul.

⑫ THE MEETING THEN ADJOURNED to a date to be fixed by the Local Members.

1899년 1월 4일 회의록

·· – 번역문 – ··

① 신동공사 회의록 사본. 1899년 1월 4일 제물포에서 1차 정기 회의를 개회하였다. 라인스도르프 씨(회장), 샌즈 씨, 시데하라 씨, 감리, 볼터 씨, 타운젠드 씨(서기)가 참석하였다.[88] 지난 번 회의록을 낭독하고 승인하였다.

② 1898년 12월 20일 회의 때 나왔던 세금 관련 제안에 대하여 의논하였다. 시데하라 씨와 타운젠드 씨는 기존의 발의를 철회하고 다시 발의하였다. "영사들께 요청합니다. 각국 조계의 토지소유주인 각자의 자국민들에게 매년 1월에 세금을 내지 않으면 이자를 붙여 내야 한다고 알려 주십시오." 만장일치로 통과되었다.

③ 서기는 회의에서 안건을 논의할 때 어떤 안건을 논의할 것인지 말로써 알려 달라는 요청을 받았다. 다음 회의에서는 은화 대신 일본 금화로 세금을 납부하는 문제와 관련하여 관련 협정을 고치자는 제안이 있을 것이라고 공지하였다.

④ 타운젠드 씨가 발의하고 샌즈 씨가 재청하였다. "1899년도 세금을 은화로 내는 것을 허용합시다. 회계께 요청합니다. 은화로 받은 세금을 일본 금화로 바꾸고 잔고도 최대한 일본 금화로 바꾸어 주십시오." 만

---

88) 1899년도 신동공사 임원은 회장 라인스도르프, 부회장은 1898년 11월 5일 부임한 제물포주재영국부영사 선디우스, 회계 볼터, 서기 타운젠드였다. 시데하라는 1898년 11월 14일부터 이듬해 5월 11일까지 제물포주재일본대리부영사로 복무하였다.

장일치로 통과되었다.

⑤ 볼터 씨가 발의하고 샌즈 씨가 재청하였다. "회계가 일시적으로 부재중일 경우 수표에 서명하고 지불할 권한을 서기에게 줍시다." 만장일치로 통과되었다.

⑥ 현지 위원들의 결정에 따라 휴회하였다.

서기 타운젠드 (서명)

‥ – **원문** – ‥

① Copy of Minutes, Municipal Council. Chemulpo, Jan. 4th, 1899. First Ordinary Meeting 1899. Present: Mr. Reinsdorf President, Messrs. Sands, Shidehara, Kamni, Wolter & Townsend Hon. Secy. Minutes of last meeting were read & confirmed.

② Discussion to place on the motion re collection of rents, moved at the meeting of Dec. 20th 1898. Messrs. Shidehara & Townsend withdrew their motion of Dec. 20 98 and proposed the following motion. That Consuls be requested to inform their Nationals, who are land renters in the Gen. Foreign Settlement that, unless rents are paid in Jan. of each year, legal proceedings will be instituted to enforce payment of the respective amounts with interest. Carried unanimously.

③ The Hon. Secy was requested to mention, as far as possible the subjects to be brought up at meetings, where issuing the Notice. Notice was given, that at the next meeting a motion would be made to alter the Agreement as to taxes, making them payable in Gold Yens instead of silver as at present.

④ Moved by Mr. Townsend, seconded by Mr. Sands that as rents for 1899 are payable in silver, that the Hon. Treasurer be requested to receive same and change Silver into Gold Yens to the best advantage possible, keeping his balance, as far as possible, in Gold Yens. Carried unanimously.

⑤ Moved by Mr. Wolter, seconded by Mr. Sands that in case of the temporary absence of the Hon. Treasurer, the Hon. Secretary be empowered to sign checks and make payments. Carried unanimously.

⑥ The meeting then adjourned, subject to the call of the Local Members.

(signed) W. D. Townsend. Hon. Secretary.

1899년 1월 30일 회의록

·· – 번역문 – ··

① 1899년 1월 30일 2차 정기 회의를 개회하였다. 정족수가 부족하여 1월 31일에 속개하기로 하고 휴회하였다.

·· – 원문 – ··

① Second Ordinary Meeting, Jan. 30th 1899. No Quorum being present, the Meeting was adjourned to the 31st inst.

1899년 1월 31일 회의록

번역문

① 1899년 1월 31일 신동공사 회의를 개최하였다. 선디우스 씨(부회장/의장), 샌즈 씨, 시데하라 씨, 감리, 볼터 씨, 타운젠드 씨(서기)가 참석하였다.[89)]

② 선디우스 씨가 제안하고 샌즈 씨가 재청하였다. "콜브란 씨와의 협정이 1월 5일자 편지에 나온 대로 신동공사 위원들의 개별 승인을 받았으니 확정합시다." 만장일치로 통과되었다.

③ 신동공사는 경찰관들이 가족과 함께 경찰서에 사는 것을 허락하였다.

④ 해관장대리 챌머스 씨가 보내 온 공문을 낭독하였다. 새로 지은 북쪽 제방 도로에 대한 브라운 씨의 공문이 동봉되어 있었다.[90)] 이에 대해서는 다음 회의 때 의논하기로 했다.

⑤ 감리는 영사들에게 편지를 써서 1차 정기 회의 때 통과된 세금 관련 제안의 내용을 알리라는 요청을 받았다. 2월 28일까지 세금을 내지 않으면 이자를 붙여 내도록 법적 절차를 집행한다는 내용이었다.

⑥ 집행위원회는 각국 조계에 가로수 400그루를 심기 위하여 일본인 정원사와 계약을 체결하는 일에 신동공사의 인가를 받았다.

---

89) 서울주재독일대리공사 라인스도르프와 선출직 위원 스즈키는 불참하였다. 주한미국공사 알렌을 대신하여 샌즈가 참석하였다.

90) 챌머스는 1898년 6월 25일부터 인천해관장대리로 복무하였다. "새로 지은 북쪽 제방 도로"란 1899년 1월 중순 폭풍우로 손상된 신축 제방을 가리킨다.

1899년 1월 31일 회의록 사본

서기 타운젠드

·· – **원문** – ··

① Jan. 31st. 1899. Present: Mr. Sundius Vice President, in the chair, Messrs. Sands, Shidehara, Kamni, Wolter and Townsend, Hon. Secretary.

② Moved by Sundius, 2nd Mr. Sands, that the Agreement made with Mr. Collbran, as per his letter of Jan. 5th, having been accepted individually by the Members of the Mun. Council, be hereby confirmed. Carried unanimously.

③ Permission was granted by the Council to the Police, to have their families live at the Police Station.

④ Despatch was read from J. L. Chalmers Esq. Acting Commissioner of Customs, enclosing despatch from J. McLeavy Brown Esq. dated Jan. re. new North Bund Road and was laid on the Table for discussion at the next meeting.

⑤ Taxes. The Kamni was requested by the Council to send letters to the Consuls, advising them of the Motion passed at 1st Ordinary Meeting re. Rents, that unless Rents were paid before Feb. 28th 1899, legal proceedings would be taken to enforce payment with interest.

⑥ The Executive Committee were authorized by the Council to contract with Japanese Gardiner for 400 trees to be planted in the streets of the General Foreign Settlement.

Copy of Minutes Meeting, Jan 31st 1899.

W. D. Townsend Hon. Secy.

1899년 2월 21일 회의록

·· – 번역문 – ··

① (사본) 1899년 2월 21일 3차 정기 회의를 개최하였다. 라인스도르프 씨(회장), 선디우스 씨, 시데하라 씨, 감리, 볼터 씨, 타운젠드 씨(서기)가 참석하였다.[91] 지난 번 회의록을 낭독하고 승인하였다.

② 해관장이 보내 온 편지를 낭독하였다. 북쪽 제방 도로에 관한 총세무사 브라운 씨의 1월 28일자 편지가 동봉되어 있었다.[92] 논의 후 타운젠드 씨가 제안하고 시데하라 씨가 재청하였다. "신동공사는 너비 15미터의 제방 도로를 각국 조계의 일부로 받아들이고 그것이 개인적으로 사용되지 않도록 보존할 준비를 갖추었습니다. 신동공사는 철도 회사가 최근의 폭풍우로 손상된 노반을 원래 높이로 회복시키는 즉시 도로에 금속 처리를 할 것입니다. 또한 신동공사는 도로의 노면을 적절하게 유지 보수할 것이지만, 제방을 복구하고 관리하는 비용은 일체 부담하지 않음을 확실하게 이해하고 있습니다. 제방 공사는 제방과 맞닿아 있으면서 제방의 일부를 소유하고 있는 한국 정부, 중국 조계, 철도 회사가 시행할 것입니다. 철도 회사는 제방에 생긴 틈 뒤편의 땅도 매립할 것입니다. 그 틈은 브라운 씨가 1월 28일자 편지에서 지적하신 대로 뒤편의 땅을 매립하지 않았기 때문에 생긴 것입니다. 또한 제방 도로 안쪽의

---

91) 주한미국공사 알렌과 선출직 위원 스즈키는 불참하였다.

92) 1899년 1월 31일 회의 때 제출된 바 있다. 영국인 브라운은 1893년부터 10년 이상 총세무사 겸 탁지부 고문으로 복무하였다.

모든 매립지는 C 부지에 해당되는 세금을 납부해야 합니다. 이는 각국 조계 장정 제7조에 따른 것이자 총세무사와 미국 기업 연합의 합의에 준거한 것입니다. 매립지에 대한 세금을 납부하지 않는다면, 신동공사는 제방 도로의 노반과 인근 토지에 들어가는 경비를 부담할 수 없습니다." 만장일치로 통과되었다. 서기는 총세무사에게 편지를 써서 이 결의안과 다음 결의안을 알리라는 요청을 받았다. 다음 결의안은 선디우스 씨가 제안하고 볼터 씨가 재청하였으며 만장일치로 통과되었다. "신동공사는 부동산 권리증이 경인선 철도 회사 앞으로 곧 발행될 것으로 알고, 원래 조계 도면에 기획된 대로 합동 조사 후 갯벌 경계를 따라 너비 15미터의 도로를 놓아야 한다는 점을 지적합니다. 이 일이 시행될 수 있도록 귀하(총세무사)께서 잘 조율해 주시기를 요청합니다."[93]

③ 새로 확장한 일본 제방 앞을 따라 너비 15미터의 도로를 놓는 문제를 의논하였다. 볼터 씨가 제안하고 타운젠드 씨가 재청하였다. "서기께 요청합니다. 새로 확장한 일본 제방 앞을 따라 너비 7미터의 기존 도로 대신 너비 15미터의 넓은 도로를 놓는 문제를 합의해 줄 수 있는지 각국외교대표단장께 문의해 주십시오." 만장일치로 통과되었다.

④ 현지 위원들의 뜻에 따라 휴회하였다.

서기 타운젠드 (서명)

---

93) 그러나 이 문제는 신속하게 조율되지 못한 것 같다. 1900년 9월 20일 서울주재독일대리총영사 바이페르트가 주한미국공사 알렌에게 보낸 편지에 따르면, 주한일본공사 하야시는 한국이 철도 회사의 이름으로 적절한 부동산 권리증을 발행하고 토지 전체를 D 부지로 편성해 주기를 희망하고 있었다. D 부지로 편성할 경우 세금은 3분의 1로 줄어드는 것이었다.

‥ – 원문 – ‥

① (Copy) THIRD ORDINARY MEETING 21st FEB. 1899. Present: Mr. Reinsdorf, President, Messrs. Sundius, Shidehara, Kamni, Wolter and Townsend, Hon. Secretary. Minutes of the last meeting were read and confirmed.

② Letter from the Commissioner of Customs was read, enclosing letter from J. McLeavy Brown Esq. Chief Commissioner of Customs, dated Jan. 28th re North Bund Road. After discussion the following motion was made by Mr. Townsend, seconded by Mr. Shidehara. That the Municipal Council is prepared to take over the 15 metre Bund Road, as a part of the General Foreign Settlement and to preserve the same from being encroached upon for any private purpose. The Council will also proceed to metal the road, as soon as the Railway Co. shall have raised the road bed to the original level at which it stood before it was damaged by the recent storm. While the Council will maintain the Surface of the Bund Road in a proper state of repair, it is clearly understood that no part of the cost of restoring the Sea-wall from end to end and of maintaining it in repair is to be borne by the Council. This work, it is assumed, will be done promptly as required, by the Korean Govt; the Chinese Settlement Authorities and the Railway Company on the Portion of the Wall which belong to them respectively or face their property and for which they are responsible. It is also understood that the Railway Company will fill in the ground behind the present breach, which breach was caused, as pointed out by the Mr. Brown in his letter of 28th Jan., by the absence of such filling. It is further taken by granted by the Council that all ground reclaimed from the foreshore inside the new Bund Road shall pay sent to the Municipal Council as C. Lots. being reclaimed foreshore ground, in accordance with Article 7 of the General Foreign Settlement Regulation and as arranged by the Chief Commissioner with American Syndicate. Until such rent shall have been paid the Council cannot bind itself to incur any expenditure in connection with the Bund Road bed and attached grounds, etc., now taken over beyond the minimum amount required to guard such Road bed, etc., as an integral part of General Foreign Settlement. Carried unanimously. The Hon. Secty was requested to communicate the above motion to the Commissioner of Customs and to add the following motion which was moved by Mr. Sundius and seconded by Mr. Wolter and carried unanimously. In connection with my (Hon. Secy) letter of today and as the Municipal Council presumes that Title Deeds will be issued to the Seoul and Chemulpo Railway Company shortly, the Council begs to point out that the inside 15 metre Road should be laid out by joint survey along the foreshore line according to the original plan of the Settlement and the Council request that you (Commr- of Customs) will make suitable arrangements to carry this into effect.

③ Discussion took place on the matter of a 15 metre Road along the front of the New Japanese Bund extension. Moved by Mr. Wolter. Seconded by Mr. Townsend. That the Hon. Secretary be requested to write to the Doyen of the Diplomatic Corps asking him if possible to make arrangement for a 15 metre wide road instead of a 7 metre road, as at present, along the front of the New Japanese Bund Extension. Carried unanimously.

④ The Meeting then adjourned subject to the Call of the Local Members.

(signed) Hon. Secretary. W. D. Townsend.

1900년 12월 6일 회의록

·· – **번역문** – ··

① 회의록 사본. 1900년 12월 6일 한국 제물포에서 3차 정기 회의를 개최하였다. 바이페르트 박사(회장), 알렌 씨, 이주인 씨, 고프 씨, 감리의 비서, 오다카 씨, 뤼어스 씨, 타운젠드 씨(서기)가 참석하였다.[94)]

② 고프 씨가 제안하고 알렌 박사가 재청하였다. "감리가 답장을 보내지 않았으므로 바이페르트 씨는 한국인 마을의 위생에 관하여 (대한제국) 외부와 이야기를 나눠야 합니다." 만장일치로 통과되었다.

③ 선거위원회에서 온 편지를 낭독하였다. 12월 5일 선거 결과 뤼어스 씨가 12표, 오다카 씨가 9표, 허치슨 씨가 6표를 얻었다는 내용이었다. 신동공사 회장 바이페르트 박사는 1901년 1월 1일부터 3년간 뤼어스 씨가 선출직 위원으로 복무할 것이라고 선언하였다. 오다카 씨는 2년 임기의 선출직 위원이 되었다.[95)]

④ 알렌 박사가 제안하고 고프 씨가 재청하였다. "신동공사의 선거 규정을 200부 인쇄하여 돌립시다." 만장일치로 통과되었다.

⑤ 경찰관 봉급과 관련하여 타운젠드 씨가 제안하고 이주인 씨가 재청하였다. "1900년 12월 31일까지 복무한 데 대하여 시마자키에게 25엔의 사례금을 주고, 다른 경찰관 2명의 월급도 12월 1일자로 2엔씩 인상

94) 서울주재독일총영사 바이페르트, 주한미국공사 알렌, 제물포주재영국부영사 고프, 제물포주재일본영사 이주인, 성명을 알 수 없는 감리의 비서, 선출직 위원 오다카, 선출직 위원 겸 회계 뤼어스, 선출직 위원 겸 서기 타운젠드가 참석하였다.

95) 이렇게 하여 타운젠드, 뤼어스, 오다카가 1901년도 선출직 위원으로 복무하게 되었다.

합시다.” 만장일치로 통과되었다.

⑥ 철도 회사가 매립한 땅에 대한 세금과 관련하여 바이페르트 박사가 공지하였다. 주한일본공사가 아직 답장을 보내지 않았으나 곧 보낼 것으로 기대한다는 내용이었다.[96)]

⑦ 회계 뤼어스 씨가 1900년 11월 30일까지의 신동공사 수입 및 지출 내역을 제출하였다. 타운젠드 씨가 제안하고 알렌 박사가 재청하였다. “연말까지의 회계 내역을 감사하기 위하여 고프 씨와 이주인 씨를 감사위원회로 임명합시다.”

⑧ 1901년도 임원 선거와 관련하여 알렌 박사가 제안하고 이주인 씨가 재청하였다. “회장에 바이페르트 박사, 서기 겸 부회장에 고프 씨, 회계에 뤼어스 씨를 선출합시다.” 만장일치로 통과되었다. 알렌 박사가 제안하고 고프 씨가 재청하였다. “이주인 씨, 뤼어스 씨, 타운젠드 씨를 1901년도 집행위원회로 구성합시다.” 만장일치로 통과되었다.

⑨ 바이페르트 박사가 제안하고 뤼어스 씨가 재청하였다. “1897년 1월부터 서기로 복무해 준 타운젠드 씨에게 공식적인 감사 인사를 전합시다.” 만장일치로 통과되었다.[97)]

⑩ 1901년도 기금 책정과 관련하여 고프 씨가 제안하고 이주인 씨가 재청하였다. 도로에 3,000엔, 경찰에 3,500엔, 제복에 200엔, 잡화에 500엔, 석탄에 200엔, 청소에 1,500엔, 가로등에 500엔, 도합 9,400엔이 만장일치로 통과되었다.

---

96) 1899년 2월 21일 회의록을 참고할 것.

97) 제물포주재영국부영사는 신동공사 출범 이래 줄곧 서기직을 맡았으나 1897년부터는 부회장으로 선출되는 일이 많아졌던 것 같다. 선출직 위원 타운젠드는 1897년부터 3년간 서기 업무를 맡았으며 이후에는 제물포주재영국부영사가 부회장 겸 서기로 복무하였다.

⑪ 현지 위원들의 결정에 따라 휴회하였다.

서기 타운젠드 (서명)

·· – 원문 – ··

① Copy of Minutes, Chemulpo, Korea, December 6th, 1900. THIRD REGULAR MEETING. Present: Dr. Weipert, President, Messrs. Allen, Ijuin, Goffe, the Kanmi's Secretary, Messrs. Odaka, Luhrs and Townsend, Hon. Secretary.

② Moved by Mr. Goffe, seconded by Dr. Allen, That in view of no reply having been received from the Kamni, that Dr. Weipert be asked to communicate with the Foreign Office re Sanitation of the Corean Town. C. U.

③ Letter was read from Official Election Committee announcing that at the election held on Dec. 5th. Mr. Carl Luhrs had 12 votes. Mr. G. Odaka had 9 votes. Mr. W. du F. hutchison had 6 votes. Dr. Weipert, President of the Council, then declared that Mr. Carl Luhrs had been elected a member of the Municipal Council to serve three years from Jan. 1st, 1901, and Mr. G. Odaka to serve two years from Jan. 1901.

④ Moved by Dr. Allen, Seconded by Mr. Goffe, That 200 copies of the Election Rules be printed by the Council for distribution. C. U.

⑤ Police Wages. Moved by Mr. Townsend, seconded by Mr. Ijuin, That Shimazaki be granted a gratuity of 25 Yen for services up to Dec. 31st, 1900, and that the other policemen (2) be granted an increase of 2 Yen per month from Dec. 1st, 1900. C. U.

⑥ R. R. Foreshore Taxes. Dr. Weipert informed the Council that no answer had yet been received from the Japanese Minister at Seoul, but one was expected shortly.

⑦ Mr. Luhrs, Hon. Treasurer, presented a statement of Expenditures and Receipts by the Municipal Council up to Nov. 30th, 1900. Moved by Mr. Townsend, seconded by Dr. Allen, That Messrs. Goffe and Ijuin be appointed a Committee of 2 to audit the Hon. Treasurer's account at the end of the year.

⑧ Officers of the Council for 1901. Moved by Dr. Allen, seconded by Mr. Ijuin, That the following Officers of the Council be elected for the year 1901. Dr. Weipert — President. Mr. Goffe — Hon. Secretary and Vice President. Mr. Luhrs — Hon. Treasurer. C. U. Moved by Dr. Allen, Seconded by Mr. Goffe, That the Executive Committee for 1901 consist of Messrs. Ijuin, Luhrs and Townsend. C. U.

⑨ Moved by Dr. Weipert, seconded by Mr. Luhrs, That the thanks of the Council be given to Mr. Townsend for his services as Hon. Secretary since Jan. 1897. C. U.

⑩ Appropriations for 1901. Moved by Mr. Goffe, seconded by Mr. Ijuin, That the following amounts be appropriated for the year 1901. Roads ¥3,000, Police ¥3,500, Uniforms ¥200, Miscl. ¥500, Coal ¥200, Scavenging ¥1,500, Lighting ¥500, Total ¥9,400. C. U.

⑪ The Council then adjourned, subject to the call of the Local Members.

(signed) W. D. Townsend. Hon. Secretary.

1913년 11월 12일 회의록

·· – **번역문** – ··

① 1913년 11월 12일 제물포 각국 조계 신동공사 회의록. 1913년 11월 12일 수요일 오전 10시 15분 신동공사 회관에서 5차 정기 회의를 개회하였다. 크뤄거 박사(회장/의장), 시드모어 씨, 히사미즈 씨, 이와사키 씨, 바우만 씨, 베넷 씨가 참석하였다.[98] 지난 번 회의록을 낭독하고 승인하였다.

② 서기와 인천부가 대청소 문제에 대하여 교환한 편지를 회장이 낭독하였다. 인천부윤이 신동공사가 제출한 문제와 관련하여 아직 답변을 주지 않았기 때문에 이 문제는 당분간 보류한다.

③ 각국 조계의 폐지 및 외국인 묘지 관리와 관련하여, 크뤄거 박사는 10월 30일 조선의 새로운 부(府)에 대하여 반포된 법령을 보고하였다. 이 법령 제34조에는 '일본 조계, 각국 조계, 서울의 위생국에 대한 법령과 조례를 폐지할 것이다'라고 되어 있고, 제33조에는 '이 법령을 집행하는 시기는 총독이 결정할 것이다'라고 되어 있다. 제35조에는 '성진을 제외한 각국 조계의 모든 문제, 권리, 의무는 부로 이관되나, 각국 조계 안에 있는 묘지는 이관되지 않는다. 제물포 각국 조계 신동공사 기금 20,000엔은 인천부로 이관하지 않는다는 규정을 두었다'라고 되어 있

---

98) 제물포 각국 조계의 폐지와 외국인 묘지 관리에 대하여 논의한 이 날 회의에는 서울주재 독일총영사 크뤄거, 서울주재미국총영사 시드모어, 인천부윤 히사미즈, 선출직 위원으로는 일본인 이와사키, 독일인 바우만, 영국인 베넷이 참석하였다.

다. 1913년 3월 17일에 열린 5차 회의 때 이 기금에 대한 초안을 만들면서, 고마츠 씨는 각국 조계의 공원을 부 당국이 잘 관리해야 한다고 발언하였다. 제10조는 다음과 같다. “각국 조계의 외국인 묘지는 외국인 주민들에 의하여 관리되어야 한다. 그들은 묘지, 화장지, 매장, 화장에 대한 법령과 조례를 준수해야 하며 세금과 요금은 면제된다. 제물포 각국 조계 신동공사 기금 20,000엔의 대부분은 이 일에 책정될 것이다.” 이와 관련하여 크뤼거 박사는 묘지기금관리인 3명이 공동으로 사직서를 내고 신탁자금위원회로 돌아가야 한다고 제의하였다. 이는 신동공사가 스스로 편리하다고 생각하는 방향으로 기금을 처리하기 위해서이다.

·· – **원문** – ··

① MUNICIPAL COUNCIL, GENERAL FOREIGN SETTLEMENT, CHEMULPO. Minutes, Chemulpo, 12th November 1913. Fifth ordinary general meeting held at the Council Hall on Wednesday 12th November 1913 at 10.15 a. m. Present: Dr. Krüger, President in the Chair, and Messrs. Scidmore, Hisamidzu, Iwasaki, Baumann and Bennett. Minutes of the previous meeting were read and approved.

② House Cleaning. Correspondence between the Secretary and the Prefect read by the Chairman; but no answer having yet been received from the Governor of the Province to whom the question was submitted, the matter must remain over in the meantime.

③ Abolition of General Foreign Settlements, Control of Cemeteries &c. Dr. Krüger reported to the Council that on the 30th of October an Order (Seirei) was promulgated regarding the new “Fu’s” in Chosen, and in Article 34 it states that “the Laws and ordinances with regard to the Japanese Municipalities, the

General Foreign Settlements, and the Sanitary Association in Seoul will be abolished." Article 33 states that the time when this Seirei will be put into force will be decided by the Governor General. Article 35 states that all matters, rights, and obligations of the General Foreign Settlements with exception of Songchin will be taken over by the new "Fu" Prefectures, but that this will not be the case with regard to Cemeteries which are inside the boundaries of the General Foreign Settlements, and that with regard to the reserve fund of 20,000 Yen of the Municipal Council of the General Foreign Settlement of Chemulpo, a provision is made that this reserve fund is not to be handed over to the new Jinsen Fu Prefecture. In the protocols with regard to this reserve fund, at the Fifth meeting held on March, 17th 1913 Mr. Komatsu proposed that the existing public garden in the Foreign Settlement be maintained in good order and condition by the Authorities. Article 10 reads as follows:- "The existing Foreign Cemeteries in the Foreign Settlements shall be maintained by local Foreign Residents in conformity with the Laws and Ordinances governing Cemeteries, Crematories, Burial, Cremation &c free of all taxes and rates. The sum of Yen 20,000- or so much thereof as may be necessary shall be appropriated for this purpose out of the property belonging to the Municipal Council of the General Foreign Settlement at Chemulpo." In respect of this arrangement Dr. Krüger suggested that the three Trustees of the Cemetery-fund should jointly send in to our Council their resignations and return to the Council the Trust-fund so that by this action the Council would be subsequently enabled to handle the fund in a way which they may deem expedient in order to fulfill the above conditions.

기타 문서

1884년 5월 10일
제물포 각국 조계의 준비를 위한 협정서[99)]

·· – 번역문 – ··

제물포 각국 조계의 준비를 위한 협정서

1884년 5월 10일

(1) 중국 조계 앞에 남쪽으로 펼쳐진 토지는 각국 조계 부지의 일부이다. 이는 첨부한 도면에 빨간색 선으로 표시한 대로 한국 정부에 의하여 매립될 것이다. 이 토지 앞에는 제물포 절벽의 남동쪽까지 이어지는 제방 도로를 쌓고, 제물포 절벽에는 화물선이 왕래할 수 있는 큰 부두를 세울 것이다. 제방 도로는 밀물이 가장 높은 날의 수위보다 2피트 높게 건설할 것이다.

(2) 추후 각국 조계가 더 많은 부지를 필요로 하게 될 경우, 일본 조계와 각국 조계 앞에 있는 갯벌을 매립함으로써 남쪽으로 확장할 수 있다. 확장한계선은 현재 일본인 묘지가 있는 제물포 절벽이다.

(3) 첨부한 도면에 빨간색 선으로 표시한 중국 조계 북쪽의 토지 역시 각국 조계를 위하여 남겨둔다.[100)]

99) 제물포 각국 조계의 조성에 필요한 부지 확보와 제방 및 부두 건설에 대한 합의안이다. 〈인천제물포각국조계장정〉은 이 협정서가 만들어지고 6개월 뒤인 1884년 11월 7일 최종 조인되었다.

100) 이 도면(부록 참조)에는 영국 영사관 부지(British Consular Ground), 부두 윗부분(Head of Jetty), 해관 경계(Customs Boundary), 해관(Custom House), 마부 숙소(Gigmen's Quarters), 검사관보 사무실(Tidewaiter's Office), 해관 창고(Customs Godown), 일본 조계(Japanese Settlement) 등이 표시되어 있다. '아직 매립되지 않은 땅(Space not yet

·· – **원문** – ··

Arrangements for the Preparation of a
General Settlement for All Foreigners at Chemulpo

10 May 1884.

16d. 4m. K. S.

(1) The ground in front of & lying to the south of the Chinese Settlement will be filled in by the Korean Government within the limits shown by the red line on the annexed plan as a portion of the site of the General Foreign Settlement. A road with a seawall will be constructed in front of this ground and will be continued to the S. W. angle of the Chemulpo Bluff where a substantial jetty for the use of Cargo boats will be built. This road will be two feet above the highest spring tides.

(2) The above ground will afterwards be extended from time to time in a southerly direction whenever more lots are required for General Foreign occupation by filling in the foreshore in front of the Japanese & so called General Settlement. The limit of this extension is the Bluff where the Japanese cemetery now is.

(3) The ground north of the Chinese Settlement as far as the red line shown on the annexed plan is also reserved for the purpose of a General Settlement for all Foreigners.

---

filled in)'이라고 기록되어 있는 부분이 협정서 제1조에 나오는 매립대상지이다. 하단에 공용 도로(Public Road)와 제방(Sea Wall)이 쓰여 있는 빨간색 선은 제1조, 해관 창고와 연결되어 있는 빨간색 선은 제3조를 참고할 것.

1891년 1월 1일 제물포 각국 조계 토지소유주 명단[101)]

·· – 번역문 – ··

제물포 각국 조계 1891년 1월 1일 현재 토지소유주 명단

성명	국적	세액($)	성명	국적	세액($)
슈타인벡	오스트리아	120.90	알마허	독일	171.00
영국 정부	영국	201.80	뫼르젤	〃	347.70
스트리플링	〃	487.98	오다	일본	60.90
홀링스워스	〃	26.24	이나미	〃	125.22
허치슨	〃	44.54	아소	〃	54.00
우리탕	중국	266.98	도사	〃	40.92
리페이첸	〃	55.14	신도	〃	46.20
한국 해관	한국	626.32	호리	〃	168.48
한국인 경찰관	〃	22.44	시마우치	〃	60.12
라포르트	프랑스	22.10	호리구치	〃	54.00
마이어	독일	597.12	오하시	〃	24.00
볼터	〃	495.34	타운젠드	미국	72.90
뤼어스	〃	40.14	쿠퍼의 유언집행자들	〃	36.00
고르샬키	〃	42.30			
브링크마이어	〃	47.70	합계		4,358.48

101) 1891년 1월 1일 현재 제물포 각국 조계 토지소유주의 성명과 국적, 매년 납부하는 세금의 액수를 기재한 표이다. 총 28명의 토지소유주 중 일본인이 9명으로 가장 많았지만 넓은 토지를 소유하고 많은 세금을 낸 것은 독일인 마이어, 볼터, 뫼르젤과 영국인 스트리플링 등 유럽인이었다.

·· ― 원문 ― ··

Chemulpo General Foreign Settlement

List of Land renters etc. for 1st Jany, 1891.

Holder	Nationality	Full tax		Holder	Nationality	Full tax	
J. Steinbeck	Austrian	$120	₵90	J. M. Allmacher	German	$171	₵00
H. B. M's Government	Brit.	201	80	F. H. Mörsel	〃	347	70
A. B. Stripling	〃	487	98	Ota Richitaro	Jap.	60	90
T. Hollingsworth	〃	26	24	Yenami Tetsuo	〃	125	22
W. D. F. Hutchison	〃	44	54	S. Aso	〃	54	00
Woo Li-tang	Chin.	266	98	K. Tosa	〃	40	92
Li Pei-chien	〃	55	14	S. Shindo	〃	46	20
Corean Customs	Corean	626	32	Hori Kintaro		168	48
Corean Magistrate	〃	22	44	Shimauchi Yoshio	〃	60	12
E. Laporte	French	22	10	Horiguchi Kayemon	〃	54	00
H. C. E. Meyer	German	597	12	Ohashi Taro	〃	24	00
C. Wolter	〃	495	34	W. D. Townsend	Am.	72	90
C. Lührs	〃	40	14	Cooper's Executors	〃	36	00
A. Gorschalki	〃	42	30				
R. Brinckmeier	〃	47	70	Total		4,358	48

1891년 1월 12일
제물포 각국 조계 구역별 토지 매각 목록[102)]

·· – 번역문 – ··

①	②	③	④	⑤		⑥		⑦	⑧	⑨	⑩	⑪	⑫	⑬	⑭
A	1	1884/00/00 (기록 없음)	1888/11/15	한국 해관	한국	한국 해관	한국	682	654.72	654.72	0	136.40	2.05	134.35	
〃	2		〃	〃	〃	〃	〃	705	676.80	676.80	0	141.00	2.11	138.89	
〃	3		〃	〃	〃	〃	〃	674	47.04	647.04	0	134.80	2.02	132.78	
B	1 & 2	1884/11/07	1888/04/04	볼터	독일	뤼어스	독일	669	41.14	40.14	1.00	40.14	2.01	38.13	
〃	4	1886/05/07	1887/12/02	스트리플링	영국	스트리플링	영국	4,240	254.40	254.40	0	254.40	12.72	241.68	
C	1	1884/11/07	1888/04/04	마이어상사	독일	마이어	독일	1,335	80.10	80.10	0	80.10	4.01	76.09	
〃	2	〃	〃	〃	〃	〃	〃	1,305	78.30	78.30	0	78.30	3.92	74.38	
〃	3	1886/07/15	〃	〃	〃	〃	〃	1,350	122.17	81.00	41.17	81.00	4.05	76.95	

102) 1891년 1월 12일 현재 제물포 각국 조계의 토지 매각 및 소유 현황을 기재한 표이다. ① 등급(Class), ② 번호(No.), ③ 매입일 또는 획득일(Date of purchase or Acquisition), ④ 권리증 발행일(Date of issue of Title deed), ⑤ 권리증 발행 당시 토지소유주(Title deed originally issued to whom), ⑥ 1891년 1월 12일 현재 토지소유주(Name of present holder (12 January 1891)), ⑦ 면적(Square Metres), ⑧ 양도가액(Amount realized by sale), ⑨ 한국 정부가 정한 최저경매가(Upset price retained by Corean Govt.), ⑩ 당시 신동공사에 전달된 잔액(Balance handed to Municipality), ⑪ 연간 세금(Full rent due per annum), ⑫ 한국 정부에 납부하는 연간 왕립세(100제곱미터당 30센트)(Crown Tax to Government per annum 30 cents per 100 sq metres), ⑬ 연간 신동공사에 전달된 잔액(Balance to Municipality per annum), ⑭ 비고(Remarks)

①	②	③	④	⑤		⑥		⑦	⑧	⑨	⑩	⑪	⑫	⑬	⑭
〃	4	1886/09/27	〃	〃	〃	〃	〃	1,250	115.62	75.00	40.62	75.00	3.75	71.25	
〃	5	1886/10/05	1884/04/04	〃	〃	볼터	〃	1,410	142.41	84.60	57.81	84.60	4.23	80.37	
〃	6	1889/03/11	1889/03/11	자이츠	〃	〃	〃	1,440	216.00	86.40	129.60	86.40	4.32	82.08	
〃	7	1889/04/08	1889/04/08	볼터	〃	〃	〃	1,320	300.30	79.20	221.10	79.20	3.96	75.24	
〃	8	〃	〃	〃	〃	〃	〃	1,320	318.12	79.20	238.92	79.20	3.96	75.24	
〃	9	1886/03/31	1887/12/28	쿠퍼	미국	리페이친	중국	919	172.31	55.14	117.17	55.14	2.76	52.38	
〃	10 & 11	1884/11/07	1890/04/14	슈타인벡	오스트리아	슈타인벡	오스트리아	2,015	120.90	120.90	0	120.90	6.05	114.85	
									3,940.33	3,092.94	847.39	1,526.58	61.92	1,464.66	
C	12	1888/05/16	1888/05/16	리키타케	일본	리키타케	일본	1,015	124.85	60.90	63.95	60.90	3.04	57.86	
〃	13	1888/09/03	1888/09/07	이나미	〃	이나미	〃	1,020	714.00	61.20	652.80	61.20	3.06	58.14	
〃	14	〃	〃	〃	〃	〃	〃	1,067	736.23	64.02	672.21	64.02	3.20	60.82	
〃	15	〃	〃	〃	〃	요시다	〃	682	429.66	40.92	388.74	40.92	2.05	38.87	
〃	16	1890/12/12	1890/12/12	신도	〃	신도	〃	770	2,286.90	46.20	2,240.70	46.20	2.31	43.89	
〃	17	1886/06/11	1888/04/04	뫼르젤	독일	뫼르젤	독일	900	54.45	54.00	0.45	54.00	2.70	51.30	
〃	18	1888/05/19	1888/05/21	호리	일본	호리	일본	900	587.25	54.00	533.25	54.00	2.70	51.30	
〃	19	〃	〃	이나미	〃	시마우치	〃	1,002	672.84	60.12	612.72	60.12	3.01	57.11	
〃	20	〃	〃	뫼르젤	독일	뫼르젤	독일	900	542.70	54.00	488.70	54.00	2.70	51.30	
〃	〃	〃	〃	호리구치	일본	나카이	일본	900	553.50	54.00	499.50	54.00	2.70	51.30	
〃	22	1884/11/07	1888/04/04	뫼르젤	독일	뫼르젤	독일	915	54.90	54.90	0	54.90	2.75	52.15	
〃	23	1888/05/19	1888/05/21	우리탕	중국	우리탕	중국	855	600.21	51.30	548.91	51.30	2.56	48.74	
〃	24	1888/03/19	1888/04/04	〃	〃	〃	〃	408	67.32	24.48	42.84	24.48	1.22	23.26	
〃	25	1888/05/19	1888/05/21	이나미	일본	아소	일본	900	342.00	54.00	288.00	54.00	2.70	51.30	

①	②	③	④	⑤		⑥		⑦	⑧	⑨	⑩	⑪	⑫	⑬	⑭
〃	26	〃	〃	〃	〃	호리	〃	900	297.00	54.00	243.00	54.00	2.70	51.30	
〃	27	〃	〃	호리	〃	〃	〃	1,008	322.56	60.48	262.08	60.48	3.02	57.46	
〃	28	1884/11/07	1888/04/04	볼터	독일	우리탕	중국	900	54.00	54.00	0	54.00	2.70	51.30	
〃	29	1886/05/28	〃	뫼르첼	〃	뫼르첼	독일	900	54.45	54.00	0.45	54.00	2.70	51.30	
〃	30	〃	〃	〃	〃	〃	〃	915	55.36	54.90	0.46	54.90	2.74	52.16	
〃	31	〃	〃	〃	〃	〃	〃	930	56.26	55.80	0.46	55.80	2.79	53.01	
C	32	1887/12/05	1887/12/20	우리탕	중국	우리탕	중국	810	648.00	48.60	599.40	48.60	2.43	46.17	
D	1	1884/11/07	1888/04/04	볼터	독일	볼터	독일	4,300	129.00	129.00	0	86.00	12.90	73.10	
〃	2	1886/05/28	1887/12/02	스트리플링	영국	스트리플링	영국	9,156	274.68	274.68	0	183.12	27.47	155.65	
〃	3	1886/04/06	1888/04/04	고르샬키	독일	고르샬키	독일	2,115	63.45	63.45	0	42.30	6.34	35.96	
〃	4	1886/05/07	1887/12/02	스트리플링	영국	스트리플링	영국	2,523	75.69	75.69	0	50.46	7.57	42.89	
〃	5	1887/04/00	1888/11/15	한국 해관	한국	한국 해관	한국	6,344	190.32	190.32	0	126.88	19.03	107.85	
〃	6	1884/00/00	〃	〃	〃	〃	〃	1,497	44.91	44.91	0	29.94	4.49	25.45	
〃	7	1888/04/30	〃	브링크마이어	독일	브링크마이어	독일	975	30.23	29.25	0.98	19.50	2.92	16.58	
〃	8	1888/09/03	〃	〃	〃	〃	〃	1,017	100.17	30.51	69.66	20.34	3.05	17.29	
〃	9	1890/04/22	1890/04/22	〃	〃	〃	〃	393	11.79	11.79	0	7.86	1.18	6.68	
〃	10	1890/10/28	1890/10/28	홉킨스	영국	홉킨스	영국	656	33.46	19.68	13.78	13.12	1.97	11.15	
〃	11 & 12	1886/05/28	1887/12/02	허치슨	〃	허치슨	〃	2,227	69.04	66.81	2.23	44.54	6.68	37.86	
〃	13	〃	1888/04/04	뫼르첼	독일	뫼르첼	독일	1,005	31.16	30.15	1.01	20.10	3.01	17.09	
〃	14	1886/04/19	1887/12/29	오하시	일본	오하시	일본	1,200	36.00	36.00	0	24.00	3.60	20.40	
〃	15	1888/04/11	1888/04/12	홀링스워스	영국	홀링스워스	영국	656	33.45	19.68	13.77	13.12	1.97	11.15	
〃	16 & 17	1886/05/07	1887/12/20	우리탕	중국	우리탕	중국	1,790	107.40	53.70	53.70	35.80	5.37	30.43	

①	②	③	④	⑤		⑥		⑦	⑧	⑨	⑩	⑪	⑫	⑬	⑭
〃	18	1884/11/07	1888/04/04	볼터	독일	볼터	독일	1,207	36.21	36.21	0	24.14	3.62	20.52	
〃	19	〃	〃	〃	〃	〃	〃	1,020	30.60	30.60	0	20.40	3.06	17.34	
〃	20	1887/12/05	1887/12/26	타운젠드	미국	타운젠드	미국	900	270.00	27.00	243.00	18.00	2.70	15.30	
〃	21	1887/03/31	〃	〃	〃	〃	〃	915	27.45	27.45	0	18.30	2.74	15.56	
									14,789.78	5,405.64	9,384.14	3,440.32	237.37	3,202.95	
D	22	1884/11/07	1887/12/26	타운젠드	미국	타운젠드	미국	930	27.90	27.90	0	18.60	2.79	15.81	
〃	23	〃	〃	〃	〃	〃	〃	900	27.00	27.00	0	18.00	2.70	15.30	
〃	24	1889/04/20	1889/04/20	라포르트	프랑스	라포르트	프랑스	1,105	33.26	33.15	0.11	22.10	3.32	18.78	
〃	25	1884/11/07	1888/04/04	마이어상사	독일	마이어(A)	독일	885	26.55	26.55	0	17.70	2.66	15.04	
〃	26	〃	〃	〃	〃	〃	〃	885	26.55	26.55	0	17.70	2.66	15.04	
〃	27 & 28	〃	〃	〃	〃	〃	〃	2,962	88.86	88.86	0	59.24	8.89	50.35	
〃	29	〃	〃	볼터	〃	볼터	〃	1,770	53.10	53.10	0	35.40	5.31	30.09	
〃	30	〃	〃	〃	〃	우리탕	중국	2,640	79.20	79.20	0	52.80	7.92	44.88	
〃	31	1888/05/14	1888/05/14	알마허	〃	알마허	독일	1,560	47.58	46.80	0.78	31.20	4.68	26.52	
〃	32	〃	〃	〃	〃	〃	〃	1,500	45.15	45.00	0.15	30.00	4.50	25.50	
〃	33	1888/09/03	1888/09/13	〃	〃	〃	〃	1,800	177.30	54.00	123.30	36.00	5.40	30.60	
〃	34	〃	〃	〃	〃	타운젠드	미국	1,830	183.00	54.90	128.10	36.60	5.49	31.11	
〃	35	〃	〃	〃	〃	〃	〃	1,860	186.93	55.80	131.13	37.20	5.58	31.62	
〃	36	1888/12/20	1888/12/20	쿠퍼	미국	〃	〃	1,800	54.00	54.00	0	36.00	5.40	30.60	
〃	37	1887/06/17	1888/04/04	마이어상사	독일	마이어(A)	독일	9,404	286.82	282.12	4.70	188.08	28.21	159.87	
〃	38	1884/05/10	1887/12/02	영국 정부	영국	영국 정부	영국	10,090	302.70	302.70	0	201.80	30.27	171.53	
〃	39	1884/10/23	1887/12/28	쿠퍼	미국	한국 해관	한국	2,865	85.95	85.95	0	57.30	8.59	48.71	

①	②	③	④	⑤		⑥		⑦	⑧	⑨	⑩	⑪	⑫	⑬	⑭
〃	40	기록 없음	미발행	미발행		한국인 경찰관	한국	1,122	33.66	33.66	0	22.44	3.37	19.07	
									16,555.29	6,782.88	9,772.41	4,358.48	375.11	3,983.37	
D	42	1891/03/24	1891/03/25	마이어(B)	독일	마이어(B)	독일	7,700	308.00	231.00	77.00	154.00	23.10	130.90	
〃	43	1891/04/03	1891/04/09	복음전도 협회	영국	복음전도협회	영국	3,780	257.37	113.40	137.97	75.60	11.34	64.26	
〃	44	1891/05/07	1891/10/22	신동공사		신동공사		3,780	1,082.97	113.40	969.57	75.60	11.34	64.26	
〃	45	1891/07/00	1891/11/18	한국 해관	한국	한국 해관	한국	3,256	96.68	97.68	0	65.12	9.77	55.35	
〃	48	1891/08/17	1891/08/18	라포르트	프랑스	라포르트	프랑스	1,807	55.11	54.21	0.90	36.14	5.42	30.72	
B	3	*1891/12/07	1891/12/08	로저스	영국	로저스	영국	1,906	638.50	114.36	524.15	114.36	5.72	108.64	
		* 합의에 따라 신동공사가 전액을 받았다.													
MS															
C	12					리키타케	일본								
〃	13 & 14					구마모토	〃								
〃	15					신도	〃								
〃	18					호리	〃								
〃	19					히구치	〃								
〃	21					나카이	〃								
〃	25					니시와키	〃								
〃	26					호리	〃								
D	14					뤼어스	독일								
〃	18					보리오니	이탈리아								
〃	24					홉킨스	영국								
〃	29			라포르트에게 이전될 예정		라포르트	프랑스								

①	②	③	④	⑤		⑥		⑦	⑧	⑨	⑩	⑪	⑫	⑬	⑭
					Nationality		Nationality								
A	1	No record sometime in 1884.	1888/11/15	Corean Customs	Corean	Corean Customs	Corean	682	654.72	654.72	0	136.40	2.05	134.35	
〃	2		〃	〃	〃	〃	〃	705	676.80	676.80	0	141.00	2.11	138.89	
〃	3		〃	〃	〃	〃	〃	674	647.04	647.04	0	134.80	2.02	132.78	
B	1 & 2	1884/11/07	1888/04/04	Carl Wolter	German	Carl Lührs	German	669	41.14	40.14	1.00	40.14	2.01	38.13	
〃	4	1886/05/07	1887/12/02	A. B. Stripling	British	A. B. Stripling	British	4,240	254.40	254.40	0	254.40	12.72	241.68	
C	1	1884/11/07	1888/04/04	E. Meyer & Co.	German	H. C. E. Meyer	German	1,335	80.10	80.10	0	80.10	4.01	76.09	
〃	2	〃	〃	〃	〃	〃	〃	1,305	78.30	78.30	0	78.30	3.92	74.38	
〃	3	1886/07/15	〃	〃	〃	〃	〃	1,350	122.17	81.00	41.17	81.00	4.05	76.95	
〃	4	1886/09/27	〃	〃	〃	〃	〃	1,250	115.62	75.00	40.62	75.00	3.75	71.25	
〃	5	1886/10/05	1884/04/04	〃	〃	C. Wolter	〃	1,410	142.41	84.60	57.81	84.60	4.23	80.37	
〃	6	1889/03/11	1889/03/11	R. Seitz	〃	〃	〃	1,440	216.00	86.40	129.60	86.40	4.32	82.08	
〃	7	1889/04/08	1889/04/08	C. Wolter	〃	〃	〃	1,320	300.30	79.20	221.10	79.20	3.96	75.24	
〃	8	〃	〃	〃	〃	〃	〃	1,320	318.12	79.20	238.92	79.20	3.96	75.24	
〃	9	1886/03/31	1887/12/28	C. H. Cooper	American	Li Pei-chin	Chinese	919	172.31	55.14	117.17	55.14	2.76	52.38	
〃	10 & 11	1884/11/07	1890/04/14	J. Steinbeck	Austrian	J. Steinbeck	Austrian	2,015	120.90	120.90	0	120.90	6.05	114.85	
									3,940.33	3,092.94	847.39	1,526.58	61.92	1,464.66	
C	12	1888/05/16	1888/05/16	Rikitaki Heihachi	Japanese	Rikitaki Heihachi	Japanese	1,015	124.85	60.90	63.95	60.90	3.04	57.86	
〃	13	1888/09/03	1888/09/07	Yenami Tetsuo	〃	Yenami Tetsuo	〃	1,020	714.00	61.20	652.80	61.20	3.06	58.14	
〃	14	〃	〃	〃	〃	〃	〃	1,067	736.23	64.02	672.21	64.02	3.20	60.82	

①	②	③	④	⑤		⑥		⑦	⑧	⑨	⑩	⑪	⑫	⑬	⑭
〃	15	〃	〃	〃	〃	J. Yoshida	〃	682	429.66	40.92	388.74	40.92	2.05	38.87	
〃	16	1890/12/12	1890/12/12	S. Shindo	〃	S. Shindo	〃	770	2,286.90	46.20	2,240.70	46.20	2.31	43.89	
〃	17	1886/06/11	1888/04/04	F. H. Mörsel	German	F. H. Mörsel	German	900	54.45	54.00	0.45	54.00	2.70	51.30	
〃	18	1888/05/19	1888/05/21	Hori Kintaro	Japanese	Hori Kintaro	Japanese	900	587.25	54.00	533.25	54.00	2.70	51.30	
〃	19	〃	〃	Yenami Tetsuo	〃	Shimauchi Yoshio	〃	1,002	672.84	60.12	612.72	60.12	3.01	57.11	
〃	20	〃	〃	F. H. Mörsel	German	F. H. Mörsel	German	900	542.70	54.00	488.70	54.00	2.70	51.30	
〃	〃	〃	〃	Horiguchi Kayemon	Japanese	K. Nakai	Japanese	900	553.50	54.00	499.50	54.00	2.70	51.30	
〃	22	1884/11/07	1888/04/04	F. H. Mörsel	German	F. H. Mörsel	German	915	54.90	54.90	0	54.90	2.75	52.15	
〃	23	1888/05/19	1888/05/21	Woo Litang	Chinese	Woo Litang	Chinese	855	600.21	51.30	548.91	51.30	2.56	48.74	
〃	24	1888/03/19	1888/04/04	〃	〃	〃	〃	408	67.32	24.48	42.84	24.48	1.22	23.26	
〃	25	1888/05/19	1888/05/21	Yenami Tetsuo	Japanese	S. Aso	Japanese	900	342.00	54.00	288.00	54.00	2.70	51.30	
〃	26	〃	〃	〃	〃	Hori Kintaro	〃	900	297.00	54.00	243.00	54.00	2.70	51.30	
〃	27	〃	〃	Hori Kintaro	〃	〃	〃	1,008	322.56	60.48	262.08	60.48	3.02	57.46	
〃	28	1884/11/07	1888/04/04	C. Wolter	German	Woo Litang	Chinese	900	54.00	54.00	0	54.00	2.70	51.30	
〃	29	1886/05/28	〃	F. H. Mörsel	〃	F. H. Mörsel	German	900	54.45	54.00	0.45	54.00	2.70	51.30	
〃	30	〃	〃	〃	〃	〃	〃	915	55.36	54.90	0.46	54.90	2.74	52.16	
〃	31	〃	〃	〃	〃	〃	〃	930	56.26	55.80	0.46	55.80	2.79	53.01	
									12,546.77	4,160.16	8,386.61	2,593.80	115.27	2,478.53	
C	32	1887/12/05	1887/12/20	Woo Litang	Chinese	Woo Litang	Chinese	810	648.00	48.60	599.40	48.60	2.43	46.17	
D	1	1884/11/07	1888/04/04	C. Wolter	German	C. Wolter	German	4,300	129.00	129.00	0	86.00	12.90	73.10	
〃	2	1886/05/28	1887/12/02	A. B. Stripling	British	A. B. Stripling	British	9,156	274.68	274.68	0	183.12	27.47	155.65	

①	②	③	④	⑤		⑥		⑦	⑧	⑨	⑩	⑪	⑫	⑬	⑭
〃	3	1886/04/06	1888/04/04	A. Gorschalki	German	A. Gorschalki	German	2,115	63.45	63.45	0	42.30	6.34	35.96	
〃	4	1886/05/07	1887/12/02	A. B. Stripling	British	A. B. Stripling	British	2,523	75.69	75.69	0	50.46	7.57	42.89	
〃	5	1887/04/00	1888/11/15	Corean Customs	Corean	Corean Customs	Corean	6,344	190.32	190.32	0	126.88	19.03	107.85	
〃	6	1884/00/00	〃	〃	〃	〃	〃	1,497	44.91	44.91	0	29.94	4.49	25.45	
〃	7	1888/04/30	〃	R. Brinckmeier	German	R. Brinckmeier	German	975	30.23	29.25	0.98	19.50	2.92	16.58	
〃	8	1888/09/03	〃	〃	〃	〃	〃	1,017	100.17	30.51	69.66	20.34	3.05	17.29	
〃	9	1890/04/22	1890/04/22	〃	〃	〃	〃	393	11.79	11.79	0	7.86	1.18	6.68	
〃	10	1890/10/28	1890/10/28	L. A. Hopkins	British	L. A. Hopkins	British	656	33.46	19.68	13.78	13.12	1.97	11.15	
〃	11 & 12	1886/05/28	1887/12/02	W. D. F. Hutchison	〃	W. D. F. Hutchison	〃	2,227	69.04	66.81	2.23	44.54	6.68	37.86	
〃	13	〃	1888/04/04	F. H. Mörsel	German	F. H. Mörsel	German	1,005	31.16	30.15	1.01	20.10	3.01	17.09	
〃	14	1886/04/19	1887/12/29	Ohashi Taro	Japanese	Ohashi Taro	Japanese	1,200	36.00	36.00	0	24.00	3.60	20.40	
〃	15	1888/04/11	1888/04/12	T. Hollingsworth	British	T. Hollingsworth	British	656	33.45	19.68	13.77	13.12	1.97	11.15	
〃	16 & 17	1886/05/07	1887/12/20	Woo Litang	Chinese	Woo Litang	Chinese	1,790	107.40	53.70	53.70	35.80	5.37	30.43	
〃	18	1884/11/07	1888/04/04	C. Wolter	German	C. Wolter	German	1,207	36.21	36.21	0	24.14	3.62	20.52	
〃	19	〃	〃	〃	〃	〃	〃	1,020	30.60	30.60	0	20.40	3.06	17.34	
〃	20	1887/12/05	1887/12/26	W. D. Townsend	American	W. D. Townsend	American	900	270.00	27.00	243.00	18.00	2.70	15.30	
〃	21	1887/03/31	〃	〃	〃	〃	〃	915	27.45	27.45	0	18.30	2.74	15.56	
									14,789.78	5,405.64	9,384.14	3,440.32	237.37	3,202.95	
D	22	1884/11/07	1887/12/26	W. D. Townsend	American	W. D. Townsend	American	930	27.90	27.90	0	18.60	2.79	15.81	
〃	23	〃	〃	〃	〃	〃	〃	900	27.00	27.00	0	18.00	2.70	15.30	

①	②	③	④	⑤		⑥		⑦	⑧	⑨	⑩	⑪	⑫	⑬	⑭
〃	24	1889/04/20	1889/04/20	E. Laporte	French	E. Laporte	French	1,105	33.26	33.15	0.11	22.10	3.32	18.78	
〃	25	1884/11/07	1888/04/04	E. Meyer & Co.	German	E. Meyer & Co.	German	885	26.55	26.55	0	17.70	2.66	15.04	
〃	26	〃	〃	〃	〃	〃	〃	885	26.55	26.55	0	17.70	2.66	15.04	
〃	27 & 28	〃	〃	〃	〃	〃	〃	2,962	88.86	88.86	0	59.24	8.89	50.35	
〃	29	〃	〃	C. Wolter	〃	C. Wolter	〃	1,770	53.10	53.10	0	35.40	5.31	30.09	
〃	30	〃	〃	〃	〃	Woo Litang	Chinese	2,640	79.20	79.20	0	52.80	7.92	44.88	
〃	31	1888/05/14	1888/05/14	F. M. Allmacher	〃	F. M. Allmacher	German	1,560	47.58	46.80	0.78	31.20	4.68	26.52	
〃	32	〃	〃	〃	〃	〃	〃	1,500	45.15	45.00	0.15	30.00	4.50	25.50	
〃	33	1888/09/03	1888/09/13	〃	〃	〃	〃	1,800	177.30	54.00	123.30	36.00	5.40	30.60	
〃	34	〃	〃	〃	〃	W. D. Townsend	American	1,830	183.00	54.90	128.10	36.60	5.49	31.11	
〃	35	〃	〃	〃	〃	〃	〃	1,860	186.93	55.80	131.13	37.20	5.58	31.62	
〃	36	1888/12/20	1888/12/20	C. H. Cooper	American	〃	〃	1,800	54.00	54.00	0	36.00	5.40	30.60	
〃	37	1887/06/17	1888/04/04	E. Meyer & Co.	German	E. Meyer & Co.	German	9,404	286.82	282.12	4.70	188.08	28.21	159.87	
〃	38	1884/05/10	1887/12/02	British Government	British	British Government	British	10,090	302.70	302.70	0	201.80	30.27	171.53	
〃	39	1884/10/23	1887/12/28	C. H. Cooper	American	Corean Customs	Corean	2,865	85.95	85.95	0	57.30	8.59	48.71	
〃	40	No record	None issued	None issued		Corean Magistrate	Corean	1,122	33.66	33.66	0	22.44	3.37	19.07	
									16,555.29	6,782.88	9,772.41	4,358.48	375.11	3,983.37	

①	②	③	④	⑤		⑥		⑦	⑧	⑨	⑩	⑪	⑫	⑬	⑭
D	42	1891/03/24	1891/03/25	Capt. F. Meyer	German	Capt. F. Meyer	German	7,700	308.00	231.00	77.00	154.00	23.10	130.90	
〃	43	1891/04/03	1891/04/09	Soc. Prop. Gospel	British	S. P. G.	British	3,780	257.37	113.40	137.97	75.60	11.34	64.26	
〃	44	1891/05/07	1891/10/22	Municipal Council		M. C.		3,780	1,082.97	113.40	969.57	75.60	11.34	64.26	
〃	45	1891/07/00	1891/11/18	Customs	Corean	Customs	Corean	3,256	96.68	97.68	0	65.12	9.77	55.35	
〃	48	1891/08/17	1891/08/18	E. Laporte	French	E. Laporte	French	1,807	55.11	54.21	0.90	36.14	5.42	30.72	
B	3	* 1891/12/07	1891/12/08	E. Rogers	British	E. Rogers	British	1,906	638.50	114.36	524.15	114.36	5.72	108.64	
		* By arrangement M. C. gets all price.													
C	12					H. Rikitake	Japanese								
〃	13 & 14					Kumamoto	〃								
〃	15					S. Shindo	〃								
〃	18					K. Hori	〃								
〃	19					S. Higuchi	〃								
〃	21					W. Nakai	〃								
〃	25					C. Nishiwaki	〃								
〃	26					K. Hori	〃								
D	14					W. Lührss	German								
〃	18					R. Borioni	Italian								
〃	24					L. A. Hopkins	British								
〃	29			Is to be transferred to E. Laporte		French									

1892년 1월 1일 제물포 각국 조계 신동공사 회계 내역[103)]

.. – 번역문 – ..

제물포 각국 조계 신동공사 수입 및 지출의 일반 회계

차변				
1891				
1월	1일	전년도 잔액 $6,658.55		
		전년도 세금 잔액 $1,341.70		
		전년도 이월금 소계 $8,000.25		
		한국 정부가 신동공사에 갚은 돈 $1,400.00	$9,400	25
5월	28일	예금 이자	216	00
6월	17일	〃	54	00
8월	8일	나가사키에 보낸 6,000달러에 대한 할증료	16	00
11월	11일	D42, D43, D44, D48 구역 매각의 순수익	1,185	44
12월	31일	다이이치은행 예금 이자	55	29
〃	〃	〃		30
〃	〃	금년도 세금 잔액		
		금년도 세금 $1,871.23		
		경찰 제반 비용 $894.58		
		잔액	976	65
			$11,903	93

103) 1891년 12월 11일 임원 선거를 통하여 1892년도 제물포 각국 조계 신동공사 회계로 선출된 볼터의 영문 및 일문 회계 내역이다.

대변				
1891				
1월	1일	한국 정부가 신동공사에 갚아야 할 돈		
		1890년도 도로평탄화 작업	$1,400	00
8월	29일	상하이의 할인 어음	88	67
11월	11일	D44 구역의 원가	1,082	97
〃	〃	D44 구역에 대한 1891년도 세금	24	65
12월	31일	1891년도 배수 처리와 도로 건설	1,719	07
〃	〃	한국 정부가 신동공사에 갚아야 할 돈		
		1891년 도로평탄화 작업	1,156	22
〃	〃	B4, D2, D4 구역의 1891년도 세금 미납분		
		받은 돈 $243.99-$47.76	196	23
〃	〃	홍콩상하이은행 예금		
		상하이 소재 은행	5,911	33
〃	〃	경찰국장이 사용한 돈	1	37
〃	〃	다이이치은행 잔액		
		제물포 소재 은행	323	42
			$11,903	93

1892년 1월 1일 제물포

회계 볼터

·· – 원문(영문) – ··

General Account of Receipts and Expenditure of

Municipal Council, General Foreign Settlement, Chemulpo.

Debt.				
1891				
January	1	To Balance $6,658.55		
		Balance taxes $1,341.70		
		1890 $8,000.25		
		Govt. owing Council $1,400.00	$9,400	25
May	28	Interest on Deposit	216	00
June	17	〃	54	00
August	8	Premium of $6,000 to Nagasaki	16	00
November	11	Net proceeds of Land Sales of D42, 43, 44 and 48	1,185	44
December	31	Interest Current A/C F. N. Bk.	55	29
〃	〃	〃 do		30
〃	〃	Balance Taxes for 1891		
		Taxes $1,871.23		
		Expenses of Policing $894.58		
		Balance	976	65
			$11,903	93

Credit.				
1891				
January	1	By Corean Govt. owing to Municipal Council,		
		Grading Streets in 1890	$1,400	00
August	29	Discount of draft of Shanghai	88	67

November	11	Cost price of M. C. Lot D44	1,082	97
〃	〃	Rent for this lot, for 1891	24	65
December	31	Drains, Roads made in 91.	1,719	07
〃	〃	Corean Govt. owing to Municipal Council,		
		Grading Streets in 1891	1,156	22
〃	〃	Taxes for 1891 on Lots B4, D2, D4 not yet		
		Received $243.99-$47.76	196	23
〃	〃	Deposit, Hongkong and Shanghai		
		Bank Corp. Shanghai	5,911	33
〃	〃	In hand of Police Supt.	1	37
〃	〃	Bank balance 1st national		
		Bank, Chemulpo	323	42
			$11,903	93

Chemulpo, 1st January 1892

Carl Wolter

Hon. Treasurer

明治廿四年度仁川各國居留地會收支決算報告

收入ノ部				
前年度越高	六、六五八	五五		
仝　税金餘剩越高	一、三四一	七〇		
小　計	八、〇〇〇	二五		
朝鮮政府勘定越高	一、四〇〇	〇〇		
			九、四〇〇	二五
各銀行預ケ金利息			三二五	五九
長崎爲替打歩			一六	〇〇
土地賣却代金			一、一八五	四四
但D第四十二号四十三号四十四号四十八号分				
本年度税金殘高				
本年度税金	一、八七一	二三		
警察諸費	八七四	五八		
			九七六	六五
合　計			一一、九〇三	九三
支出ノ部				
朝鮮政府勘定			一、四〇〇	〇〇
但前年度中道路修築分				
上海爲替割引料			八八	六七
各國居留地會所有地所代金			一、〇八二	九七
但D第四十四号分				
仝　上　本年度地税金			二四	六五
本年度道路溝渠開築費			一、七一九	〇七
朝鮮政府勘定			一、一五六	二二
但本年度中道路修築分				
本年度未納税金			一九六	二三
香港上海銀行預ケ金			五、九一一	三三
警察署手許有金			一	三七
第一國立銀行當座預ケ金			三二三	四二
合　計			一一、九〇三	九三

右之通相違無之候也

明治廿五年一月

仁川港
各國居留地議會
名譽會計役
シー、ウオルター

1892년 5월 12일 가지야마가 허드에게 보낸 편지[104)]

·· — **번역문** — ··

한국 서울 주한일본공사관

1892년 5월 12일

허드 씨께,

어제 날짜로 보내 주신 귀하의 메모를 잘 받았습니다. 귀하께서는 지난 번 외교 회의 때 일본 갯벌에 대한 제 발언과 관련하여 문의하셨습니다. 당시 저는 일본 갯벌이 제물포 조약에 따라 자연스럽게 일본 조계의 소유라는 일본 정부와 제 신념을 밝혔습니다. 또한 한국 정부가 우리의 시각에 동의하고 있다는 점도 진술하였습니다. 힐리어 씨가 제안하신 내용과 관련하여 저는 오로지 이의가 없다고만 말하였습니다. 저는 다른 나라 정부의 결정에 대해서는 발언하지 않았으며 어떤 결정이든 기꺼이 따를 것입니다.

진심을 담아서,

가지야마

104) 1892년 5월 12일 주한일본공사 가지야마가 주한미국공사 허드에게 보낸 편지이다. 제물포 각국 조계와 관련된 문제인 것 같으나 정확히 어떤 내용인지 알아내지 못했다.

·· – **원문** – ··

H. I. J. M.'s Legation, Seoul, Corea.
12 May 1892.

Hon. Mr. Heard,

I have with pleasure received your note of yesterday's date inquiring me about what I have said on the last diplomatic meeting on the subject of Japanese foreshore. I remember I have expressed at that time my conviction & of my government that by our Chemulpo treaty Japanese foreshore belongs naturally to Japanese Settlement; I also stated that in fact the Corean Government have assented to our views. As to the suggestion & proposal of Mr. Hillier, I simply said that I had no objection; I did mention nothing about the decision of the different Governments by which I would be willing to abide.

Yours truly,

T. Kajiyama

1893년 9월 15일 모건이 드미트레프스키에게 보낸 편지[105)]

번역문

1893년 9월 15일 서울

주한러시아대리공사 드미트레프스키 귀하

친애하는 드미트레프스키 씨께,

갯벌 매립의 한계선을 보여 드리기 위하여 해관이 준비한 도면의 사본을 귀하께 보내 드립니다. 매우 유능한 기술자의 의견에 따르면 제물포 갯벌 매립 공사는 내항을 해치지 않는 범위 내에서 안전하게 시행될 수 있다고 합니다.

귀하께서 알고 계시다시피 한계선 안에 있는 갯벌을 다 매립할 필요는 없지만 한계선을 넘어가면 확실히 횡력(橫力)이 떨어질 것입니다. 횡력은 모래톱의 침투로부터 정박지를 지키기 위해서 반드시 필요합니다. 그리고 한계선을 약간 변형하는 것은 항구를 위해서도 나쁘지 않습니다.

도면에 기록된 내용 중 매립에 관한 합의를 암시하는 것은 없습니다. 제가 이 점을 굳이 첨언할 필요는 없겠지요.

진심을 담아서,

모건

105) 1893년 9월 15일 총세무사대리 모건이 주한러시아대리공사 겸 각국외교대표단장 드미트레프스키에게 보낸 편지이다. 제물포 각국 조계 부지 매립과 관련하여 해관이 준비한 도면을 전달하기 위하여 작성하였다.

·· — 원문 — ··

Seoul, 15th Sept. 1893

To the Honorable, P. A. Dmitrevsky,

H. I. R. M.'s Charge d'Affaires

etc., etc., etc.

Dear Mr. Dmitrevsky,

I send you herewith a copy of a plan that has been prepared by the Customs to show the limit to which, in the opinion of very competent engineer, filling in of the foreshore at Chemulpo can be safely carried without danger of injury to the Inner Harbour.

Of course you will understand that it is not necessary to fill in all, or any part of the foreshore within the line, but that filling in beyond, it is considered, will most certainly restrain and diminish the side forces it is desired to utilize in order to keep the very limited anchorage fill from the sandbanks which are encroaching on it; and it is possible that experience may get show that some slight modification of this line may become advisable in the interest of the Port.

It is hardly necessary for me to add that no agreement as to filling in is implied by anything delineated on the plan.

Yours very sincerely,

F. A. Morgan

1894년 5월 3일 유경환이 실에게 보낸 편지[106)]

·· – 번역문 – ··

조선 개조 503년 음력 3월 28일

1894년 5월 3일

귀하께,

일본 영사로부터 공문을 받았음을 귀하께 알려 드립니다. 그것은 일본 상인들이 제물포 각국 조계 D 부지 북서쪽의 5개 구역을 매입할 수 있는지 문의하는 내용이었습니다. 그는 신동공사가 새로 설계한 도면에 5개 구역을 표시하여 제게 보냈습니다. 저는 이 구역들을 측량하고 경계석을 세웠습니다. D65 구역은 넓이가 1,080㎡이고 D50 구역의 남쪽에 있습니다. D62 구역은 1,100㎡, D63 구역은 1,020㎡, D67 구역은 880㎡, D68 구역은 1,050㎡이며 모두 D50 구역의 북쪽에 있습니다.

이 5개 구역에 대한 경매는 음력 4월 8일(5월 12일) 오후 2시 검사관보 사무실에서 열립니다. 검사관보 사무실 문에 이미 공고가 붙었습니다만, 귀하께서도 이 소식을 미국 시민들에게 알려서 경매에 참여할 수 있도록 협조해 주시기를 요청합니다.

106) 1894년 5월 3일 서리감리인천항통상사무 유경환이 주한미국공사 실에게 보낸 편지이다. 발신자의 이름은 영문 원문의 'You Kieng Hwan'에서 유추한 것이다. 한문 원본에는 '유(俞)'라고만 기록되어 있다.

서리감리인천항통상사무 유경환

주한미국총영사 실 귀하

·· — **원문(영문)** — ··

28 day, 3 Moon, 503 Yr.

May 3 1894.

Sir,

I have the honor to inform you that I am in receipt of a despatch from the Japanese Consul, stating that the Japanese Merchants asking for sale of 5 pieces of Lots on the West-North side of D lot which situated in the General Foreign Settlement at Chemulpo and also be sent me a plan for the said 5 lots drawn out according to the new plan which made by the Municipal Council.

I have measured the said 5 lots and erected boundary stones on each lot as following;-

D lot No. 65 - 1,080 sq. metres, this lot is on the South side of D lot no. 50.

D lots No. 62 - 1,100 sq. m. No. 63 - 1,020 sq. m. No. 67 - 880 sq. m. and No. 68 - 1,050 sq. m. these 4 lots are on the North side of D lot No. 50.

I have now to inform you that the above 5 lots shall be sold by public auction at the Tidesurveyor's Office on the 8th of 4th Moon at 2 P. M. (May 12), therefore the notice for sale has put up at the gate of Tidesurveyor's Office. And I would request you will notify the American Citizens who would purchase the said lots, in order that they may present at auction at certain time.

I have, etc.

You Kieng Hwan

Acting Superintendent of Trade, Jenchuan

Honorable,

John M. B. Sill.

U. S. Consul General.

.. – **원문(한문)** – ..

照會

大朝鮮署理監理仁川港通商事務兪 爲

照會事照得接准 日本領事照會以日商大谷正誠等請將仁川濟物浦各國租界第四等西北邊之基地五址照章拍租弁按公司新繪之圖繪送該五址圖前來本監理照章勘明該五址地丈量淸晰各竪界石其第四等六十五號地一千八十丁方米突此一址係在第四等五十號地南邊其第四等六十二號地一千一百丁方米突第四等六十三號地一千二十丁方米突第四等六十七號地八百八十丁方米突第四等六十八號地一千五十丁方米突此四址均在第四等五十號地北邊玆擇收(我曆本年四月初八西曆本年五月十二)日午後二點鍾時在海關理船廳內將該五址照章公拍除出示收理船廳及公司兩門前俾衆悉知外相應備文照會

貴總領事請煩査照傳知貴商欲租賃該地者卽收屆期隨帶銀元到理船廳聽拍出價永租可也須至照會者

右照會

大美欽命駐箚朝鮮總領事施

開國五百三年三月二十八日

美第二十二号

1894년 5월 4일 윌킨슨이 실에게 보낸 편지[107)]

-- 번역문 --

1894년 5월 4일 제물포

귀하께,

저는 서리감리인천항통상사무로부터 이번 달 12일 각국 조계의 5개 구역을 경매에 붙인다는 내용의 안내문을 받았습니다.

이 안내문의 번역문을 동봉합니다. 신동공사 회관에도 붙였습니다.

귀하의 충복,

서기 윌킨슨

서울, 각국외교대표단장 실 귀하

번역문 :

5월 12일 오후 2시 항무장 사무실에서 각국 조계 북서쪽에 위치한 5개 구역에 대한 경매를 실시하게 된 것을 알려 드립니다. 대금은 구입할 때 지불하면 됩니다. 대상 구역은 D62(1,100㎡), D63 (1,200㎡), D65(1,800㎡), D67(880㎡), D68(1,500㎡)입니다.

1894년 5월 4일 감리 (인)

107) 1894년 5월 4일 신동공사 서기였던 제물포주재영국부영사 윌킨슨이 주한미국공사 실에게 보낸 편지이다. 서리감리인천항통상사무 유경환에게 받은 안내문의 번역문을 전달하기 위하여 작성하였으며 내용은 전날 유경환이 실에게 보낸 편지와 같다.

-- 원문 --

Chemulpo, May 4 1894.

Sir,

The Acting Superintendent of Trade at this Port has sent to me a Notice of Auction of Five Lots in the General Foreign Settlement, to be held on the 12th instant.

This Notice, of which I have the honour to enclose a translation, I have caused to be posted at the Municipal Buildings.

I have the honour to be, Sir,

Your obedient servant,

W. H. Wilkinson

Hon. Secretary

Hon. Jno. M. B. Sill

etc., etc., etc.

Doyen of the Foreign Representatives.

Söul

Translation. Notice is hereby given that an Auction will be held on the 12th May next at 2 o'clock in the afternoon at the Harbour Master's Office of Five lots of land situated in the northwest of the General Foreign Settlement, the price to be paid at time of purchase.

Lots are as follows:

D62 measuring 1100 square metres,

D63 〃 1200 〃 〃

D65 〃 1800 〃 〃

D67 〃 880 〃 〃

D68 〃 1500 〃 〃

May 4th 1894, Seal of Kamni

1894년 6월 26일
윌킨슨이 제안하여 통과된 결의안[108)]

·· – **번역문** – ··

제안한 결의안

일본 당국은 일본 조계와 각국 조계 근처에 주둔한 병력을 철수시켜 달라는 신동공사의 긴급한 항의를 거절 내지 무시하였습니다. 최근에 일어난 몇몇 사건들은 일본 군인들이 개항장에 주둔하는 것과 그들이 무기를 소지하고 자유롭게 돌아다니는 것이 신동공사 주민들의 생명에 중대한 위협이 된다는 것을 보여 주었습니다.

신동공사는 개항장에 군함을 정박하고 있는 사령관들께 요청합니다. 신동공사의 도장이 찍힌 허가증이 없이는 어떤 사람도 무기를 소지하고 각국 조계를 지나다니지 못하도록 조치를 강구해 주시기 바랍니다.

·· – **원문** – ··

Proposed Resolution

Whereas the Japanese Authorities have, in spite of the urgent representations made to them, refused or neglected to withdraw the troops stationed in the Jap. Settlement & upon the Bund of the G. F. S.; and whereas certain recent

---

108) 1894년 6월 26일 신동공사 회의 때 제물포주재영국부영사 윌킨슨이 제안하고 서울주재 독일부영사 라인스도르프가 재청하여 통과된 결의안이다.

occurrences have shown the grave danger to the lives & persons of residents on the G. F. S. arising from the presence of those troops in the port area and their practice of moving freely about it carrying arms;

The Council to request commrs of the vessels of war now in the port to take such measure as shall prevent persons equipped with weapons of any description from passing through the General F. S. unless provided with a permit issued by this Council & stamped with its seal.

1894년 12월 7일 윌킨슨이 이노우에에게 보낸 편지[109)]

-- 번역문 --

1894년 12월 7일 제물포 신동공사

귀하께,

어제 신동공사 회의에서 통과된 두 가지 결의안을 각국 외교 대표들께 제출해 주시기를 요청합니다.

(1) 각국 외교 대표들께 요청합니다. 제방 끝에 있는 일본우선회사 옆에서부터 제방을 따라 부두에 이르는 지점에 너비 15미터의 도로를 건설하는 문제를 한국 정부와 조율해 주십시오. 그래서 빠르면 1895년 3월 평탄화 작업과 포장 공사를 시작할 수 있게 해 주십시오.

(2) 각국 외교 대표들께 요청합니다. 전술한 도로와 해관 창고 앞 사이에 있는 모든 화물 창고에 대하여 최대한 빨리 한국 정부와 합의하셔서 신동공사가 그곳에 포장 공사와 배수 처리를 시작할 수 있게 해 주십시오.

귀하의 충복,

서기 윌킨슨

서울, 각국외교대표단장 이노우에 백작 귀하

---

109) 1894년 12월 7일 신동공사 서기였던 제물포주재영국부영사 윌킨슨이 주한일본공사이자 각국외교대표단장이었던 이노우에에게 보낸 편지의 사본이다. 원본은 윌킨슨이 이노우에게 12월 6일 신동공사 회의에서 결의된 내용을 전달하기 위하여, 사본은 이노우에가 실에게 자신이 받은 편지를 전달하기 위하여 작성하였을 것이다. 1894년 12월 6일 신동공사 회의록을 참고할 것.

·· – **원문** – ··

Municipal Council.

Chemulpo, December 7th 1894.

Sir,

I have the honor to request that Your Excellency will be good enough to bring before the Foreign Representatives the two following resolutions, passed by the Council at its meeting of yesterday:

(1) That the Foreign Representatives be requested in concert with the Corean government, to have a road laid out from the end of the bund next to the Nippon Yusen Kaisha, along the bund to the jetty, 15 metres wide, so that the Municipal Council can metal and grade this road early in March 1895.

(2) That the Foreign Representatives be requested to confer with the Corean government with a view to the metalling and draining, as soon as possible, of all the Cargo space between 15 metre road referred to in the resolution just carried, and the front of the Customs Godowns.

I have the honor to be, Sir,

Your Excellency's most obedient servant,

W. H. Wilkinson

Hon. Secretary

His Excellency

Count Inouye

Doyen of the Foreign Representatives, Seoul.

1894년 12월 19일 이노우에가 각국 외교 대표들에게 보낸 편지[110)]

-- **번역문** --

주한일본공사관

1894년 12월 19일 서울

귀하들께,

제물포 신동공사 서기 윌킨슨 씨로부터 받은 편지의 사본을 귀하들께 제출합니다. 1894년 12월 6일 신동공사 회의 때 통과된 결의안들에 대한 내용입니다. 귀하들께서 해당 문제들을 심의하신 후 제게 의견을 알려 주시면 이 사건을 적절하게 처리하겠습니다.

이 기회를 빌려 귀하들께 다시 한 번 최고의 경의를 표합니다.

이노우에

서울,

주한미국공사 겸 총영사 실,

주한러시아대리공사 베베르,

서울주재영국총영사 힐리어,

서울주재독일총영사 크린,

주한프랑스대리공사 르페브르 귀하

---

110) 1894년 12월 9일 주한일본공사 겸 각국외교대표단장 이노우에가 주한미국공사 실, 주한러시아대리공사 베베르, 서울주재영국총영사 힐리어, 서울주재독일총영사 크린, 주한프랑스대리공사 르페브르에게 보낸 편지이다.

·· – **원문** – ··

H. I. J. M's Legation.

Seoul, December 19, 1894.

Sirs;

I have the honor to lay before you a copy of a communication which I have received from W. H. Wilkinson Esq., Honorary Secretary of the Municipal Council of Chemulpo regarding the resolutions passed by the Council meeting of December 6, 1894, with the desire that you will be good enough to give full consideration to the questions therein contained and inform me of the views that you entertain respecting them, so as to enable me to make proper disposition of this affair.

I avail myself of this occasion to renew to you the assurances of my highest consideration.

K. Inouye

Hon. J. M. B. Sill

Minister Resident and Consul General of the United States.

C. Waeber Esq.

H. I. R. M's Charge d'affaires.

W. C. Hillier Esq.

H. B. M's Consul General.

F. Krien Esq.

H. I. G. M's Consul with functions of Imperial Commissioner.

G. Lefévre Esq.

sérvant du Commissariat de France.

Seoul.

1895년 4월 19일
실이 각국 외교 대표들에게 보낸 편지[111)]

·· – **번역문** – ··

회람

신사이자 동료이신 귀하들께,

제물포 각국 조계 신동공사의 회장인 저는 외무대신과 각국 외교 대표들로부터 중국 조계의 치안, 조명, 미화를 신동공사가 일시적으로 맡아 주면 좋겠다는 제의를 받았습니다. 비용은 중국 조계 주민들이 부담할 것입니다. 현재 아무 준비가 되어 있지 않아 모든 제물포 주민들의 건강과 평안에 위협이 되고 있습니다.

외무대신이 이에 동의하였으므로 이제 귀하들께서 각각 승인해 주시는 일만 남았음을 덧붙입니다.

승인 여부를 알려 주시겠습니까?

1895년 4월 19일 귀하들의 충복, 실

이노우에, 전적으로 승인합니다.

베베르, 전적으로 동의합니다.

힐리어, 전적으로 승인합니다.

---

111) 1895년 4월 19일 신동공사 회장이었던 주한미국공사 실이 주한일본공사 이노우에, 주한러시아대리공사 베베르, 서울주재영국총영사 힐리어, 서울주재독일총영사 크린, 주한프랑스대리공사 르페브르에게 보낸 회람이다. 신동공사가 중국 조계를 관리하는 일에 대하여 각국 외교 대표들의 승인 여부를 묻기 위하여 작성되었다. 수신자 성명 옆의 "전적으로 승인합니다" 등은 수신자가 회람을 읽은 후 답변을 기록한 것이다.

크린, 동의합니다.

르페르브, 승인합니다.

·· ─ **원문** ─ ··

Circular

Gentleman and Colleagues;-

As President of the Municipal Council of the General Foreign Settlement of Chemulpo, I have been asked by that body to propose to the Minister for Foreign Affairs and to the Foreign Representatives, that said Council be allowed, temporarily, to police, light and scavenger the Chinese Settlement at that place, the expense of this work to be born by the Chinese Residents. The absence of any such provision at present is a menace to the health and peace of every resident of Chemulpo.

I may add that the Minister for Foreign Affairs agrees to this proposition and it now awaits your individual sanction.

Will you kindly suggest your approval or disapproval hereupon.

I have the honor to be,

Your obedient servant,

Seoul April 19, 1895. John M. B. Sill.

To

His Excellency Count Inouye, I fully approve.

Honorable C. Waeber, I fully agree.

W. C. Hillier Esquire, I entirely approve.

F. Krien Esquire, I agree.

G. Lefevre Esquire, Approved.

1895년 4월 24일 월킨슨이 실에게 보낸 편지[112)]

·· – 번역문 – ··

신동공사

1894년 4월 24일 제물포

귀하께,

이번 달 22일자 귀하의 공문을 받았음을 알려 드립니다. 외무대신과 서울에 주재하는 모든 각국 외교 대표들이 제물포 각국 조계 신동공사가 중국 조계의 치안, 조명, 미화를 일시적으로 담당해야 한다는 제안을 승인하였다는 내용이었습니다.

저는 신동공사 집행위원회에 귀하의 공문을 제출하였습니다. 집행위원회는 오늘부로 중국 조계의 도로 정비와 배수 공사에 착수할 것입니다.

귀하의 충복,

서기 월킨슨

주한미국공사 실 귀하

---

112) 1895년 4월 24일 제물포주재영국부영사 월킨슨이 주한미국공사 실에게 보낸 편지이다. 4월 19일 실이 각국 외교 대표들에게 보낸 편지에서 다루어진 문제 즉, 신동공사가 중국 조계의 치안, 조명, 미화를 일시적으로 담당하는 것에 대하여 이야기하고 있다. 생산일자와 관련하여 월킨슨은 1894년이라고 썼으나 주한미국공사관 수령인(印)에는 1895년 4월 25일(Apr 25, 1895)이라고 쓰여 있다.

·· — 원문 — ··

Municipal Council,

Chemulpo, April 24, 1894.

Chempo.

Sir,

I have the honour to acknowledge receipt of your Despatch of the 22nd instant informing me that the Minister for Foreign Affairs and all the Foreign Representatives at Söul heartily approve of the proposal that this Council should temporarily police, light, and scavenger the Chinese Settlement at Chemulpo.

I have laid your Despatch before the Executive Committee of the Council, who are today commencing to put in order the streets and drains of that Settlement.

I have the honour to be, Sir,

Your obedient servant,

W. H. Wilkinson

Hon. Secretary

Hon. J. M. B. Sill

United States Minister

etc., etc., etc.

1895년 4월 30일 후루타가 월킨슨에게 보낸 편지[113)]

·· – 번역문 – ··

1895년 4월 30일 제물포, 시장 사무실

사본

귀하께,

이번 달 5일 귀하께서 보내신 편지를 받았음을 알려 드립니다. 일본 우선회사 사무실 앞의 땅을 매립함으로써 현재 제방을 따라 건설 중인 도로와 잘 이어지게 하는 일에 협조를 요청하신다는 내용이었습니다. 저는 일본 조계 자치 의회 임시 회의를 소집하고 귀하께서 말씀하신 문제를 제출하였습니다.

회의는 대체로 대중의 편의를 증진시키고자 하는 욕구에 의하여 진행되었습니다. 그 결과 일본 조계는 귀하께서 요청하신 대로 매립을 수행할 뿐 아니라 제방을 따라 놓여 있는 도로를 넓히기로 결의하였습니다. 제방은 두 조계와 해관 부두 사이에 있는 아주 평평한 길이자 인파와 화물로 붐비는 가장 분주한 곳입니다. 이곳에 놓여 있는 도로의 너비는 규정에 따르면 12미터가 되어야 하지만 실제로는 6미터가 안 됩니다. 따라서 대중은 늘 불편을 느껴 왔습니다. 해관 창고 근처에 도

113) 1895년 4월 30일 제물포 일본 조계 자치 의회 회장 후루타가 각국 조계 신동공사 서기 월킨슨에게 보낸 편지의 사본이다. 1895년 5월 2일 월킨슨이 주한미국공사 실에게 편지를 보내면서 이 편지를 동봉하였다.

로가 생기고 나면 그 불편은 더욱 심해질 것입니다.

자치 의회는 이 긴급 사태에 맞서 해당 도로를 다른 도로보다 넓게 확장하기로 결의하였습니다. 이 공사가 완료되면 두 조계의 상호 편의가 크게 증진될 것이라고 믿어 의심치 않습니다. 다만 이를 준비하는데 다소 시간이 걸린다는 점을 이해해 주시기 바랍니다.

끝으로 많은 위원들이 불참하여 정족수를 채우지 못한 관계로, 저는 귀하께 마땅히 드려야 할 공식적인 대답을 드릴 수 없었습니다.

이만 줄입니다.

일본 조계 시장 후루타 (서명)

제물포 각국 조계 신동공사 서기 윌킨슨 귀하

·· – **원문** – ··

Mayor's Office, Chemulpo, April 30th, 1895

Copy.

Sir,

I have the honor to acknowledge the receipt of your letter of the 5th inst. in which you request up to co-operate with you in filling up the ground in front of Nippon Yusen Kaisha's office, so as to properly connect with the road you are constructing along the bund. I called an extraordinary meeting of the Council of our Settlement and submitted for consideration the subject of your communication under reply.

The meeting, actuated by the desire of promoting the convenience of the public in general, resolved that the Settlement shall undertake the work of not only filling up the ground as requested by you, but also of extending the width of the road all along the bund. The bund, being the most level passage between the two Settlements and the Custom's jetty, is the busiest place, where men and cargoes pass most frequently. But the width of the street, which according to the regulation should be 12 metres, as is the case with other streets, is really not more than 6. As the consequence, the public has always been subjected to the inconvenience of obstructions, which will be felt more keenly after the construction of the road near the Customs Godowns.

In order to meet with these exigencies, the Municipal Council has resolved to extend the road in question to a width somewhat more spacious compared with other streets, and I fully trust that the work, when completed, will greatly promote the mutual convenience of the two Settlements. In consequence, however, of the extension of the plan, you will please understand that more or less time will be require for the preparation of the work.

In conclusion, I beg to state that, for want of the quorum in the Council owing to the absence of many members, I have not been able to reply to your communication as promptly as I ought to have done.

I have, etc.

(signed) J. Furuta,

Mayor of Japanese Settlement.

To W. H. Wilkinson Esq.

Hon. Secretary,

the Municipal Council of the General Foreign Settlement, Chemulpo.

1895년 5월 2일
윌킨슨이 실에게 보낸 편지[114)]

·· – 번역문 – ··

신동공사

1895년 5월 2일 제물포

실 씨께,

동봉한 편지는 어제 일본 조계 자치 의회로부터 받은 것으로, 지난 달 5일 우리가 보낸 편지에 대한 답장입니다. 저는 타운젠드 씨에게 이 편지를 보여 주었고 그들의 제안이 훌륭하다는 데 동의하였습니다. 그러나 한두 가지 고려해야 할 점이 있습니다.

1893년 가을 한국 정부는 각국 외교 대표들에게 각국 조계와 일본 조계 남쪽의 모든 갯벌은 각국 조계의 소유라고 하였습니다. 그러므로 일본인들은 엄밀히 말하자면 후루타 씨의 공문에 언급된 12미터만 매립할 수 있습니다. 남쪽 토지는 우리 땅입니다.

그러므로 일본의 제안에 무조건적으로 찬성하는 것은 우리가 장래의 권리들을 거저 주는 것처럼 비춰질 수 있습니다. 한편 부두와 한국인 마을을 잇는 너비 15미터의 도로는 공익을 위하여 요긴합니다.

각국 조계가 일본인들에게 3미터든 얼마든 땅을 늘려 준다면 그들이

---

114) 1895년 5월 2일 제물포주재영국부영사 겸 신동공사 서기였던 윌킨슨이 당시 각국외교 대표단장이었던 주한미국공사 실에게 보낸 편지이다. 제물포 일본 조계 자치 의회 회장 후루타의 편지를 전달하고 관련 문제를 의논하기 위하여 작성하였다.

무조건적인 도로 폐쇄에 동의할까요? 귀하께서는 이러한 조율이 가능하다고 생각하십니까? 제 두 번째 요점을 말씀드리겠습니다. 일본인들은 전염병의 위협이 있을 때에는 격리 규정을 집행하기 위하여 열심히 노력하는 편입니다. 일전에 저는 그들이 일부 또는 모든 도로를 폐쇄하고 보행자들에게 강제 소독을 시켰다는 이야기를 들었습니다.

진심을 담아서,

윌킨슨

·· – **원문** – ··

Municipal Council,
Chemulpo, May 2nd 1895.

Dear Mr. Sill,

I received yesterday from the Japanese Municipal Council the enclosed reply to our letter of the 5th ultimo.

I have shown the despatch to Mr. Townsend, and we are both agreed that in itself the proposal of the Japanese Council is excellent. There would seem, however, one point, or rather two, to be considered.

In the autumn of 1893 the Corean Government officially informed the Foreign Representatives that all the foreshore south of the General Foreign and the Japanese Settlements appertained [or would when filled in appertain] to the General Settlement. The Japanese therefore are strictly speaking, only entitled to fill in to the width of the 12 metres mentioned in Mr. Furuta's despatch. All ground beyond [that is, south] of that appertains to us.

In agreeing unconditionally, therefore, to the Japanese proposal we might seem to be giving away certain perspective rights: on the other hand, a 15 metre road from the jetty right through to Corea town would be a public boon.

Would it be possible, do you think, to arrange that in consideration of the increase of 3 metres [or whatever it is to be] acceded by the General Settlement to the Japanese, the latter agree under no circumstances to close the road? I ought to have brought in first my second point, which is, that the Japanese are apt when there is any suspicion of an epidemic, to endeavour to enforce quarantine regulations, one of which on the last occasion (as I am informed) consisted in stopping some, or all, of their streets, & forcibly disinfecting passers-by.

Yours very truly,

W. H. Wilkinson

1895년 12월 9일
윌킨슨이 실에게 보낸 편지[115)]

·· – 번역문 – ··

신동공사

1895년 12월 9일 제물포

귀하께,

이번 달 6일에 열린 회의에서 다음 결의안이 반대자 없이 통과되었습니다. "신동공사는 제물포 토지 규칙 제6절에 언급된 '조약국 영사들'이 실제로 제물포에 거주하는 영사관원들을 뜻한다고 믿으며, 한 사람이 당연직 위원과 정부 대표를 겸할 경우 많은 불편이 생기는 것을 인지하고 있습니다. 한국 정부에 출입하는 정부 대표 말고 다른 사람이 신동공사 회의에 참석하게 해 주시기를 정중하게 요청합니다."

따라서 저는 귀하께서 각국 외교 대표들과 이 결의안에 대하여 소통해 주시기를 정중하게 요청합니다.

귀하의 충복,

서기 윌킨슨

서울, 각국외교대표단장 실 귀하

---

115) 1895년 12월 9일 제물포 각국 조계 신동공사 서기였던 제물포주재영국부영사 윌킨슨이 주한미국공사 겸 각국외교대표단장 실에게 보낸 편지이다. 며칠 전 신동공사 회의에서 통과된 결의안을 각국 외교 대표들과 의논해 달라고 요청하는 내용이다.

·· — **원문** — ··

Municipal Council,

Chemulpo, Dec. 9th, 1895.

Sir,

At a meeting of the Council held on the 6th instant the following resolution was passed without a dissentient vote: "This Council believing it to have been the intention of the signatories to the Chemulpo Land Regulations that the 'Consuls of the Treaty Powers' referred to in §6 should be Consular Officers actually resident in Chemulpo, and recognizing the many inconveniences that have arisen from the same persons acting both as Official Members of the Council and as Foreign Representatives at Söul, respectfully requests, through the several Representatives, the attention of the Governments of the Treaty Powers to this matter, to the end that in each case a special Officer, not being the Representative of the Government at the Corean Court, may be appointed to attend the meetings of the Council."

I have accordingly the honour to respectfully request that you will be good enough to communicate the above resolution to the Foreign Representatives.

I have the honour to be, Sir,

Your most obedient humble servant,

W. H. Wilkinson

Hon. Secretary

Hon. J. M. B. Sill

Doyen of the Foreign Representatives

Söul

1895년 12월 27일 실이 각국 외교 대표들에게 보낸 편지[116)]

·· – **번역문** – ··

친애하는 동료들께,

괜찮으시다면 이번 달 30일 월요일 오후 3시 제 개인 사무실에서 귀하들을 뵙고 싶습니다. 제물포 신동공사 서기가 보내 온 편지에 언급된 문제를 논의하기 위해서입니다.

존경을 담아서,

실

1895년 12월 27일 주한미국공사관

승인 여부를 알려 주십시오.

(판독 불가—서명)

좋습니다. (판독 불가—서명)

좋습니다. (판독 불가—서명)

좋습니다. 크린

좋습니다. 고무라.

---

116) 1895년 12월 27일 각국외교대표단장을 맡고 있던 주한미국공사 실이 서울주재영국총영사 힐리어, 서울주재독일총영사 크린, 주한러시아대리공사 베베르, 주한프랑스대리공사 르페브르, 주한일본공사 고무라에게 보낸 편지이다. 12월 9일 신동공사 서기 윌킨슨으로부터 받은 편지와 관련하여 모임을 제안하기 위하여 작성하였다.

·· – 원문 – ··

Dear Colleagues,

I will be happy to meet with you in my private office at 3 p. m. on Monday the 30th Instant, to discuss the matter mentioned in the enclosed letter from the Honorary Secretary of the Chemulpo Municipal Council, if convenient and agreeable to you.

Yours very respectfully,

JOHN M. B. SILL

U. S. Legation, Dec. 27/95

Please indicate approval or otherwise.

(판독 불가—서명)

Yes. (판독 불가—서명)

Yes. (판독 불가—서명)

Yes. Kr.

Yes. Komura

1896년 1월 20일 윌킨슨이 실에게 보낸 편지[117]

- 번역문 -

신동공사

1896년 1월 20일 제물포

귀하께,

지난 달 9일 저는 당연직 위원들에 대한 신동공사의 결의안을 귀하께 제출하였습니다. 이제 귀하께서 보내 주신 12월 30일자 공문을 받았음을 알려 드립니다. 공문의 내용은 신동공사가 해당 결의안을 회람에 기록하지 않음으로써 규칙을 위반하였고 따라서 각국 외교 대표들이 그것을 무효화하기로 결정하였다는 것이었습니다.

이번 달 16일에 열린 신동공사 임시 회의에서 "신동공사는 우리가 심사숙고하여 만든 규칙 아래 발생한 모든 문제들을 결정할 특권을 누군가가 침해하는 것에 대하여 정중하게 이의를 제기합니다"라는 결의안이 통과되었을 때, 저는 귀하께서 보내 주신 공문을 회의장에 제출하였습니다.

귀하의 충복,

서기 윌킨슨

서울, 각국외교대표단장 실

1월 21~22일 모든 대표들이 돌려 읽음

---

117) 1896년 1월 20일 제물포주재영국부영사 겸 신동공사 서기 윌킨슨이 당시 각국외교대표단장이었던 주한미국공사 실에게 보낸 편지이다.

·· – **원문** – ··

Municipal Council,

Chemulpo, January 20, 1896.

Sir,

With reference to my letter of the 9th ultimo submitting a resolution of the Council in regard to Official Members, I have had the honour to receive your Despatch of the 30th December informing me that the Foreign Representatives had decided that the resolution in question was invalid because, in contravention of Sect. B § 12 of the Rules for regulating the Council's Proceedings, no notice of the motion had been given in the circular conveying the meeting.

This Despatch I laid before an extraordinary meeting of the Council on the 16th instant, when the following resolution was passed: "The Council respectfully demurs to any infringement of the privilege, reserved to it under Section 1 § 2 (a), of determining all questions arising under the Rules appertaining to the deliberations of the Council."

I have the honour to be, Sir,

Your most obedient servant,

W. H. Wilkinson

Hon. Secretary

Hon. J. M. B. Sill

Doyen of the Foreign Representatives.

Söul.

Circulated & seen by all the Representatives. Jan 21, 22.

1897년 2월 15일 이재정이 실에게 보낸 편지[118)]

·· – 번역문 – ··

인천감리 이재정이

주한미국공사 겸 제물포 신동공사 회장 실에게 보낸 편지

1897년 2월 15일 인천

귀하께,

귀하께 알려 드립니다. 저는 지난 달 23일 신동공사 서기에게 802.90달러짜리 수표를 동봉한 편지를 보냈습니다. 이 돈은 제물포 각국 조계의 토지소유주 4명으로부터 받은 1895년도 세금의 일부이고, 그 중 54.50달러는 일본 은행에 예금되어 있었던 1896년도 세금에 대한 이자로서 신동공사 기금입니다. 저는 이 수표에 대한 영수증의 원본과 사본도 서기에게 보냈습니다. 애초에 그의 서명을 받으려고 영수증을 보냈으나 그가 영수증에 서명하지 않고 돌려보냈기 때문입니다. 아울러 저는 통역관이 없으므로 서기에게 받은 영문 편지를 반송하고 평소처럼 번역본을 첨부해 달라고 요청하였습니다.

귀하께서는 서기에게 지시하여 영수증에 서명하여 제게 보내라고 해 주십시오. 그러면 저는 신동공사 기금을 위하여 작년 세금 일부를 액수

---

118) 1897년 2월 15일 인천감리 겸 인천부윤 이재정(李在正)이 당시 신동공사 회장이었던 주한미국공사 실에게 보낸 편지이다. 편지 하단의 메모 "번역관들은 이 편지를 (…) 외국인이 썼는지도 모르겠다"는 당시 주한미국공사관 서기관이었던 알렌이 쓴 것이다.

에 맞게 신동공사에 전달하겠습니다.

이만 줄입니다.

이재정 (서명과 인장)

번역관들은 이 편지를 영어로 옮기느라 애를 먹었다. 표현 방식이 보통 한국인의 것 같지 않았다. 외국인이 썼는지도 모르겠다.

–원문(영문)–

Superintendent of Trade Ye Chai Chung to
Mr. Sill U. S. Minister & President of the Chemulpo Municipal Council

Jenchuan 15th Feb. 1897

Sir,

I have the honor to inform you that I have sent a letter to the Secretary of the Municipal Council on the date of 23rd ult. with the enclosures of a check of sum $802.90 which was extracted from the rent of 1895 paid by the four land holders of the Chemulpo Foreign Settlement and $54.50, the interests of one year last for all the rents which was deposited at the Japanese Bank, for the fund of the Municipal Council; and also sent him the original and duplicate copies of said check's receipt which were provided by my office in need of his signature and to be sent back to my office. In further I beg to inform you that I have received an answer from him written by English, but without the signed receipt. So I returned the same English letter to him as I had no translator, and requested him to communicate with me hereafter in accompany of a translation as usual.

I trust your Excellency will kindly instruct the Secretary to have the said receipt to be signed and send back to me and then I will deliver, to the Municipal Council, the certain account for the Municipal funds which are extracted from the annual rents of last year to settle that accounts.

I have etc.

(signed) Chai Chung & official seal

Interpreters had quite difficulty in translating his letter. The form of expression not being as usual with Koreans. It may have been written by a foreigner.

·· – **원문(한문)** – ··

照會第二号

大朝鮮仁川港監理李

爲照會事照得本年五月二十三日本監理備函附送紳董公司文案本港各國租界內四租戶未完已繳到一千八百九十五年之年稅款內公司應存備金八百二元九角並自一千八百九十六年五月初一日起至十二月三十一日止之陸續繳到各年稅收存日本第一銀行之利息銀內公司應得銀五十四元五角合共銀八百五十七元四角銀票一張連代繕收到該銀正副收單二張等因嗣於正月二十五日接到紳董公司文案送來洋文書函一件而收到該銀之正副收單未見盖印畫押送還本署因無繙譯之負是以當將該洋文書函備文送還一向請該紳董公司文案以後几有於本署文件仍請照舊以英漢二文合璧自公司之設迄令旣將已九載之久紳董公司文案向用英漢二文合璧在案査本港各國租界內各租戶陸續繳到一千八百九十六年之年稅內尾款公司應得之存備金早已備便可以撥交該公司收存以便

將該年之年稅款項淸訖爲此備文請煩

貴公司議長査照懇請設法將前經附送紳董公司文案存備金之正副收單盖印畫押送還存案備査是所至望一俟將該收單送還之後當可將一千八百九十六年之年稅內公司應得存備金款送交公司收存淸款湏至照會者

右照會

大美國總領事兼仁川港各國租界公司議長施閣下

建陽二年二月十五日

1898년 8월 22일 포네가 알렌에게 보낸 편지[119)]

·· ─ **번역문** ─ ··

1898년 8월 22일 진남포 신동공사 사무실

귀하께,

귀하께 알려 드립니다. 오늘 회의를 개최하고 진남포 각국 조계 신동공사를 출범하였습니다. 회장에 포네, 회계에 야스노스케가 선출되었습니다.

귀하의 충복,

포네

서울, 주한미국공사 알렌 귀하

·· ─ **원문** ─ ··

Municipal Council's Office, Chinnampo,
22nd August 1898.

Sir,

I have the honor to inform Your Excellency, that at a meeting held to-day, that the Municipal Council for the Foreign Settlement of Chinnampo, has been inaugurated, and that the following officers have been elected, Eugene Peugnet,

---

119) 1898년 8월 22일 진남포주재러시아부영사 포네가 주한미국공사 알렌에게 보낸 편지이다. 진남포 각국 조계 신동공사의 출범을 알리기 위하여 작성하였다.

President, and Yasunosuke Ohki, Honorary Treasurer.

I am, Sir,

Your Excellency's obedient servant,

Eug. Peugnet

To His Excellency

Horace N. Allen

Ministers Resident and Consul General of the United States of America.

etc., etc., etc.,

Seoul.

1900년 9월 20일 바이페르트가 알렌에게 보낸 편지[120)]

·· – 번역문 – ··

1900년 9월 20일 서울

알렌 박사께,

오늘 아침 저는 하야시 씨에게 경인선 철도역의 세금 문제가 어떻게 진행되고 있는지 문의하였습니다. 그는 부동산 권리증 양식의 6번째 문단을 지적하면서 자신은 우리의 요구를 지지하고 이 일을 합의하기 위하여 일본 정부를 설득할 것이라고 대답하였습니다. 그는 곧 각국 외교 대표 회의 때 철도 회사의 제안서들을 제출할 것인데, 그 내용은 한국이 철도 회사의 이름으로 적절한 부동산 권리증을 발행하고 토지 전체를 D 부지로 편성한다면 철도 회사는 기꺼이 세금을 납부하겠다는 것입니다. 이는 세금이 3분의 1로 줄어드는 것을 의미합니다. 부동산 권리증은 한국 정부가 발행하고 제약 조건은 권리증 폐기시의 제약 조건과 같습니다. 철도 이권의 경우와 같습니다.

하야시 씨는 우리에게 자세한 성명서를 보내 준 후 절차를 진행하겠다고 이야기하였습니다. 그러나 저는 이 내용을 귀하께 즉각 알리는 것이 좋다고 생각하였습니다. 귀하가 현재 제물포에서 타운젠드 씨나

---

120) 1900년 9월 20일 신동공사 회장이었던 서울주재독일대리총영사 바이페르트가 주한미국공사 알렌에게 보낸 편지이다. 경인선 철도역의 소유권 및 세금과 관련하여 주한일본공사 하야시와 나눈 대화 내용을 전달하기 위하여 작성하였다.

기타 관계자들과 이 문제를 의논할 기회가 있을까 해서입니다.

귀하와 알렌 부인의 건강을 기원하며 인사를 전합니다.

진심을 담아서,

바이페르트

·· ─ **원문** ─ ··

Söul, Sept. 20th 1900

Dear Dr. Allen,

This morning I asked Mr. Hayashi about the present condition of the Chemulpo ― Railway ― Station ― Rent ― question. He said that by pointing out the 6th paragraph of the Title deed form, which according to his opinion was in favour of our demand, he has proceeded in persuading his government that something had to be done in order to arrive at a compromise. He would therefore very soon lay the proposals of the Railway Company before the meeting of the Representatives. The chief features of these proposals would be, that the Company was willing to pay the tax, provided that a proper title deed would be issued in the name of the Company and that the whole ground in question would be placed as D lots. This would mean a reduction of the rent to 1/3 of the rent paid by C lots and demanded hitherto in view of Art. 7 of the Land Regulations. As to the title deed, it will have to be issued by the Corean authorities and ought to be limited by the same conditions as to its termination, as the Railway concession itself.

Mr. Hayashi said he would communicate to us a detailed statement before having the proceeding, but I thought it would be better to inform you about the main features at once because you may perhaps have an opportunity now in Chemulpo to speak about the matter with Mr. Townsend and other parties interested.

Hoping that you and Mrs. Allen are in good health, I am with kind regards.

Yours very sincerely,

H. Weipert

제물포 각국 조계 도면(전체)[121]

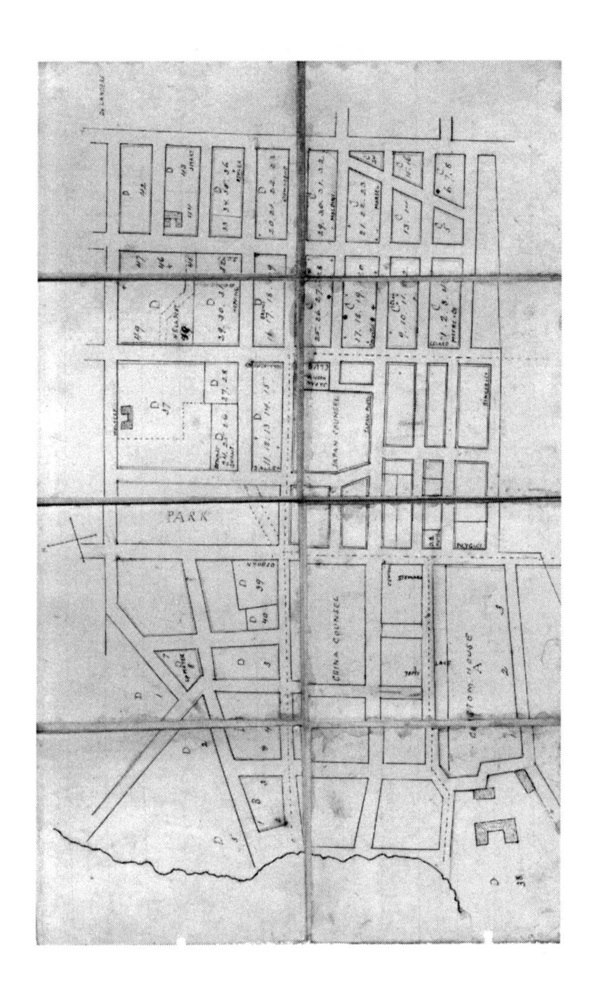

121) 각국 조계 뿐 아니라 중국 조계와 일본 조계도 간단히 그려져 있다. 공원(park), 중국 영사관(China Counsel), 일본 영사관(Japan Counsel), 해관(Custom House)은 큰 글씨로 표시되어 있고 건물명과 일부 토지소유주들의 이름은 작은 글씨로 표시되어 있다. 1890년대 후반에 작성된 것으로 추정된다.

제물포 각국 조계 도면(일부)[122]

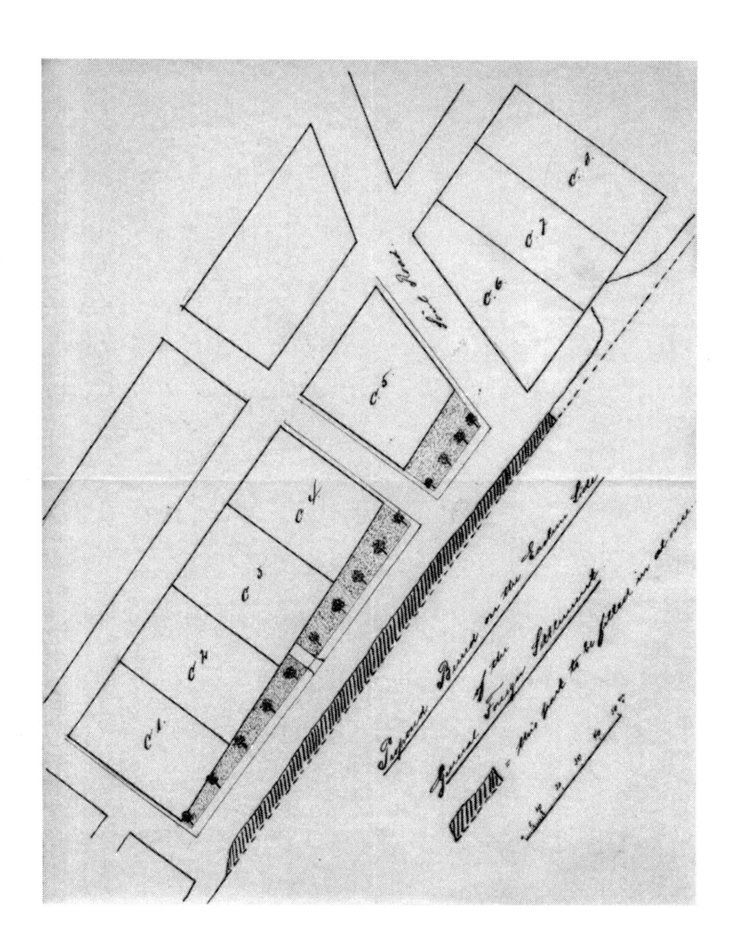

122) 각국 조계의 C1~C8 구역과 그 사이를 지나가는 서울행 도로(Söul Road)가 그려져 있으며, '각국 조계 동쪽 끝에 건설하자고 제안한 제방 도로(Proposed Bund on the Eastern Side of the General Foreign Settlement)'라는 문구가 쓰여 있다. 빗금으로 표시된 부분에는 '즉시 매립해야 할 부분(this part to be filled at once)'이라고 쓰여 있다.

제물포 각국 조계 장정 및 토지 규칙 개정을 위한 제안서[123)]

번역문

새로운 제물포 각국 조계 장정 및 토지 규칙을 위한 제안서

(1) 기존의 법규들을 폐지하되 현재의 장정과 규칙에 포함되는 것들은 그대로 둔다.

(2) 신동공사의 구성원은 조약국—각국 조계에 토지를 소유한 사람들의 조국—의 영사들과 제물포에 있는 왕립 해관의 수장, 그리고 토지 소유주 3명이다.

(3) 조약국의 영사들 또는 각국 외교 대표들로 구성된 법정을 개설한다.

(4) 한국 정부는 각국 조계라는 이름으로 알려진 토지를 신동공사에 영구 임대한다. 이 토지는 새롭게 정의된 것으로 북쪽 및 남쪽 갯벌을 포함한다. 한국 정부는 이 토지 안에 있는 한국인 주택과 묘지를 정해진 날짜 안에 철거할 책임이 있다.

(5) 신동공사는 과거 1년간 매각한 모든 구역에 대하여 매년 2월 1일 100제곱미터당 30센트의 세금을 납부한다.

(6) 세금은 매년 1월 1일에 징수한다. 혹자가 납세를 무시하거나 거부할 경우 그의 담당 영사 앞에서 절차에 따라 징수한다.

123) 제물포 각국 조계 장정과 토지 규칙을 개정하기 위하여 작성한 생산일자 미상의 제안서이다.

(7) 부동산 권리증은 첨부한 양식에 따라 신동공사가 발행한다.

(8) 한국 정부는 현재 소유하고 있는 구역을 앞으로도 소유할 수 있고 공적인 목적에 한하여 다른 구역을 매입할 수도 있다. 한국 정부의 소유지는 각국 조계의 다른 구역들과 마찬가지로 납세의 의무를 지며 각국 조계의 규정과 통제에 따라야 한다.

·· – **원문** – ··

Suggestions for a new agreement and

Land Regulations for the General Foreign Settlement of Chemulpo.

(1) The old Regulations are hereby abolished, excepting in so far as they are embodied in the present agreement and Regulations.

(2) The Municipal Council shall consist of the Consuls of the Treaty Powers, where subjects or citizens hold land in the settlement, the chief officer of the Royal Customs at Chemulpo and three land-holders.

(3) A court shall be established, consisting of the Consuls, or Representatives of all the Treaty Powers, before which it may be sued.

(4) The Korean Government shall lease in perpetuity to the Municipal Council the land known as the General Foreign Settlement, which shall be newly defined and which shall include the foreshore north and south. The Korean Government will undertake to remove the Korean dwellings and graves within the limits of the Settlement as speedily as possible and certainly before the expiration of form the date hereof.

(5) The Municipal Council shall pay as rent on the 1st of February of each year a sum equal to 30 cents per 100 square metres upon all lots sold to that

date.

(6) Rents shall be payable on 1st of January of each year at half the present rates (to be previously specified) which may be increased at the dictation of the Foreign Representatives. In case of neglect or refusal to pay, they may be collected by necessary process before the Consul of the delinquent.

(7) Title deeds shall be issued by the Municipal Council in the form attached.

(8) The Korean Government may hold the lots of which it is now in possession, and may acquire other lots by purchase, but only for strictly official purposes connected with the Settlement. Such lots shall be subjected to taxation, municipal regulation and control, precisely as other lots in the Settlement.

부록

1. 신동공사 역대 위원

다음은 제물포 각국 조계 신동공사의 역대 위원 명단이다. 1889~1895년, 1898~1900년, 1913년은 회의록이 일부라도 남아 있어 큰 문제가 없었으나, 1896~1897년과 1901~1912년은 회의록이 전혀 남아 있지 않아 명단을 파악하기 어려웠다. 이에 불가피하게 1889~1900년과 1913년 명단만 수록하였다. 독자들께 양해를 구한다.

〈1889년〉

당연직: 딘스모어(미국), 크린(독일), 풀포드(영국), 리나이룽→홍즈빈(중국), 스즈키→하야시(일본), 김○○→존스턴(한국)

선출직: 타운젠드(미국), 이나미(일본), 라포르트(프랑스)

임원진: 딘스모어(의장 대행), 풀포드(서기 대행)

〈1890년〉

당연직: 딘스모어→허드(미국), 크린(독일), 풀포드→스캇→캠벨→스캇(영국), 홍즈빈(중국), 하야시(일본), 존스턴(한국), 플랑시(프랑스)

선출직: 타운젠드(미국), 이나미(일본), 볼터(독일)

임원진: 플랑시(회장), 하야시(부회장), 존스턴(회계), 풀포드→스캇→캠벨→스캇(서기)

〈1891년〉

당연직: 허드(미국), 크린(독일), 스캇→프레이저(영국), 홍즈빈(중국), 하야시(일본), 존스턴(한국)

선출직: 타운젠드(미국), 이나미(일본), 볼터(독일)

임원진: 허드(회장), 하야시(부회장), 스캇→프레이저(회계·서기)

〈1892년〉

당연직: 허드(미국), 크린(독일), 프레이저→스캇→존슨(영국), 홍즈빈(중국), 하야시→노세(일본), 존스턴→우경선(한국)

선출직: 니시와키(일본), 스트리플링(영국), 볼터(독일)→뤼어스(독일)

임원진: 허드(회장), 하야시→크린(부회장), 볼터(회계), 프레이저→스캇→존슨(서기)

〈1893년〉

당연직: 허드→헤롯→알렌(미국), 크린(독일), 존슨→폭스(영국), 홍즈빈→류자충(중국), 노세(일본), 우경선(한국)

선출직: 니시와키(일본), 스트리플링(영국), 타운젠드(미국)

임원진: 크린(회장), 존슨→노세(부회장), 타운젠드(회계), 존슨→폭스(서기)

〈1894년〉

당연직: 알렌→실(미국), 크린(독일), 폭스→윌킨슨(영국), 류자충(중국), 노세→에이타키(일본), 우경선→감리(한국)

선출직: 니시와키(일본), 우리탕(중국), 타운젠드(미국)

임원진: 크린(회장), 노세(부회장), 니시와키(회계), 폭스→윌킨슨(서기)

〈1895년〉

당연직: 실(미국), 크린(독일), 윌킨슨(영국), 류자충(중국), 에이타키 → 진다 → 야마자 → 하시구치 → 하기와라(일본), 감리(한국)

선출직: 니시와키(일본), 우리탕(중국), 타운젠드(미국)

임원진: 크린(회장), 진다(부회장), 니시와키(회계), 윌킨슨(서기)

〈1896년〉

당연직: 실(미국), 크린(독일), 윌킨슨(영국), 하기하라 → 이시이(일본), 감리(한국)

선출직 및 임원진: 미상

〈1897년〉

당연직: 실 → 알렌(미국), 크린(독일), 윌킨슨 → 윌리스 → 졸리(영국), 이시이(일본), 감리(한국)

선출직 및 임원진: 미상

〈1898년〉

당연직: 알렌(미국), 크린 → 라인스도르프(독일), 졸리 → 오트윌 → 선디우스(영국), 이시이 → 시데하라(일본), 감리(한국)

선출직: 볼터(독일), 타운젠드(미국), 스즈키(일본)

임원진: 알렌 → 이시이(회장), 졸리 → 오트윌 → 선디우스(부회장), 볼터(회계), 타운젠드(서기)

〈1899년〉

당연직: 알렌(미국), 라인스도르프(독일), 선디우스 → 고프(영국), 시데하라 → 이주인(일본), 감리(한국)

선출직: 볼터(독일), 타운젠드(미국), 스즈키(일본)

임원진: 라인스도르프(회장), 선디우스(부회장), 볼터(회계), 타운젠드(서기)

〈1900년〉

당연직: 알렌(미국), 바이페르트(독일), 고프(영국), 이주인(일본), 감리(한국)

선출직: 타운젠드(미국), 오다카(일본), 뤼어스(독일)

임원진: 바이페르트(회장), 고프(부회장), 뤼어스(회계), 타운젠드(서기)

〈1913년〉

당연직: 시드모어(미국), 크뤼거(독일), 레이(영국), 히사미즈 사부로(일본)

선출직: 이와사키(일본), 바우만(독일), 베넷(영국)

임원진: 크뤼거(회장) 외 미상

2. 신동공사 관련 인물

다음은 제물포 각국 조계 신동공사 관련 인물들의 명단이다. 신동공사 역대 위원과 등록된 토지소유주, 그밖에도 회의록에 언급된 외국인들의 인적 사항을 가급적 균일한 분량으로 수록하였다. 한자를 알아내지 못한 중국 및 일본 인명은 불가피하게 원문에 나온 대로 표기하였으며, 한국 대표로 참석한 경찰관과 감리 등은 본문에 각주를 내어 소개하였으므로 여기에는 싣지 않았다. 독자들께 양해를 구한다.

〈ㄱ〉

가지야마 데이스케(梶山鼎介): 1848년에 태어난 일본인이다. 1891~1892년 주한일본공사를 역임하였다. 1933년 사망하였다.

고프(Herbert Goffe): 1870년에 태어난 영국인이다. 1899~1902년 제물포주재영국대리부영사로 복무하였다. 한국을 떠난 후 중국에서 외교관으로 활동하였으며 1937년 사망하였다.

고르샬키(A. Gorschalki): 생몰년 미상의 독일인이다. 1884년 내한하여 상인, 묘목장 관리인, 잠상공사 감독관으로 활동하였으며 제물포 각국 조계의 등록된 토지소유주였다.

고무라 주타로(小村壽太郎): 1855년에 태어난 일본인이다. 1895~1896년 주한일본공사를 역임하였다. 1901~1906년 외무대신에 임명되었으며 여러 국가에서 외교관으로 활동하였다. 1911년 사망하였다.

구로다(Y. Kurota): 생몰년 미상의 일본인이다. 신동공사 회관 건축 입찰에 참여하였다.

구마모토(E. Kumamoto): 생몰년 미상의 일본인이다. 제물포 각국 조계의 등록된 토지소유주였다.

기무라(J. Kimura): 생몰년 미상의 일본인이다. 제물포 각국 조계의 등록된 토지소유주였다.

〈ㄴ〉

에이타키 큐키치(永瀧久吉): 1866년에 태어난 일본인이다. 1893~1894년 부산주재일본부영사와 1894~1895년 제물포주재일본영사를 역임하였다. 한국을 떠난 후 여러 국가에서 외교관으로 활동하였으며 1942년 사망하였다.

나카이(K. Nakai): 생몰년 미상의 일본인이다. 제물포 각국 조계의 등록된 토지소유주였다.

노세 다스고로(能勢辰五郎): 생몰년 미상의 일본인이다. 1891~1894년 제물포주재일본부영사와 1899~1901년 부산주재일본영사, 1910~1911년 전라남도장관 등을 역임하였다.

니시와키 초타로(西脇長太郎): 생몰년 미상의 일본인이다. 1890년대에 다이이치은행 제물포지점 지배인으로 활동하였으며 제물포 각국 조계의 등록된 토지소유주였다.

〈ㄷ〉

도미타(S. Tomita): 생몰년 미상의 일본인이다. 1892년도 해외 거주 외국인 명부의 일본인 상인 명단에 이름을 올렸으며 제물포 각국 조계의 등록된 토지소유주였다.

도사(K. Tosa): 생몰년 미상의 일본인이다. 1889년도 해외 거주 외국인 명부에 따르면 일본우선회사 사무원이었으며 제물포 각국 조계의 등록된 토지소유주였다.

드미트레프스키(Pavel A. Dmitrevsky): 1851년에 태어난 러시아인이다. 1891~1893년 주한러시아대리공사를 역임하였다. 1899년 같은 직위에 재임명되었으나 몇 달 후 사망하였다.

딘스모어(Hugh A. Dinsmore): 1850년에 태어난 미국인이다. 1887~1890년 주한미국공사를 역임하였다. 한국을 떠난 후 미국에서 변호사 및 정치인으로 활동하였으며 1930년 사망하였다.

〈ㄹ〉

라인스도르프(F. Reinsdorf): 생몰년 미상의 독일인이다. 1887~1892년 서울주재독일영사관 통역관과 1892~1900년 서울주재독일부영사를 역임하였다.

락스데일(William H. Ragsdale): 생몰년 미상의 미국인이다. 1890년 제물포 각국 조계 경찰관 겸 공사감독관으로 고용되었다. 1890년대 후반 운산금광에 취직하기 전까지 수년간 경찰국장으로 복무하였다.

라포르트(Emile Laporte): 생몰년 미상의 프랑스인이다. 1883~1898년 인천해관 방판, 1898~1901년 부산해관장대리, 1901~1905년 인천해관장을 역임하였다. 제물포 각국 조계의 등록된 토지소유주였다.

랜디스(Eli B. Landis): 1865년에 태어난 미국인이다. 1890년 영국국교회 한국선교부 소속 의료선교사로서 내한하였다. 1898년 사망하였으며 인천외국인묘지에 묻혀 있다.

레이(Arthur H. Lay): 1865년에 태어난 영국인이다. 1904~1911년 제물포주재영국부영사와 1914~1927년 서울주재영국총영사를 역임하였다. 1934년 사망하였다.

뤼어스(G. F. W. Lührss): 생몰년 미상의 독일인이다. 1890년대 초 인천해관 항무장으로 복무하였으며 제물포 각국 조계의 등록된 토지소유주였다. 한국을 떠난 후 중국에서 해관원 생활을 계속하였다.

뤼어스(Carl Lührs): 생몰년 미상의 독일인이다. 1885년경 마이어상사 제물포지점 직원으로 내한하여 20년 이상 상업에 종사하였으며 제물포 각국 조계의 등록된 토지소유주였다.

로저스(Edward Rogers): 생몰년 미상의 영국인이다. 제물포 각국 조계의 등록된 토지소유주였다.

루이리링(Lui Li Ling): 생몰년 미상의 중국인이다. 신동공사 회관 건축 입찰에 참여하여 선정된 건설업자였다.

류자충(劉家驄): 생몰년 미상의 중국인이다. 1893~1894년 제물포주재중국부영사로 복무하였다.

르페브르(Georges Lefevre): 생몰년 미상의 프랑스인이다. 1893년 주한프랑스공사관 서기관으로 내한하여 1894~1896년과 1899~1901년 주한프랑스대리공사를 역임하였다.

리나이룽(李乃榮): 생몰년 미상의 중국인이다. 1883~1889년 제물포주재중국부영사로 복무하였다.

리윈눈(Li Yün Noon): 생몰년 미상의 중국인이다. 제물포 각국 조계의 등록된 토지소유주였다.

리페이친(Li Pei Chin): 생몰년 미상의 중국인이다. 제물포 각국 조계의 등록된 토지소유주였다.

리키타케 헤이하치(力武平八): 생몰년 미상의 일본인이다. 1892년도 해외 거주 외국인 명부의 일본인 상인 명단에 이름을 올렸으며 제물포 각국 조계의 등록된 토지소유주였다.

〈ㅁ〉

마다(Mada): 생몰년 미상의 일본인이다. 제물포 각국 조계의 등록된 토지소유주였을 가능성이 있다.

마이어(H. C. Eduard Meyer): 1841년에 태어난 독일인이다. 1884년 마이어상사 제물포지점을 개설하였으나 실제로 내한한 적은 없는 것 같으며 제물포 각국 조계의 등록된 토지소유주였다. 1926년 사망하였다.

마이어(Franz Meyer): 생몰년 미상의 독일인이다. 1880년대 말부터 수년간 선장으로 활동하였으며 제물포 각국 조계의 등록된 토지소유주였다.

모건(F. A. Morgan): 생몰년 미상의 영국인이다. 1892년 인천해관장과 1892~1893년 총세무사대리를 역임하였다. 한국을 떠난 후 중국에서 해관원 생활을 계속하였다.

몬디니(Ph. Mondini): 생몰년 미상의 이탈리아인이다. 1880년대부터 중국에서 해관원으로 활동하다가 1890년대 말 내한하여 인천해관 검사관보로 복무하였다. 제물포 각국 조계의 등록된 토지소유주였다.

뫼르젤(Ferdinand H. Mörsel): 생몰년 미상의 독일인이다. 1883년 내한하여 인천해관에서 항해사와 항무장 등으로 복무하였다. 1890년대부터는 상업, 중개업, 임대업 등 다양한 일에 종사하였으며 제물포 각국 조계의 등록된 토지소유주였다.

〈ㅂ〉

바우만(Paul F. Baumann): 1874년에 태어난 독일인이다. 1890년대 후반 마이어상사 제물포지점 직원으로 내한하였다. 1904년 주한벨기에공사의 딸과 결혼하였다. 한국을 떠난 후 필리핀으로 이주하였으며 1965년 사망하였다. 제물포 각국 조계의 등록된 토지소유주였다.

바이페르트(Heinrich Weipert): 1855년에 태어난 독일인이다. 1900년 서울주재독일대리총영사와 1900~1903년 서울주재독일총영사를 역임하였다. 1905년 사망하였다.

베넷(Walter G. Bennett): 1868년에 태어난 영국인이다. 1890년대 후반 내한하여 홈링어상사 제물포지점을 개설하고 수십 년간 상업에 종사하였다. 1937년 아내가 죽은 후 한국을 떠났으며 1944년 사망하였다. 제물포 각국 조계의 등록된 토지소유주였다.

베베르(Carl I. Waeber): 1841년에 태어난 러시아인이다. 1885~1891년과 1894~1897년 주한러시아대리공사를 역임하였다. 1910년 사망하였다.

보리오니(F. R. Borioni): 생몰년 미상의 이탈리아인이다. 1883년 내한하여 인천해관에서 10년 이상 활동하고 1900년대 후반에는 부산해관에서도 복무하였다. 한국을 떠난 후에는 중국에서 해관원 생활을 계속하였다. 제물포 각국 조계의 등록된 토지소유주였다.

볼터(Carl A. Wolter): 1858년에 태어난 독일인이다. 1884년 마이어상사 제물포지점 직원으로 내한하여 수십 년간 상업에 종사하였다. 1907

년 귀국하였으며 1916년 사망하였다. 제물포 각국 조계의 등록된 토지소유주였다.

브라운(J. McLeavy Brown): 1835년에 태어난 영국인이다. 1893년 내한하여 10년 이상 총세무사를 역임하고 탁지부 고문으로도 복무하였다. 1905년 한국을 떠났으며 1926년 사망하였다.

브링크마이어(Robert H. C. Brinckmeier): 1840년에 태어난 독일인이다. 1880년대 말 내한하여 인천해관 검사관보로 복무하고 이후 서울주재독일영사관에서 일하였다. 1930년 사망하였으며 인천외국인묘지에 묻혀 있다. 제물포 각국 조계의 등록된 토지소유주였다.

〈ㅅ〉

선디우스(Ambrose J. Sundius): 1864년에 태어난 영국인이다. 1898~1899년 제물포주재영국부영사를 역임하였다. 1899년 한국을 떠난 후 중국에서 외교관으로 활동하였으며 1924년 사망하였다.

샌즈(William F. Sands): 1874년에 태어난 미국인이다. 1898~1899년 주한미국공사관 서기관과 1899~1901년 궁내부 고문을 역임하였다. 한국을 떠난 후 여러 국가에서 외교관으로 활동하였으며 1946년 사망하였다.

세레진-사바친(Afanasy I. Seredin-Sabatin): 1860년에 태어난 우크라이나(당시에는 러시아)인이다. 1883년 내한하여 인천해관 검사관보로 활동하고 서울과 인천의 근대 건축에 깊이 관여하였다. 러일전쟁 후 한국을 떠났으며 1921년 사망하였다.

쉐니크(J. F. Schoenicke): 생몰년 미상의 독일인이다. 1886~1889년 인천해관장대리와 1889~1892년 총세무사대리를 역임하였다. 한국을 떠난 후 중국에서 해관원 생활을 계속하였다.

슈타인벡(J. Steinbeck): 생몰년 미상의 오스트리아인이다. 1884년 내한하여 제물포 각국 조계의 토지를 매입하고 1880년대 후반 한국호텔(Hotel de Corée)을 운영하였다. 1889년 제물포 각국 조계의 등록된 토지 소유주가 되었다.

스에나가(T. Suyenaga): 생몰년 미상의 일본인이다. 제물포 각국 조계의 등록된 토지소유주였다.

스즈키(A. Suzuki): 생몰년 미상의 일본인이다. 제물포 각국 조계의 등록된 토지소유주였다.

스즈키 미츠요시(鈴木充美): 1854년에 태어난 일본인이다. 1886~1888년 제물포주재일본영사로 복무하였으며 1930년 사망하였다.

스캇(James Scott): 1850년에 태어난 영국인이다. 1886년부터 1892년까지 제물포주재영국부영사 또는 대리부영사로 복무하였다. 한국을 떠난 후 중국에서 외교관으로 활동하였으며 1920년 사망하였다.

스트리플링(Alfred B. Stripling): 1838년에 태어난 영국인이다. 1883년 내한하여 인천해관장과 경무청 고문을 역임하였고 제물포 각국 조계의 등록된 토지소유주였다. 1904년 사망하였으며 양화진외국인묘지에 묻혀 있다.

시데하라 기주로(幣原喜重郎): 1872년에 태어난 일본인이다. 1898~1899년 제물포주재일본대리부영사와 1901~1902년 부산주재일본영사를 역임하였다. 한국을 떠난 후 여러 국가에서 외교관으로 활동하였으며 제2차 세계대전이 끝난 후 총리를 지냈다. 1951년 사망하였다.

시드모어(George H. Scidmore): 1854년에 태어난 미국인이다. 1909~

1913년 서울주재미국총영사로 복무하였다. 한국을 떠난 후 일본에서 외교관으로 활동하다가 1922년 사망하였다.

시마우치 요시오(Shimauchi Yoshio): 생몰년 미상의 일본인이다. 1889년도 해외 거주 외국인 명부에 따르면 다이이치은행 제물포지점 직원이었으며 제물포 각국 조계의 등록된 토지소유주였다.

시마자키(Shimazaki): 생몰년 미상의 일본인이다. 제물포 각국 조계 경찰관으로 복무하였다.

신도(S. Shindo): 생몰년 미상의 일본인이다. 제물포 각국 조계의 등록된 토지소유주였다.

실(John M. B. Sill): 1831년에 태어난 미국인이다. 1894~1897년 주한미국공사를 역임하였다. 1901년 사망하였다.

〈ㅇ〉

아사오카(Asaoka): 생몰년 미상의 일본인이다. 신동공사 회관 건축 입찰에 참여하였다.

아사이다 류우치(Asayida Riuchi): 생몰년 미상의 일본인이다. 신동공사 회관 건축 입찰에 참여하였다.

아소(S. Aso): 생몰년 미상의 일본인이다. 1899년도 해외 거주 외국인 명부에 따르면 다이이치은행 제물포지점 직원이었으며 제물포 각국 조계의 등록된 토지소유주였다.

알렌(Horace N. Allen): 1858년에 태어난 미국인이다. 1884년 내한하여 의료선교사로 활동하다가 외교관으로 전업하여 1897~1905년 주한미국공사를 역임하였다. 1905년 한국을 떠났으며 1932년 사망하였다.

알마허(Fr. Allmacher): 생몰년 미상의 독일인이다. 1889년도 해외 거주 외국인 명부에 따르면 증기선 해룡호의 수석 기술자였으며 제물포 각국 조계의 등록된 토지소유주였다.

야마자 엔지로(山座圓次郎): 1866년에 태어난 일본인이다. 1894년 부산주재일본대리영사, 1895년 제물포주재일본대리영사, 1899~1901년 주한일본공사관 서기관을 역임하였다. 1914년 사망하였다.

야스노스케 오기(Yasunosuke Oki): 생몰년 미상의 일본인이다. 1898~1899년 진남포주재일본대리영사로 복무하였다.

야와시타(R. Yawashita): 생몰년 미상의 일본인이다.

에클런드(Eklundh): 생몰년 미상의 미국인이다. 1890년대 말 제물포 각국 조계 경찰국장으로 복무하였다.

오스본(William McC. Osborne): 생몰년 미상의 영국인이다. 중국에서 해관원으로 활동하다가 내한하여 1892~1894년 인천해관장대리와 1901~1907년 부산해관장을 역임하였다.

오다 리키타로(Ota Richitaro): 생몰년 미상의 일본인이다. 제물포 각국 조계의 등록된 토지소유주였다.

오다카(G. Odaka): 생몰년 미상의 일본인이다. 제물포 각국 조계의 등록된 토지소유주였다.

오트윌(H. A. Ottewill): 생몰년 미상의 영국인이다. 1898년 내한하여 서울주재영국영사관 보조와 제물포주재영국대리부영사, 주한영국공사관 서기관을 역임하였다.

오하시 타로(Ohashi Taro): 생몰년 미상의 일본인이다. 제물포 각국 조계의 등록된 토지소유주였다.

와이어스(Wyers): 1894년 신동공사의 토지 매각을 알선한 경매업자이다. 영국국교회 평신도 선교사로 내한하였다가 제물포주재영국부영사관 경찰관이 된 와이어스(John M. Wyers)와 동일인일 가능성이 있다.

요시다(J. Yoshida): 생몰년 미상의 일본인이다. 제물포 각국 조계의 등록된 토지소유주였다.

요시다 와주(Yoshida Waju): 생몰년 미상의 일본인이다. 신동공사 회관 건축 입찰에 참여하였다.

우리탕(吳禮堂): 1843년에 태어난 중국인이다. 1883년 인천해관 방판으로 내한하였으며 제물포 각국 조계의 등록된 토지소유주였다. 1912년 사망하였으며 인천외국인묘지에 묻혀 있다.

윌킨슨(William H. Wilkinson): 1858년에 태어난 영국인이다. 1893~1894년 서울주재영국대리총영사와 1894~1897년 제물포주재영국부영사를 역임하였다. 한국을 떠난 후 중국에서 외교관으로 활동하였으며 1930년 사망하였다.

이시이 기쿠지로(石井菊次郎): 1866년에 태어난 일본인이다. 1896~1898년 제물포주재일본영사로 복무하고 1897년부터는 진남포의 영사업무를 겸하였다. 한국을 떠난 후 여러 국가에서 외교관으로 활동하였으며 1945년 사망하였다.

이나미 데스오(Tetsuo Yenami): 생몰년 미상의 일본인이다. 제물포 각국 조계의 등록된 토지소유주였다.

이노우에 가오루(井上馨): 1836년에 태어난 일본인이다. 1894~1895년 주한일본공사를 역임하였다. 1915년에 사망하였다.

이와사키(Iwasaki): 생몰년 미상의 일본인이다. 제물포 각국 조계의 등록된 토지소유주였다.

이주인 히코키치(伊集院彦吉): 1864년에 태어난 일본인이다. 1899~1901년 제물포주재일본영사와 1896~1899년 부산주재일본영사를 역임하였다. 1924년 사망하였다.

〈ㅈ〉

자이츠(Robert Seitz): 생몰년 미상의 독일인이다. 해외 거주 외국인 명부에 따르면 1885년경부터 마이어상사 제물포지점의 직원이었으며 제물포 각국 조계의 등록된 토지소유주였다.

존스턴(John C. Johnston): 생몰년 미상의 영국인이다. 중국에서 해관원으로 활동하다 1889~ 1892년 인천해관장대리로 복무하였다. 한국을 떠난 후 중국에서 해관원 생활을 계속하였다.

존슨(Octavius Johnson): 생몰년 미상의 영국인이다. 1892~1893년 제물포주재영국대리부영사를 역임하였다. 한국을 떠난 후 중국에서 외교관으로 활동하였다.

졸리(Henry B. Joly): 1858년에 태어난 영국인이다. 1880년대부터 중국에서 외교관으로 활동하다가 1897년 제물포주재영국부영사로 부임하였다. 복무 중이던 이듬해 한국에서 사망하였다.

진다 스테미(珍田捨巳): 1857년에 태어난 일본인이다. 샌프란시스코주재일본영사로서 복무를 마친 후 1895년 1~5월 제물포주재일본영사로 복무하였다. 한국을 떠난 후 여러 국가에서 외교관으로 활동하였으며 1929년 사망하였다.

〈ㅊ〉

챌머스(J. L. Chalmers): 생몰년 미상의 영국인이다. 1880년대부터 중국에서 해관원으로 활동하다가 1898~1901년 인천해관장대리와 1901~1905년 총세무사 비서를 역임하였다. 한국을 떠난 후 중국에서 해관원 생활을 계속하였다.

〈ㅋ〉

캠벨(Charles W. Campbell): 1861년에 태어난 영국인이다. 1887~1891년 서울주재영국영사관 보조로 있으면서 1888년 4~5월과 6~11월 제물포주재영국대리부영사를 역임하였다. 한국을 떠난 후 중국에서 외교관으로 활동하였으며 1927년 사망하였다.

코지마(Dr. Kojima): 생몰년 미상의 일본인 의사이다. 1894년도 해외거주 외국인 명부의 코조(K. Kojio), 1897년도 명부의 코지마(K. Kojima)와 동일인일 가능성이 있다.

코프(Charles J. Corfe): 1843년에 태어난 영국인이다. 1890년 내한하여 영국국교회 한국선교부를 개설하고 선교에 종사하였다. 1905년 한국을 떠났으며 1921년 사망하였다.

콜브란(Henry Collbran): 1852년 영국에서 태어난 미국인이다. 1890년대 말 내한하여 경인선 철도 건설 계약을 필두로 전기, 수도, 광업 이권을 획득하였다. 은퇴한 후에는 영국에서 여생을 보냈으며 1925년 사망하였다.

쿠리가와(Kurikawa): 생몰년 미상의 일본인이다. 제물포 각국 조계의 등록된 토지소유주였다.

쿠퍼(Charles H. Cooper): 1835년에 태어난 미국인이다. 1883년 내한하여 상업에 종사하였으며 제물포 각국 조계의 등록된 토지소유주였다. 1889년 사망하였으며 인천외국인묘지에 묻혀 있다.

크뤼거(Fr. Krüger): 생몰년 미상의 독일인이다. 마닐라와 홍콩 등지에서 외교관으로 활동하다가 1907~1914년 서울주재독일총영사를 역임하였다.

크린(Ferdinand Krien): 1850년에 태어난 독일인이다. 1887년 서울주재독일대리영사로서 내한하여 1889~1898년 서울주재독일영사를 역임하였다. 한국을 떠난 후 일본에서 외교관으로 활동하였으며 1924년 사망하였다.

키지야마(Kijiyama): 생몰년 미상의 일본인이다. 제물포 각국 조계 경찰관으로 복무하였다.

키츠키(Kitsuki): 생몰년 미상의 일본인이다. 제물포 각국 조계 경찰관으로 복무하였다.

〈ㅌ〉

타운젠드(Walter D. Townsend): 1856년에 태어난 미국인이다. 1885년 내한하여 모스타운젠드상사를 열고 수십 년간 상업에 종사하였으며 제물포 각국 조계의 등록된 토지소유주였다. 1918년 사망하였으며 인천외국인묘지에 묻혀 있다.

〈ㅍ〉

패덕(Gordon Paddock): 1865년에 태어난 미국인이다. 1901년 내한하여 주한미국공사관 서기관, 부총영사, 총영사 등을 역임하였다. 1909년 한국을 떠난 후 여러 국가에서 외교관으로 활동하였으며 1932년 사망하였다.

포네(Eugene Peugnet): 생몰년 미상의 러시아인이다. 1897~1899년 진남포해관 책임자를 역임하였다. 1899년도 해외 거주 외국인 명부에 따르면 진남포주재러시아부영사를 겸하고 있었다.

폭스(H. H. Fox): 생몰년 미상의 영국인이다. 1893~1894년 제물포주재영국대리부영사로 복무하였다.

풀포드(Henry E. Fulford): 1859년에 태어난 영국인이다. 1887~1890년 제물포주재영국대리부영사를 역임하였다. 한국을 떠난 후 중국에서 외교관으로 활동하였으며 1929년 사망하였다.

플랑시(V. Collin de Plancy): 1853년에 태어난 프랑스인이다. 1888~1891년 주한프랑스공사를 지냈다. 1896년 주한프랑스대리공사로서 다시 내한하였고 1901년 주한프랑스공사로 재임명되었다. 1906년 한국을 떠났으며 1924년 사망하였다.

〈ㅎ〉

하기와라 슈이치(萩原守一): 1868년에 태어난 일본인이다. 1895~1896년 제물포주재일본대리영사와 1901~1906년 주한일본공사관 서기관을 역임하였다. 1911년 사망하였다.

하시구치 나오에몬(橋口直右衛門): 생몰년 미상의 일본인이다. 1887~1891년 서울주재일본부영사와 1895년 제물포주재일본영사를 역임하였다.

하야시 곤스케(林權助): 1860년에 태어난 일본인이다. 1888~1892년 제물포주재일본영사를 거쳐 1899~1906년 주한일본공사로 복무하였다. 한국을 떠난 후 여러 국가에서 외교관으로 활동하였으며 1939년 사망하였다.

허드(Augustine F. Heard, Jr.): 1827년에 태어난 미국인이다. 어거스틴 허드상사 창립자의 조카로서 광둥에서 오래 활동하였다. 1890~1893년 주한미국공사를 역임하였으며 1905년 사망하였다.

허치슨(William D. Hutchison): 생년 미상의 영국인이다. 1885~1887년 우체국장과 인천해관장대리 비서를 지냈다. 1890년대 초 다시 내한하여 통제영학당과 한성영어학교에서 교사로 활동하였다. 1901년 사망하였으며 양화진외국인묘지에 묻혀 있다.

헤롯(Joseph R. Herod): 생몰년 미상의 미국인이다. 1892~1895년 주일미국공사관 서기관으로 복무하였고 1893년 허드가 한국을 떠난 후 잠깐 주한미국대리공사를 겸임하였다.

호리구치 카에몬(Horiguchi Kayemon): 생몰년 미상의 일본인이다. 1886년도 해외 거주 외국인 명부의 일본인 상인 명단에 이름을 올렸으며 제물포 각국 조계의 등록된 토지소유주였다.

호리 리키타로(堀力太郎): 생몰년 미상의 일본인이다. 1883년 내한하여 다이부츠호텔을 운영하였으며 제물포 각국 조계의 등록된 토지소유주였다.

홀링스워스(Thomas Hollingsworth): 1840년대 초 영국에서 태어난 미국인이지만 제물포 각국 조계 문서에는 영국인으로 기록되어 있다. 내한 초기에는 숙박업에 종사하다가 1887년 인천해관에 고용되었으며 제물포 각국 조계의 등록된 토지소유주였다. 1899년 사망하였으며 인천외국인묘지에 묻혀 있다.

홉킨스(Leonard A. Hopkins): 생몰년 미상의 영국인이다. 내한 초기에는 제물포주재영국부영사관 경찰관으로 일하다가 1886년경 인천해관에 고용되었으며 제물포 각국 조계의 등록된 토지소유주였다. 1900년대에는 진남포해관과 목포해관에서도 책임자로 복무하였다.

후루타(J. Furuta): 생몰년 미상의 일본인이다. 1895년도 제물포 일본조계 자치 의회 회장이었다.

후지와라(Fujiwara): 생몰년 미상의 일본인이다. 제물포 각국 조계의 등록된 토지소유주였다.

훙즈빈(洪子彬): 생몰년 미상의 중국인이다. 1889~1893년 제물포주재중국부영사로 복무하였다.

히구치(S. Higuchi): 생몰년 미상의 일본인이다. 제물포 각국 조계의 등록된 토지소유주였다.

히사미즈 사부로(久水三郎): 1857년에 태어난 일본인이다. 1883~1889년 제물포주재일본영사관 서기관, 1889~1892년 원산주재일본대리영사, 1897~1899년 목포주재일본영사를 역임하고 여러 국가에서 외교관으로 활동하였다. 1910~1916년 인천부윤으로 복무하였다.

힐리어(Walter C. Hillier): 1849년에 태어난 영국인이다. 1888년 서울주재영국대리총영사로 내한하여 1891~1896년 서울주재영국총영사를 역임하였다. 1927년 사망하였다.

FOREIGN SETTLEMENT C 36
Chemulpo minutes
Vol II
U.S. Legation Seoul

134

distribute them amongst all other landholders.

At the request of the Council Mr. Nishiwaki undertook also to have 50 more copies printed.

Adjournment The Meeting then adjourned until 3 o'clock the same day.

Adjourned Meeting of 11th May. 1892.

Present Same Members.

Road leading from D.39 to B.2.

All members having gone over this road it was general opinion that the same ought to be cut down a good deal more at D39. the depth was however left an open question; Mr. Krien kindly undertook to bring this matter before the Gov. Repp.

Corean Graves. Proposed by Mr. Morse & Seconded by Mr. Nishiwaki;

" that a letter be addressed by the Hon. Secr.
" to the Kamni asking him to have the
" Graves in the G. S. 3. especially those in
" Public Garden and the cemetery removed
" within 3 weeks or else the M. C.
" would have them removed without
" further notice after the expiration of
" that period.—

Taxes on Lots B.4. D.2 & 4 for 1891 Mr. Wolter raised the question of taxes per 91 on Lots B. 4. D.2 & D.4 which so far he had not yet received

from Mr. Johnston he wanted money and he could not understand why it had not been paid yet.-
The taxes were for these lots = $243.99.
of which the Cor. Govt Bpp 47.76
So we ought to have received: $.196.23.

Mr. Stripling mentioned that the amount had been paid at the beginning of March.

Finally Mr. Wolter proposed and Mr. Stripling seconded:

„ that a letter be written to Mr.
„ Johnston asking him to send the amount
„ of 196.23. to the Hon. Treasurer as the
„ Council wanted money.„

Carried unanimously.

Prison. The question was raised by Mr. Moese whether it was advisable to have any prison at all in the Municipality had a right to imprison anybody.

Mr. Krien mentioned that with the exception of the Japanese and Chinese Authorities no other ones had a prison here in Chemulpo. What should they do if somebody committed a crime? In Kobe in the Foreign Settlement they had a proper prison adjoining the Municipal Buildings; prison regulations and daily charges for the keeping of prisoners were made out. He would certainly like to see the Council building a proper prison, what name they gave to the place was quite immaterial but they ought to have a good and strong room where a prisoner could be kept for a night or for a longer period. if the

136

proper Authorities should wish it. In his opinion the Council had of course not the right to imprison offenders, but they had certainly the right and not only the right but it was their duty, to detain such offenders until taken over by the proper Authorities.

Funds in Hong Kong & Shanghai Bank, Shanghai

Mr. Nosse wished to discuss the question of withdrawl of money now in this bank but as this was a very important question, it was generally thought that proper notice should be given to all Members.

Mr. Nosse then asked to have the following inserted into the Minutes of this meeting:
" Mr. Nosse expressed his wished that notice
" be given to the members to the effect that
" the Municipal fund amounting to something
" to something Five thousand Dollars at
" present deposited with the Hg kg & Shai
" Bank shall be withdrawn and deposited
" with the local Bank in Chemulpo. He
" deems this course be more reasonable and
" convenient; besides he does not see any
" necessity of depositing the money at
" Shanghai while there are several Banks
" here which are as good as any Bank
" in Shanghai."

Seawall & Jetty. Mr. Wolter said that Mr. Stripling and he had called on Mr. Johnston and asked him to begin the work that was still to be done at an early date; they had also asked Mr. Johnston to use when building the outer edge of the seawall, well dressed stones. They thought this absolutely necessary, as in the present state of this outer edge all boats got their bows smashed in, if there were only a moderate sea. if no dressed stones were used, then the Government

138

ought to put wooden balks as fenders in front.

Mr. Krien kindly undertook to mention at a meeting of the For. Repps. the necessity of having dressed stones at the outer edge of seawall and jetty.—

Next Meeting. Mr. Kosse proposed and Mr. Stripling seconded;

„ that the next meeting be held some „ time in the first week of June on a „ day to be decided upon by the Local „ members of the Council."—

Carried unanimously.

The meeting then adjourned.—

Sigd. F. Krien.
Vice President and Chairman p. t.

Sigd. J. Scott.
Hon. Secretary.

Meeting of Local members of Municipal Council 25th Augt. 1892. for the purpose of considering and accepting estimates for erection of Municipal Building in terms of Municipal resolution of 7th June 1892.

Present Messrs Hung. Kosse, Wolter, Stripling & Scott.

First	estimate by	Y. Murata	$ 4273.608
Second	„ „	Yoshida Wajiu	3975„40
Third	„ „	Asayida Riuchi	5271.
Fourth	„ „	Asaoka	3442„25
Fifth	„ „	Lui Li Ling	3200„

The estimate of $ 3200 by Lui Li Ling accepted and executive Committee requested to complete arrangement for the final

139

contract unanimously.

White despatch Box recovered by Police from Corean under suspicious circumstances on night of 11th July was opened and as it was found to belong to A. Yamashita the box and contents were handed to Mr. Nosse.

Sigd Nosse, Chairman p.t.
Sigd James Scott Hon. Secr.
Chemulpo 25th 1892 Aug.

Meeting of Municipal Council of 23. Sept. 1892.

Present

Messrs Nosse, Wolter, Stripling & Scott but not being a quorum the meeting was adjourned from day to day until 28th Sept. 1892 at 10 a.m.

Sigd T. Nosse Chairman p.t.
Sigd James Scott Hon. Secr.

Meeting of M. C. of 27th Sept. 1892.

Present

Messrs Stripling, Scott and Wolter but there being no quorum the meeting was further adjourned from day to day until next week for a date to be afterwards fixed by the Local Members.

Woo the Corean Magistrate afterwards appeared.

Sd T. Nosse, Chairman, p.t.
Sd James Scott. Hon Secretary.

140

Meeting of Municipal Council of 5th Oct. 1892.

Present.

Messrs Stripling. Nosse. Johnson. Wolter.
but there being no quorum the meeting was
further adjourned until the 6th inst. at 3. p.m.

Sd. T. Nosse. chairman p.t.

Sd. Oct. Johnson. Hon. Secretary.

Meeting of Municipal Council of 6th Oct. 1892

Present.

Messrs Stripling. Nishiwaki. Johnson.
and Wolter but there being no quorum.
the meeting was further adjourned until
the 7th inst. at 3. p.m.

Sd. T. Nosse Sd. Oct. Johnson.
chairman pt. Hon. Secr.

Meeting of Municipal Council of 7th Oct. 1892.

Present:

Messrs Stripling. Nishiwaki, Nosse.
Johnson and C. Wolter.

Minutes of last meeting & of no quorum meetings
read and signed.

Proposed by Mr. Nosse. Seconded by Mr. Nishiwaki
that Mr. Johnson be elected Secretary for
the current year - carried.

Proposed by Mr. Nosse, Seconded by Mr. Wolter,
that the Secretary be asked to convey a warm
vote of thanks to Mr. James Scott. for services
rendered to the Council during his term
of office as Secretary. — Carried.

Mr. Wolter handed in the Contract for
erection of Municipal building and stated

that the sum of $100.- for drawing out the plans for the same as ready voted by the Council had been paid although the work was not yet complete he asked that the approval of the Council to this early payment might be given.-

Mr. Stripling proposed that this early payment be approved & Mr. Nishiwaki seconded - Carried. On the motion of Mr. Nosse, seconded by Mr. Nishiwaki the sum of $20.00 Consular fee for cancelling old and issuing new title deeds for lots D. 2. & B. 4 A letter was handed in by Mr. Stripling requesting a refund of $106.04 taxes paid by him on land forming part of his property which had been utilized by the Council for making a road.- Proposed by Mr. Nosse. Seconded by Mr. Nishiwaki, that the treasurer be authorized to pay this sum if found correct. Carried.—

A long discussion took place with regard to laying out the Western end of the settlement in lots and grading road therein. Mr. Stripling proposed that steps should be taken by the Council to lay out in lots and mark on the plan of the General Foreign Settlement the whole of the western end of the same, but this found no seconder. Eventually Mr. Wolter having proposed and Mr. Nosse seconded it was carried that the Secretary should be asked to write to the Doyen of Diplomatic Body at Seoul urging him to press the Corean Government to begin grading more roads in the General Foreign

142.

settlement at once and also to refund the Council for expenses already incurred under this head. If the Corean Government refuse this it is to be suggested that the sum of 30 cents per 100 metres annual ground rent at present paid to the Corean Government be withheld and the same sum paid by the lot-proprietor to their Consul to be kept by the latter at the disposal of the Council.

Mr. Stripling handed in the following proposition signed. „ I beg to propose „that the grading of Public Road leading „South to North dividing D.2. from D.1. and „ D7. 8.9. be proceeded with without further delay.

Signed: Alfred B. Stripling.

Oct 6th 1892.

This was seconded by Mr. Wolter who at the same time wished it to be recorded that he did so in consideration of the fact that there were men & material at present at the disposal of the Council that might be employed for the purpose:— Carried

Mr. Wolter reported that a man applied to be allowed to store coal on jetty. Council unanimously disapproved.

The meeting then adjourned until the 8th inst. at 3. P.M.

8th Oct. 1892. — Present: Messrs Stripling, Nishiwaki, Nosse, Johnson & Wolter.

Proposed by Mr. Johnson, in continuation of the resolution carried by the Council on the subject at the meeting of 10th May last

that the plans having now been completed. the position of the Public Gardens in the Municipal Lot be left to the decision of the Executive Committee, seconded by Mr. Nosse. - Carried.
Road leading from D 39 to B 2. Specially from B 4 to B 2.

The unsatisfactory condition of the Chinese side of this road was again mentioned and Mr. Nosse kindly consented to call on the Chinese Consul and speak with him on the subject and also urge the necessity of a road in front of Chinese settlement from B 2 to N. W. corner of Consular Hill.

Mr. Stripling asked that notices might be sent out calling for a general meeting to be held within four weeks of this date at which he would propose „ that "in order to open up the „western part of the settlement the Council authorize „ the expenditure of $600.00 for the purpose of „ building a jetty in front of Lots B. -

Meeting of Nov. 8, 1892. Present Messrs. Krien, Hung On, Stripling Wolter, Johnson. The notice calling the meeting was read. Minutes of last meeting read and confirmed.
Mr. Johnson asked Mr. Hung whether Mr. Nosse had called on him with reference to the roads as promised. Mr. Hung said he had called and discussed the matter. Mr. Hung said that present the road could not be put in proper order as it would not be convenient for the Chinese Consular Premises, but it would be done next year. He said that the decision in the matter rested with him. About the road from the Chinese Settlement to the corner of Consular Hill, Mr. Hung said it was entirely a Chinese matter and when trade

144 was flourishing enough no doubt it would be done. Mr. Wotter suggested that perhaps the M.C. might keep with regard to funds in making this road. Mr. Hung said it was not a matter of money only nor of any other particular consideration, but of the wishes of the Chinese Consul. Mr. Krien asked if Mr. Hung would allow the —— slope of the Chinese half of the road behind the Chinese Consulate to be sloped off so that the earth would not fall into the Gen. For. Settlement part of the road. He answered No; he would not, but it would be done by Chinese if not this year, then, next year, when the whole of the Chinese part of the road would be put in order, if the road sank below the level of the Chinese Consulate foundation he would have it filled up again. Mr. Heard's letter relative to the sending of the Minute-book to the Commissioner of Customs to be copied was read. Mr. Johnson asked whether the book was to be sent in future or not.

Mr. Stripling proposed that the book should not be sent to the Commissioner of Customs but should be open to his inspection, or any land-owner's, at the convenience of the Hon. Sec. — seconded by Mr. Wotter. Mr. Wotter said that he thought the M.C. was under no obligations to the Customs, but rather the contrary. The proposition being put to the meeting was carried.

The letter of Mr. Hung referring to a row on the jetty & asking ~~that~~ the matter might be brought to the notice of the Ex. Com. was read.

Mr. Rosse's letter excusing himself from attending at this meeting was read.

Mr. Hung having other business to attend to excused himself and left.

Mr. Stripling proposed that in order to open up the Western part of the Settlement the M.C. authorize the expenditure of $600.00 for the purpose of building a jetty in front of lots B (Prop. put in voting & signed) — seconded by Mr. Wotter. After some discussion, meeting adjourned till 3 P.M.

Nov. 8, 3 P.M. Present Messrs. Krien, Wotter, Johnson, Stripling. There being no quorum, meeting adjourned until a day to be afterward fixed by the local members. (Sd) F. Krien

Vice-Pres. & Ch'man pro tem.

(Sd) Octavius Johnson. Hon. Sec.

188

Registered Land-holders
in the Chemulpo General Foreign Settlement on Dec. 7, 1893

Order of Voting	Name	Lots.
2	H.B.M. Govt.	D 38
7	Alfred Burt Stripling	D 2
	"	D 4.
	"	B 4
8	William Dutton Hutchison	D 11 & 12
13	Thomas Hollingsworth	D 15
12	Leonard Armstrong Hopkins	D 10
1	The Society for the Propagation of the Gospel in Foreign Parts London	D 43
	Head for time being of Ch. of Eng. Mission in Corea	Outside Settlement.
	Alfred Burt Stripling	D 33
	Leonard Armstrong Hopkins	D 24
Absent	Edward Rogers	B 3
17	Morse, Townsend & Co.	C. 1 2 3 4, D 20 26, D 27, 28, 37
Absent	H.C. Eduard Meyer	
"	Carl Wolter	C. 5 7 6 8, D. 11 9 33
3	Carl Fühls	B. 12
Absent	Franz Meyer	C 10 11 D 42
16	Robt. Brinckmeier	D 7 8 9
Absent	Fr. Allmacher	D 31 32
10	F. H. Mörsel	C. 17 20 22 29 30 31 D 13
4	A. Gorschalki	D 3
15	C. Nishiwaki	C. 25
Objected	S. Tomita	D 14
Absent	E. Kumamoto	C. 13
6	H. Rikitake	C. 12
18	S. Shindo	C. 15 16
	Hori Kintaro	C. 18, 26, 27
5	S Higuchi	C. 19
14	T Suyenaga	C. 21

Absent	Ko Nishiwaki	C.13
9	J Kimura	D15
19	Woolitang	C 24
	"	C 23
	"	C 32
	"	C 28
	"	D 16 17
	"	D 30
11	Romulo Borioni	D 11
Absent.	Li Yun-noon	C.9

List of those Voting at election Dec. 7 '93.

1	S.P.G.	10	Mörsel.
2	H.B.M.Gt.	11	Borioni
3	Lührs	12	Hopkins
4	Gorschalki	13	Hollingsworth
5	Higuchi	14	~~[illegible]~~ Suyenaga
6	Pikitaki	15	Nishiwaki
7	Stripling	16	Brinckmeier
8	Hutchison	17	Morse, Townsend
9	Kimura	18	Shindo
		19	Woolitang

Result of Voting

Townsend	11
Mörsel	7
Lührs	1

Dec. 6, 1892.

Present:- Messrs. Krien, Hung, Ou, Stripling, Nossé, Johnson, Allen. 145

Minutes of last meeting read and confirmed. Notice calling meeting read.
The fact that Mr. Walter had resigned the treasurership being known to most members his resignation was accepted although no letter to that effect had been received to place before the meeting.

Mr. Stripling proposed & Mr. Nossé seconded that Mr. Walter's resignation be accepted with great regret & that a hearty vote of thanks for his services to the Council be accorded him — Carried.

Election of a member pro tem. caused by resignation of Mr. Walter.
Result. C. Luhrs, 5 votes, W. D. Townsend, 2 votes. Luhrs declared elected.

Letter to the British Vice-Consul from the Kamni regarding payment of expenses of regrading roads read.

Correspondence received since last meeting — Letters from Commissioner of Customs, Brinckmeier & Hutchison — were read.

Proposed by Mr. Allen, sec. by Nossé, that Mr. Luhrs be asked to act as Treasurer pro tem. & so fill the vacancy caused by resignation of Mr. Walter: Carried unanimously.

Cemetery:— Proposed by Mr. Stripling "that a strong wall be put around the foreign cemetery & that the ground be put & kept in proper condition without delay. This proposal is made by special request of a number of landholders who are very anxious to see the ground put in proper condition." Seconded by Mr. Luhrs. Carried. Meeting adj. till 2:30 P.M.

Adjourned meeting. 12:30. P.M. Present: Messrs. Krien, Luhrs, Hung, Nossé, Stripling, Allen, Johnson.

Mr. Johnson called attention to the fact that to-morrow between 10:30 A.M. & 0.30 P.M. the presence of 3 official members is necessary for the election of one member. Mr. Ou sent his card excusing himself.

Proposed by Mr. Stripling: "That the Western end of the Settlement be at once surveyed & laid out in toto by a competent person — and that all lots, boundaries & roads be distinctly marked on the official plan of the settlement as suggested by Mr. Hutchison in his letter to the President. This proposal is strongly supported by ten land-holders."
Seconded by Mr. Nossé & carried.

146

By acclamation and consent of Mr. Lührs, Mr. Lührs was appointed member of the Exec. Com.

Proposed by Dr. Allen & seconded by Mr. Lührs "That the Exec. Com. be instructed to confer with Mr. Sabatin & ascertain for what compensation he will lay out that portion of the western end of settlement not yet laid out in conformity with the plan, & to report at next meeting." Carried.

Proposed by Mr. Johnson & sec. by Dr. Allen that Mr. Lührs be appointed auditor of the last Treasurer's, (Mr. Wolter) accounts — Carried. Discussion about filling in in front of Chinese Settlement. Mr. Hung said that all matters connected with the Chinese Settlement were for him to decide; no one could influence him.

In pursuance of Mr. Stripling's proposal concerning jetty at last meeting. Proposed as an amendment by Mr. Johnson, sec. by Dr. Allen, that until a proper estimate of the cost of the building same can be brought before the M.C. the building of it cannot be sanctioned. Discussion:- Mr. Stripling suggested that advertisement be put in local paper inviting tenders for the work.

Amended as above, carried.

Appropriation of Funds:—		$
	Ragsdale's pay @ $70 a month	840
	Rent of " house for 6 months	90
	Six police at $12 per month	864
	" Uniforms	180
	Four scavengers, $16 per month	192
	Repairs to roads	400
	Ten Lamps	90
	Contingencies	344
		$ 3000

Proposed by Dr. Allen, sec. by Mr. Hung, that the sum of $3000, as above particularized, be appropriated from the funds for the next year's expenses — carried. Discussion with regard to road from east & west passing behind Japanese Consulate in front of Commissioner of Customs House:-

147

Proposed by Mr. Stripling :— "That the main road connecting the eastern with the western ends of settlement, i.e., the road running past the back of Japanese ~~Settlement~~ Consulate & in front of the Commissioner of Customs house, be graded & made without unnecessary delay." Sec. by Mr. Lührs. Amended by Mr. Nossé :— "a competent man should be engaged to inspect the road and report to the M.C. before commencing work." Sec. by Mr. Johnson.
Discussion on amendment :— Mr. Stripling said that roads had always hitherto been made by Mr. Ragsdale, why should they not be done by him again?" Amendment carried.
The President requested the Sec. to write to Mr. S. Sabatin of Seoul on the subject. Mr. Stripling brought up the matter of taxing wheelbarrows, carts, boats :— decided that the matter should be left for further consideration. Mr. Stripling brought up the matter of fire brigade. Mr. Nossé said that there was a Japanese fire brigade that would be willing to assist at a fire in any house in Chemulpo — Japanese or foreign.
Meeting adjourned at 6 P.M. till to-morrow at 2:30 P.M.

Dec. 7th, 1892.

Meeting adjourned from yesterday 2:30 P.M. Present: Messrs. Krien, Hing, Nossé, Mahiwaki, Johnson, Lührs, Stripling.
Election of Officers for ensuing year :— President, Mr. A. Heard, Vice President, Mr. F. Krien, Secretary, Mr. Johnson, Treasurer, Mr. Townsend.
Accounts audited by Mr. Lührs & found correct, handed in to M.C.
Vote of thanks to auditor carried with cordiality.
Proposed by Mr. Krien, sec. by Mr. Johnson, "That a vote of thanks be tendered to the Chemulpo Club for allowing one of their rooms to be used by the Council — carried.
Proposed by Mr. Stripling: "That in future M.C.'s meeting be held in Daibutsu Hotel instead of at the Club where the Committee hitherto have kindly allowed it to be held." Sec. by Mr. Krien.
Amended by Mr. Johnson "That in future the meetings of M.C. be held in the room found most convenient until the M.C. building is ready, the most convenient room to be ascertained by the Sec. and notice given by him to members." Sec. by Mr. Lührs — carried.

Mr. Krien proposed, + Mr. Nossé seconded "that a sum not exceeding $200 should be appropriated as a remuneration for surveying and laying out into lots + mapping on the plan of the G.F.S. the ~~[illegible]~~ boundary of lots [illegible] that part of the G.F.S. that has not yet been laid out — and for inspecting + reporting about the grading + building of the road leading from the eastern [illegible] of the western end of the G.F.S. [illegible], the road passing the back of the Jap. Consulate + front of Commissioner of Customs' House — + that the Exec. Com. should arrange for the best terms possible." Carried.

Discussion about subscribing to the Jap. Fire Brigade. Mr. Nossé made a proposal that the M.C. should subscribe towards it, but subsequently withdrew it convinced that the M.C. had no power to do so.

Resolved that the Sec. be asked to write to the President asking him to call on the Korean authorities to provide the Sec. with a complete list of land-holders in the G.F.S. + to inform him of all such purchases + transfers. Resolved that the next meeting take place in the first week in Feby — day to be appointed by local members. Vote of thanks to Chairman closed the meeting.

(Sd) Oct. Johnson, Vice-President 7/2/93 (Sd.) Octavius Johnson, Hon. Sec.

Meeting of Dec. 29, 1893. Extraordinary meeting called in accordance with the rules, by the President, Mr. A. Heard for the election of a President for the ensuing year. — Mr. Heard himself having declined to accept the office — + to elect an Exec. Com. + to transact such other business as might properly be brought before the meeting. Present: Messrs. Hung, Johnson, Stripling, Nossé, Lührs, Nishiwaki. Notice calling meeting read. Election of President:— Mr. Krien, 6, elected unanimously. Vice-President. Mr. Johnson, 5, Mr. Nossé, 1. Mr. Johnson elected. Exec. Com. Mr. Townsend 5, Stripling 6, Nossé 5, Nishiwaki 2, Messrs. Townsend, Stripling + Nossé elected. Mr. Johnson brought the matter of the Korean Govt. offer to meet Consuls + decide liability regarding grading of roads, before the meeting, considerable discussion ensued, at length it was:

Proposed by Mr. Lührs, sec. by Mr. Stripling that the M.C. appoint the 3 local Consuls at Chemulpo, i.e. Messrs. Hung, Nossé + Johnson to meet the Kamni + the Commissioner of Customs in order to decide the amount due to the M.C. for grading roads. Carried. Communication in the sense of the above motion to be sent in due course to the Kamni.

Resolved that the Treasurer be asked to make an account, produce vouchers & provide the official members with all information with regard to expenses of grading roads.

Proposed by Mr. Lührs, sec. by Mr. Nossé, that the salary of the Chief of Police be increased by $5.00 per month from Jan. 1, 1893, the amount to be paid out of the contingency appropriation. Carried.

Land-rent memo. from Kammi received & laid before the meeting. amount $75.60

Mr. Stripling proposed, Mr. Nossé sec., that the annual ground rent for the Municipal lot be not paid on Jan. 1 & not until after the question of half taxes has been brought before a meeting of M.C. for 1893. Amendment by Mr. Johnson that until the agreement has been altered the M.C. has no right to discuss the matter of reducing the amount of ground rent stipulated to be paid in that agreement. Sec. by Mr. Nossé. Carried.

Mr. Hung, referring to an entry in Ragsdale's occurrence book, asked Mr. Nossé whether it was true that the M.C.'s Chinese policemen's lives had been threatened by Japanese & if so, whether proper measures had been taken in the matter. Mr. Nossé replied that he had heard the rumor but that there was now no cause for alarm.

Mr. Nossé produced a paper containing evidence that he had taken suitable steps regarding the late row between Jap. & Chinese policemen in the G. F. S.

Meeting closed at about 12:30.

(Sd.) Oct. Johnson
Vice-President

(Sd) Oct. Johnson
Hon. Sec.

See page 158 for List of Registered Land-holders

150

Meeting of the Municipal Council Feby 7, 1893. 10.30 A.M.
Present: Messrs. Nishiwaki, Stripling, Townsend, Nossé, Johnson (in the chair).

The minutes of the last regular meeting and of the subsequent extra-ordinary meeting were taken as read and confirmed.

Letter from China & Japan Trading Co. read, requesting to be informed whether there was any objection to the erection of a building for storage of Kerosene oil on Lot B. 3.

After some discussion it was resolved that an answer be sent as follows:

The Council at present have no power to prevent your erecting a building for the storage of Kerosene oil on Lot B. 3. provided that it is not of an inflammable nature, but at the same time they express their opinion that it is not prudent to do so.

Mr. Hung was announced and joined the meeting, but excused himself at once as a friend had arrived by the Chinese steamer and he had important business with him.

Discussion with regard to road in front of Commissioner of Customs house:—

Proposed by Mr. Townsend and seconded by Mr. Stripling "That the road in front of the Commissioner of Customs house be metalled and drained at present grade." Carried.

Resolved that the writer at the British Vice-Consulate be presented with the sum of ten dollars in recognition of his services rendered to the Council during the last few years.

Proposed by Mr. Townsend and seconded by Mr. Nossé - "That the Treasurer be authorized to withdraw the Councils money now deposited in the Hongkong and Shanghai Bank, Shanghai and deposit same and other monies received by him in the 1st National Bank of Japan, Chemulpo Branch." Carried.

Proposed by Mr. Townsend and seconded by Mr. Nossé "That the Secretary be asked to write to the Kamni requesting him to pay over to the Municipal Council the rents collected by him in 1892." Carried.

Mr. Sabatin came forward and explained, in general, the manner in which he proposed to lay out the N.W. end of the settlement the roads were sketched out on the plan but in direct lines. He was accordingly requested to sketch them out as they would be made to suit the conformation of the land.

Mr. Sabatin said he would have such a sketch ready by the next day morning (Feby 8th) and it was resolved that the Executive Committee should meet him on that day and decide what the final plan should be.

Resolved that the date of the next regular meeting should be left to be decided by the local members.

Meeting closed at 12:30 P.M.

(Sd) Oct. Johnson, Vice President. (Sd) Octavius Johnson Hon. Sec.

Meeting of April 7, 1893.

Vice-Consulate 10.30 A.M. Present Messrs. Stripling, Sin (Chinese Consul) Nishiwaki, Nossé, Ou, Townsend & Johnson (in the Chair).

Minutes of last meeting read and confirmed. Letter from Kammi read, in reply to letter requesting him to pay up as much as is due to the M.C. out of the taxes as he has already received, at once, in which he says that he cannot pay up until the full amounts due by all land-renters have been received.

Discussion on the subject: a list of landowners who had not paid was laid on the table by Mr. Townsend, procured by him from customs, as follows

Stripling	$487.98
Mörsel	347.70
Kikitaki	60.90
Shindo	87.12
Hori	222.48
Gorshalki	42.30
M. C.	75.60

152

Proposed by Mr. Stripling, 2nd by Mr. Townsend "That in the event of Messrs. + Ou, + Rossi failing to induce Kamni to pay in to the M.C. that portion of the taxes due to them already collected for 1892, the Sec. be instructed to bring the matter to the notice of the Representatives in Seoul with a view to instructions being issued to the Kamni to pay over to the M.C. the taxes on each lot within a week after the amount is paid to him — Carried.

Mr. Townsend said during the discussion on the above proposal, that there was a precedent in 1891 when the M.C., being as at present, in want of funds, Mr. J.C. Johnston acting Commissioner of Customs, paid up amounts from the rents collected on account. He said the matter was at present urgent as the funds in hand would only last 45 days more.

Proposed by Mr. Townsend 2nd by Mr. Johnson.

That the Sec. be requested to write to the Kamni requesting him to bring suits for non-payment of rent against such land-renters as should not have paid up their rents within ten days from the 8th inst. in their respective Consular Courts — Carried.

Mr. Townsend explained that his reason for bringing forward was that during the last 15 months those that had not paid had been frequently asked to pay — some of the land-renters who have not paid have reasons which should be looked into by a Law-court some have no reasons and should be forced to pay.

Discussion regarding Municipal Building — it was resolved that the Exec. Com. be requested to abide by Mr. Sabatin's advice as to the proper completion of the contract.

Proposed by Mr. Townsend, 2nd by Mr. Nishiwaki, that the Sec. be asked to write to the Body of Foreign Representatives at Seoul requesting that action be taken at once in the matter of laying out the road from the Jap. Settlement to the Jetty, to state that the plan sent herewith so far as regards the road meets the ~~appropr~~ approbation of the M.C. that with regarding to the portions of the foreshore colored green the M.C. suggest that if the proposed scheme be adopted, these should not be fenced in, that with regard to the portions colored brown they suggest that these should be left for further inquiry, that at the same time they wish to lay weight on the fact that the metalling of the road should proceed at once, not being delayed for the decision of the other matters. Carried.

Mr. Stripling requested that it should be noted that he objected on the ground that the expense of the road would have to be borne by the G. F. S. whereas seeing that it would be used mostly by the merchants living in the Jap. Settlement the Japanese should contribute a portion.

The meeting closed at 1.15 P.M.

(Sd) F. Krien, President. (Sd) Oct. Johnson, Hon. Sec.

Meeting May 20, 1893.

Present. Messrs. Krien (in chair), Johnson, Nozaé, Stripling, Townsend.
Minutes of last meeting read and confirmed.

Mr. Johnson said that a resolution had been passed at a previous meeting to build a wall around the cemetery & wished to know why it had not been done. Mr. Townsend replied that a contract had been made in 1891 with a Chinese contractor to build the said wall but before beginning the desired work the Korean graves must be removed. A letter was sent to the Kamni asking him to have the graves removed & he replied that he would do so, but up to the present it has not been done & therefore the building of the wall has been postponed. Mr. Stripling remarked that want of money prevented the work proceeding at present.

Mr. Townsend stated that Mr. Heard informed him that the Korean Govt. refused to accept title-deed for ground in front of present Customs Godowns with any limitations regarding fencing.

Proposed by Mr. Townsend & seconded by Mr. Stripling:
In view of the refusal of the Korean Govt. to guarantee that the ground along the sea-wall in front of the present Customs Godowns be always kept open, that the Secretary be requested to write to the Foreign Representatives asking them to settle the matter of this ground by adhering to the original plan of a road along the

154

sea-wall, but of a suitable width, not less than 15 metres at the same time maintaining that the rational road for traffic is by the present Customs Godowns that it would be better that the road be made that way, but that the Foreign Reps. be called on to see that the ground in front of the Customs Godowns be not inclosed by a fence at all, to interfere with the handling of cargo. Carried unanimously.

Mr. Townsend as Hon. Treasurer then stated that the amount of funds belonging to the M.C. now on hand was $1500. odd whereas our liabilities on June 1 will be approximately.

To Contractor of Municipal Building	$1300
" Mr. Sabatin for Surveying	200
" Current Expenses	170
" Arrears & rent of Constable's House	40
	$1710

Mr. Johnson then said that in view of the funds being insufficient to meet the ordinary expenses & liabilities incurred he objected to counter-signing as by the By-laws it was his duty to do, any vouchers now except for ordinary expenses, holding that it was more necessary to keep up the ordinary ~~expenses~~ services of the Settlement, i.e. police, scavengers, lighting, &c. than to overstep the limits of the funds by paying extraordinary sums rightly due.

Discussion followed & Mr. Johnson having offered to resign was requested to withdraw same until it was seen whether money matters could be settled with the Korean Govt.

Mr. Stripling said that he thought we should pay the Chinese contractor the M.C. Building amount due him as long as any money remained in the hands of the Treasurer. Mr. Johnson said that the Chinese Contractor if not paid had recourse ~~[illegible]~~ thro' his own Consul. Mr. Johnson read a letter from Mr. Heard dated May 8 stating that the President of the F.O. had written the Jenchuan Kamni to pay at once to the M.C. all money now due to them & hereafter to pay moneys received from taxpayers immediately on receipt of same, less amount due to Korean Govt.

Mr. Stripling proposed, sec. by Mr. Krien.
With regard to Mr. Heard's dispatch of May 8 the Kamni not having paid over to the M.C. any of the rent collected for 1892, & as the Hon. Sec. states that the funds in hand amount to $1500 only, whereas the liabilities due on June 1 amount to $1710 that another letter be addressed by the Hon. Sec. to the For. Reps. urging them to press the claim for immediate payment of rent collected and due to the M.C.
Discussion followed & Mr. Johnson offered to see Kamni the same day & press for payment.

Meeting of June 26, 1893.
Present Messrs. Krien (in chair) Gin, Stripling, Johnson & Townsend.
Minutes of last meeting read & confirmed.
Correspondence since last meeting read.
Mr. Townsend stated that he had paid the Chinese contractor for Municipal Buildings all monies due to him in his contract with the exception of two hundred dollars held back by him in conformance with Mr. Sabatin's letter of May 30. He suggested that contractor should be paid $100.00 in making alterations as suggested by Mr. Sabatin & the balance on Sept. 1 if roof is found to be right.
Suggestion adopted.
Proposed by Mr. Townsend, sec. by Mr. Johnson: "That Mr. Ragsdale be ordered to move into the Municipal Building on June 30th the building being now in order. Also that the constables be ordered to move into their quarters on the same date. Amendment by Mr. Stripling "that as the M.C. building is too far from the residents to be suitable for police purposes, the house & lot be advertized for sale or let to the highest bidder" not seconded.
Mr. Townsend's proposition as above carried.
Mr. Townsend stated during discussion on the subject that the question of the advisability of the Municipal Building being built could not now be discussed as the contract had been agreed to unanimously by the M.C. meeting June 7, '92 & that the building being now finished we must put it to its best use.

156

Mr. Stripling stated emphatically that the vote was not unanimous as he having been present at the meeting did not vote for it.

Mr. Townsend referring to the Police force said that two men were now off duty — one Japanese — sick (had been so for half a month) & one Chinese — wanted leave for two months to go home. The latter offered to provide a substitute.

Mr. Lin said that he would inquire into the character of the Chinese substitute. The Exec. Com. were asked to apply to the Jap. Consul Mr. Nossé for character of Jap. substitute.

Discussion with regard to road between Jap. settlement & Jetty.

Proposed by Mr. Townsend & sec. by Mr. Stripling —— "That the Sec. be requested to write to the For. Reps. that the M.C. object to accepting a road along the Customs Godowns without a definite agreement that the foreshore & sea-wall be always kept open to boats & traffic, & without such agreement they must again request that the 15 metre road be laid out along the sea-wall

Amendment by Mr. Johnson.

That the part of Mr. Townsend's proposition as above be adopted down to the words "boats & traffic" but that the road next the Customs Godowns should be pressed for & the help of the For Reps. be called for to prevent any inclosure outside this being made —— not seconded. Mr. Townsend's prop. as above carried.

The Hon. Sec. put forward a letter from the Kamni stating that altho' he handed over $2000 on account of money that he had received as land rents, there were some amounts still not paid and he did not consider himself bound to pay any until they were all paid. This payment was not to be taken as a precedent. Discussion on this letter: it was considered that urgent steps should be taken to obtain the receipt of the amount of rents due to the Council from the Korean Govt. as soon as any payment on this account was made to the Korean Govt. Mr. Krien referred to Art. 5 Para. 3. of the agreement saying that the "yearly rental of A lots &c. + + + shall belong to the Municipal Fund."

He said that the money being the property of the M.C. has to be refunded by the Kamni as soon as he receives it, & that the position at present assumed by the Kamni is utterly untenable. Proposed by Mr. Stripling, sec. by Mr. Johnson, "that referring to Mr. Heard's letter of May 8 as the Kamni has ignored the President's instructions & paid the M.C. only $2000 which the Kamni says is not to be regarded as a precedent, that another letter be addressed to the For. Reps. urging them to insist upon the immediate payment of the total amount due", carried.

Mr. Townsend said that Mr. Kimura (Lot. D. 62) wants to make a well in public road close by his lot. He proposes to make the well at his own expense, to be always open to public use & promises to fill it up at any time when so requested by the M.C.

Mr. Stripling thinks that if the M.C. agree to allow the well to be built the M.C. the M.C. should get from Mr. Kimura a document in writing to be stamped by the Jap. Consul to the effect that Mr. Kimura will build the well in a way approved by the M.C. & in such a way as not to be inconvenient to the public. Approved in principle by the M.C., the Exec. Com. however to have power to put such restrictions on the carrying out of the work as they may think necessary.

Mr. Townsend stated that he should propose an appropriation of $250 for furniture for the Municipal Building at next meeting.

Mr. Stripling gave notice that at the ~~usual~~ next meeting he would make application for the appropriation of $1000 for grading all the roads laid down in the approved plan of the settlement.

The meeting commenced at about 11 A.M. adjourned about 1.30 P.M. met again at 3:15 P.M. & closed at about 4.30 P.M.

Meeting at H. B. M's Vice Consulate.
on July 24th commencing at 11. a.m.

Present:- Mr Johnson, (Vice President) in chair; Messrs Herod, Nosse, Townsend & Stripling.

The minutes of the last meeting were read and confirmed.
The Hon. Secretary read out & afterwards handed round the following correspondence, received since the last meeting:-
(1.) Letter from the Commissioner of Customs asking for information concerning the organisation of the Municipal Police.
(2.) Letter from Mr Dmitrevsky, Doyen of the Foreign Representatives, forwarding copy of nine proposals by the President of the Foreign Office for the construction of roads in the Foreign Settlement.
(3.) Letter from the Kamni enclosing cheque for the balance of 1892 rents ($2541.93.) not yet handed over to the Council.

Discussion on No (1).-
Mr Stripling was strongly opposed to the Commissioner of Customs request being acceded to, maintaining that the Council were not obliged to furnish outsiders with information regarding their police arrangements, although every attention should of course be given to definite complaints laid before them.
Mr Johnson was of the same opinion and submitted a draft answer to that effect, for which after some discussion the following draft by Mr Herod, in the same sense, was

substituted.

"Referring to years:
I beg to inform you that the Municipal Council has concluded that it is not consistent with their policy to furnish upon your application a general outline of the system of policing the Foreign settlement. The Council is willing however to hear any complaint which may be made by a landholder relative to the negligence or inefficiency of one or more of its officers in particular cases."

Discussion on (2.)- The proposals which, it was explained, really emanated from the Chief Commissioner of Customs in Seoul were read out and the places referred to identified on the plan. The sense of the Council was that the road in question should be made, with the understanding that no vessels should be allowed to stretch ropes across it or otherwise obstruct it.

Discussion on (3.)- Mr Townsend, who had gone to the Japanese Bank to cash the Kamni's cheque returned and informed the Council that the balance in the Kamni's name was $503 odd.

Mr Nosse then proposed that the Hon. Secretary should be instructed to write to the Kamni informing him that his cheque had been dishonoured, and giving him two days within which to pay the sum in question, after which time, if it still remained unpaid, the matter would be laid before the Foreign

Representatives.
Seconded by Mr Townsend & carried.

Proposed by Mr Townsend "that the sum of two hundred and fifty dollars be appropriated for the purpose of buying furniture for Municipal buildings, to be expended under direction of the Executive Committee".-
Seconded by Mr Stripling.
Mr Townsend explained that only the public offices would be furnished out of this sum, and not the Constables quarters.-
Carried.-

Proposed by Mr Stripling "that a sum of one thousand dollars be appropriated for the purpose of grading roads and making drains in the General Foreign Settlement and that the executive members be requested to proceed with the work without delay.-
Seconded by Mr Townsend.-
Mr Stripling explained that the Corean Government refused to move a finger in the matter and that some of the roads, as for instance the one leading up to Mr Wolter's house, the road running behind Mr Gorschalki's lot were in a very bad condition and urgently needed repair.
Mr Townsend suggested that the roads running past inhabited lots should first be repaired and afterwards those farther away from the houses.- Mr Stripling's proposal was carried.
Proposed by Mr Stripling "that in view

of the fact that the Kamni has with held the sum of $2541.93, taxes due to the Council for 1892, that the Council invite a Committee of land owners to draft a revised set of Land Regulations and By-Laws to be submitted to the Council for their consideration and if approved to be forwarded by the Council to the Representatives for their favourable consideration and approval and that the Secretary be invited to inform the land-renters of the fact by circular.-

Seconded by Mr Townsend.

Mr Stripling said that many landrenters were complaining of not having a sufficient voice in the expenditure of their money and that it was only fair that they should be given some opportunity of expressing their views.

Mr Johnson suggested the words "not less than seven" should be inserted after a Committee of land owners.-

Mr Stripling accepted this suggestion and the proposal was carried.

Mr Nosse asked whether the Council had given their approval to the plan of the Foreign Settlement drawn up for them by Mr Sabatin and, if so, what steps would be taken with regard to it. He was informed that it had been conditionally approved of by the Council, but had not yet been submitted to the Foreign Representatives. The consideration of some proposed alterations in the plan was deferred to the next meeting.

Proposed by Mr Stripling "that the Hon Secretary be requested to write to the Representatives in Seoul asking them to be good enough to request the President of the Foreign Office to instruct the Kamni to furnish the Council with a full and complete list of the landowners of the General Foreign Settlement, with size of lots and amounts of taxes on each lot no attention having been paid to previous requests of a similar nature.

Seconded by Mr Townsend and carried.

Proposed by Mr Stripling "that a very cordial vote of thanks be given to the Hon. Augustine Heard, U.S. Minister and late Doyen of the Foreign Representatives in Seoul for the kind support and assistance he rendered the Council during his term of office and that the Hon. Secretary be requested to write to him to that effect.-

Seconded by Mr Townsend; carried.

Mr Johnson begged to tender his resignation as Vice President + Hon Secretary.

Proposed by Mr Townsend "that Mr Johnson's resignation be accepted with regret and that Mr Fox be elected Secretary of the

Municipal Council.
Seconded by Mr Nosse; carried.

Mr Townsend proposed that Mr Nosse be elected Vice President.
Seconded by Mr Johnson and carried unanimously.

A cordial vote of thanks to Mr Johnson was proposed and carried unanimously.

(sd) F. Krien (sd) H. H. Fox
President Hon. Secretary

Meeting held at H. B. M's vice Consulate on September 2nd 1893. at 11 a.m.

Present:- Mr Krien (in chair) Mr Nosse (Vice Pres.), Messrs Townsend, Stripling Wu and Fox (Hon Sec.)

The Acting Kammi was present under instructions from the President of the Foreign office, ostensibly at the request of Mr Krien. Mr Krien explained that he had asked the President to instruct Mr Wu, the Corean official member of the Council to attend, and not the Kammi, a mistake evidently having been made in the names. As, however, there were one or two matters which the Council wished to settle with the Kammi he suggested that the Kammi should be invited to remain and listen to the proceedings.

Mr Stripling objected on the ground that the Corean Government were already represented by Mr Wu and that on a previous occasion the Council had refused to allow a non-member to be present.

The question was then put to the vote and Mr Krien's proposal carried.

The Kammi kindly consented to remain and answer any questions the Council wished to put to him.

The minutes of the previous meeting were then read and confirmed.

The

The Hon Secretary read out a letter from the Kamni requesting information about the roads at present being graded by the Council.

Mr Stripling pointed out on the plan of the Settlement the roads that had already been graded and the ones the Executive Committee had in hand at present.

Mr Wu wished to know what authority the Council had for filling in the ground in front of lots B 1 and 2 and suggested that the Corean Authorities ought to have been consulted before undertaking the work.

It was explained that the ground in question was beyond high water mark and therefore belonged to the General Foreign Settlement. Also that the road marked in the plan could not be made unless an embankment were first built to support it and prevent the sea washing it away. The expense of the wall at present being constructed for that purpose would be borne by the Council.

Mr Stripling pointed out that the earth taken from the roads being graded must be thrown somewhere and that this was the best and almost only place available.

Mr Wu still objected to this place being filled in at present and as the other members approved of the work, begged to lodge a protest against its being

Continued.

Mr Fore drew attention to the state of the road leading from the British Vice Consulate to the Bund, past the Custom House and suggested that it should be required at once, it being of much greater importance than some of the roads at present being graded by the Executive Committee.

<u>Answer to Kammi's letter.</u> Mr Krien said it was the duty of the Corean government to grade roads in the Settlement and Mr Stripling referred to a letter from Mr Heard to the Council in which they were informed that the Kammi had been instructed to proceed with the grading at once.

Mr Krien proposed that the Kammi should be informed that it was intended to grade all the roads marked in the Official plan, but at present certain roads (to be specified) were being graded and until they were finished their length, and expense could not be given.

Seconded by Mr Noske, & Carried.

<u>Cemetery</u> Mr Krien said that he had written to the President of the Foreign Office pointing out, the disgraceful state of the Foreign Cemetery owing to the Corean Authorities having neglected to remove some Corean graves, as they had often promised, and that the President had replied that they should be removed at once.

The Kammi was informed of this and said he would have the graves removed, but that it could not be done at once, as the owners lived far away and would have to be consulted.

Mr Fox pointed out that the Kammi's predecessor had said the same thing four years ago and on several subsequent occasions, yet the graves still remained.

Mr Krien proposed that the Hon Secty request the Kammi to have the graves removed within eight days after which period, if not done the Council would do it themselves.

Seconded by Mr Fox and carried unanimously.

Mr Wu said the Kammi would have the graves removed at once, together with some in the Public Garden.

Mr Townsend gave notice of an appropriation of $500 for the purpose of building a wall round the cemetery. It was decided that the work should be taken in hand at once.

Mr Townsend proposed that the meeting be adjourned for tiffin till 2.30. p.m.

Seconded by Mr Fox & Carried.

The Kammi took his leave at this point being thanked by Mr Krien on behalf of the Council for his kindness in attending.

Meeting continued at 2.45. p.m. members present as before.

Furniture for Municipal Buildings

Mr Townsend said that the furniture was being bought and that the next meeting could probably be held in the Municipal Building.

Policing of Settlement. The Hon Secretary read out a letter from the Commissioner of Customs to the President of the Municipal Council complaining of insufficient Police protection.

After some discussion, the following answers to the Commissioner's Complaints were drafted by the Council.

(1.) that the Council will do all they can to protect property and patrol the streets in the general Foreign Settlement, but they are of opinion that it is the duty of the Customs authorities to hire watchmen for their own protection, as is done elsewhere.

(2.) The Council regrets the losses the Commissioner has sustained but cannot undertake to prevent every petty larceny that occurs in the Settlement.

(3.) The Council regrets that notice was not given at once to the Municipal police authorities, so that the Captain of the American Man-of-war could have been communicated with; this being the only recourse when dealing with sailors from man-of-war.

(4.) The man has been punished already.

The Council employs a Police

Constable and six policemen who should be applied to in cases of this kind.

Mr Stripling proposed "that all official letters emanating from the Council be drafted at the meeting of the Council."
Not seconded.
Mr Stripling was asked to withdraw his proposal, but refused.

Registration of Boats - The Hon Secretary read out a letter from the Commissioner of Customs drawing attention to the fact that some boats belonging to the Council were not registered.
As regards the legality of the Harbour Regulations which had only been approved provisionally by the Foreign Representatives, Mr Krien and Mr Nosse said they were binding so far as their nationals were concerned.
Mr Wu asked where the stones carried in the Municipal boats had come from.
He was informed that they were supplied by a Chinese contractor.
Mr Stripling explained that the boats were only used for carrying stones.
Mr Townsend admitted the right of the Customs authorities to control the "dumping" of stones but objected to the tone of the Commissioner's letter.
Messrs. Krien, Nosse and Fox concurred in this opinion.

Mr Stripling said that the stones thrown from Municipal boats were always put in places where they could not obstruct or damage other craft.

Mr Nosse remarked that boats had been damaged by stone thrown into the harbour.

Mr Wu suggested that a place should be fixed for the "dumping" of stones.

After some further discussion, Mr Krien proposed, seconded by Mr Fox "that the Customs authorities be officially informed that the boats owned by the Municipal Council had been marked "M.C. Nos 1 and 2" and that notice would be given whenever stones were to be landed".

Mr Stripling objected.

Mr Krien proposal carried.

With regard to the Municipal boats being registered, Mr Krien thought this was not necessary, other members concurring.

The Council agreed that the following clause be added to the letter "that the Council object to the action of the Customs Authorities in seizing and detaining their boats and are of opinion that a proper regard for the Municipal Council has not been shown in the matter." – Mr Wu explained that when the boats were seized, it was not known that they belonged to the Council.

Mr Stripling gave notice of a proposal for the licensing of boats by the Municipal

Council at the next meeting.

Mr Nosse proposed "that the Council give permission to the Chemulpo Japanese Fire Brigade to sink underneath the roadside wooden tubs at fourteen different places in the General Foreign Settlement to keep water all the seasons to be always ready in time of fire, there being no other reliable way to get the water.

Height of tub - $6\frac{1}{2}$ ft.
Breadth 6 ft. at top.
" $5\frac{1}{2}$ ft at bottom.

Wooden mouth to be about $2\frac{1}{2}$ ft broad (Diagram appended). Mr Nosse explained that similar wells were being placed in the Japanese Settlement and that the cost of the ones in question would be defrayed by the Fire Brigade. The holders of the lots in front of which these tubs were to be lowered would of course first be asked and obtained for their permission.

Seconded by Mr Townsend.

Proposal carried unanimously with thanks to Mr Nosse.

Mr Stripling proposed "that in view of the coming election and the fact that at previous elections votes had been cast by the Acting Commissioner of Customs, the Acting British Vice Consul and the local agent for the Society for the propagation of the Gospel - neither of whom are personally

Council at the next meeting.

Mr Nosse proposed "that the Council give permission to the Chemulpo Japanese Fire Brigade to sink underneath the roadside wooden tubs at fourteen different places in the General Foreign Settlement to keep water all the seasons to be always ready in time of fire, there being no other reliable way to get the water.

Height of tub - 6½ ft.
Breadth 6 ft at top.
" 5½ ft at bottom.

Wooden mouth to be about 2½ ft broad (Diagram appended). Mr Nosse explained that similar wells were being placed in the Japanese Settlement and that the cost of the ones in question would be defrayed by the Fire Brigade. The holders of the lots in front of which these tubs were to be lowered would of course first be asked and obtained for their permission.

Seconded by Mr Townsend.

Proposal carried unanimously with thanks to Mr Nosse.

Mr Stripling proposed "that in view of the coming election and the fact that at previous elections votes had been cast by the Acting Commissioner of Customs, the Acting British Vice Consul and the local agent for the Society for the propagation of the Gospel - neither of whom are personally registered landholders, and as voting by proxy is not allowed that the Council address a letter to the Representatives asking them to kindly favour the Council with their opinion as to whether the votes in question were, or were not, legal".

Not seconded.

Mr Wu withdrew at this point having important business to attend to.

Mr Stripling proposed "that for the benefit of the landholders a précis of the Minutes of all meetings held since the 1st of January last, and of all meetings thereafter, together with the official correspondence laid upon the table, be published in the local and other papers, or that a copy be supplied to each of the landholders".

Not seconded.

Mr Stripling proposed "that in future the summons convening the Municipal meetings be on a printed form in which only the day and dates require to be filled in and that a copy of the summons be sent to each member of the Council.

Seconded by Mr Townsend & Carried.

Trees in Foreign Settlement.

Mr Townsend said that a sum of money had been voted two years ago for trees, most of which had been stolen or destroyed. He now gave notice of an appropriation of $100. to purchase trees to be planted in the Settlement.

The meeting closed at 5.30 p.m. Next meeting was fixed for the first week in October.

Meeting held at H.B.M's. Vice Consulate on October 10th at 10.30. A.M.

Present: Mr Krien (in Chair) Messrs Nosse, Townsend, Stripling and Fox.

A letter was read from Mr Lin excusing himself on account of urgent business.

The minutes of the last meeting were read and confirmed after the words "and obtained" had been added to Mr Nosse's proposal with regard to the sinking of fire-wells in the Settlement.

Grading roads. Resolved that a letter be addressed to the Kammi pressing for payment of the $2,100, the sum agreed upon at the meeting of the Foreign Consuls & Corean local authorities as a just settlement of the Council's claim for grading roads.

Mr Nosse mentioned that copies of the agreement had been sent round to the Consuls.

It was decided to obtain one for the Municipal Council

Cemetery and trees. Mr Townsend moved that the appropriation recommended at the last meeting of $500. for building a wall round the Cemetery and $100. for trees to be planted in the Settlement, be now confirmed.

Seconded by Mr Stripling - Carried unanimously.

Repairs to road. Mr Fox drew attention to the state of the road forming the Eastern boundary of the Settlement, part of which only had been graded and drained. The upper part was being gradually washed away and rendered impassable by the rain.

He was informed that the road would be repaired immediately but could not be graded at present.

Bund road. Mr Krien informed the Council that the President of the Foreign Office agreed to a 15. metre road being made along the sea-wall.

Resolved that as there seemed no likelihood of the F. F. R.R.'s deciding where the road should be, and as its construction was of urgent necessity, a letter be addressed to the F. F. R.R.'s informing them that the Council have decided to proceed with the construction of a 15 metre broad road along the sea-wall at once, and requesting them to ask the Corean Government to build up the sea-wall, otherwise the road could not be completed.

Police. Mr Fox proposed, seconded by Mr Nosse "that in view of the inadequacy of the present force of Police employed by the Council to patrol the Settlement especially during the night-time, its number be increased from Six to twelve Constables."

Mr Fox explained that in the day time only one man was on duty, at a time for the whole Settlement, and during the night only two, one of whom remained at the Eastern end while the other patrolled the street running along the North of the Japanese & Chinese Settlement. The Bund, Jetty & Western end of the Settlement were left totally unprotected. The Japanese Settlement, about ¼ the size of the Foreign Settlement, had four men on duty every night.

Messrs. Townsend & Stripling opposed the proposal on the ground of the extra expense an increase of the force would entail, and also because they were of opinion that the present force was quite sufficient.

Mr Fox mentioned that frequent complaints had been made by residents of insufficient police protection.

Mr Townsend proposed an amendment to the effect that the wages of the Municipal Police should be raised $3 each per month and that the hours of duty be raised to twelve hours per day and the number be restricted to six at present.

Seconded by Mr Stripling.

Mr Fox maintained that this would not have the desired effect but agreed to the proposal being given a trial.

The Amendment was then carried.

Two letters from the Commissioner of Customs referring to Police and Registration were then read.

Meeting

Meeting adjourned to 2. P.M.

Members reassembled at 2.15. P.M.

Tennis Court. Mr Fox asked if the Council had any objection to a small fence being put round the lawn tennis court in the Public Garden, so as to prevent children, dogs and other nuisances spoiling the Court.

The Council had no objection.

Fire Brigade. Mr Nosse proposed that an appropriation of a sum of $300. be made towards the subscription to the Chemulpo Volunteer Fire Brigade for the purchase of one powerful pump (the cost of it being $400 and freight $30 = $430) in consideration of the great amount of work undertaken by the Brigade for the protection of property against fires in the general foreign settlement where one fire station everything complete is to be established and kept always in good order.

Mr Nosse mentioned that an opportunity presented itself for purchasing a seconded hand fire engine in Yokohama.

Mr Townsend suggested that the M.C. should take a share in the purchase and ownership of the engine.

After some discussion Mr Nosse gave notice of an appropriation of not more than $300 for the part purchase by the Council of a fire engine.

Proposed by Mr Stripling "that the boats plying for hire at the Jetties within the Foreign Settlement be licensed and regulated by the Municipal Council."

Mr Stripling said he had drawn up a table of charges, subject to alterations, which would be affixed in every licensed boat.

Mr Fox pointed out that with the present Municipal Police force it would be impossible to enforce such a regulation.

After some further discussion, the proposal was not seconded.

Mr Stripling again referred to the question of the legality of the votes of the Act. British Vice Consul Bishop Corfe and the Commissioner of Customs. He desired that the F.F. R.R.O should be asked for their opinion on the subject: Voting by proxy was not allowed by the Regulations.

Mr Fox begged to state that the vote of an accredited agent or representative of a Corporate body was not a vote by proxy within the meaning of the regulation, and that if these votes were disallowed a very considerable portion of the land in the Foreign Settlement would be unrepresented.

After some further discussion the matter was allowed to drop Mr Stripling announcing his intention of challenging the votes in question at the Next election.

Taxes. Mrs Nosse asked if anything had been done with regard to the payment of taxes for the present year. It was suggested that the money should be paid into the First National Bank instead of to the Kamni.

Mrs Stripling proposed seconded by Mrs Townsend "that as the estimated balance at the end of the year will be about $1500. with a additional amount of $2100. due (by the enclosed agreement) from the Corean Government for the grading of roads, that half rents only will be necessary, and that the Representative be asked to kindly arrange with the Corean Government that half taxes only be collected for the current year. Carried.

The next meeting was fixed for the second week in November.

The meeting closed at 4. P.m.

Meeting held at the Municipal Buildings. on November 16th at 10.30. a.m.

Present Mr Krien (in chair) Messrs Mossé, Lin, Townsend, Allen, Stripling Fox (Hon Sec.)

Mr Krien in a short speech Congratulated the Council on meeting for the first time in their own board room and thanked the British Acting Vice Consul for the loan of a room at the Consulate during the present year.

Police. Mr Townsend reported that one of the Council's Japanese police constables had just died. The Council voted a sum of $30 to defray his funeral expenses.

Plan of the Settlement. It was decided that Mr Sabatin in conjunction with the executive Committee, should be requested to complete the plan of the general Foreign Settlement, if possible before the next meeting of the Foreign Representatives.

Fire Engine. On a proposal to confirm the appropriation of a sum of $30 for the part purchase of a Fire Engine, made at last meeting.
Mr Mossé said that the Japanese Fire Brigade had not at present sufficient funds at their disposal to take part in the purchase, and afterwards maintain this fire engine. They desired that the matters should be allowed to remain over for the present.

The

The appropriation was accordingly not confirmed.

Municipal Councils Budget. Mr Townsend presented a statement shewing the expenses incurred by Council during the present year, the estimated balance in hand, and estimated expenditure for next year.

After some discussion on the subject of half taxes the Secretary was requested to forward this statement to the Foreign Representatives for their perusal in accordance with their request in a letter to the Secretary, dated Oct. 24th.

List of land-holders. The Secretary was instructed to ask the Kamni for a list of land-holders compiled up to date.

Election. The election of a member of the Council to fill the vacancy caused by the retirement of Mr Stripling was fixed for December 6th next between of 10. a.m. and 1. p.m.

Next meeting to be held on the 7th of December.

Record of the Election of one non official member of the Council on Dec. 6. 1893 from 10 a.m. to 1 p.m.

Present: Messrs. Nossé, Lin, Wu, and Fox (official members)

Messrs. Krien & Allen were prevented from attending by business in Seoul.

A letter (No 1.) from Mr Moisel was read. The official members were of opinion that three hours were sufficient for the election, and also, that the application should have been made earlier. However, in view of the exceptionable circumstances (Mr Moisel's steamer having been seen in the distance approaching Chemulpo) it was decided to reopen the ballot box at 3. p.m. for a quarter of an hour, so as to give those who were unavoidably prevented from attending earlier, a chance to vote. (Mr Moisel afterwards withdrew his letter.)

After Bishop Corfe had recorded his vote (as representative of the Society for the Propagation of the Gospel), and Mr Fox, H. M's Acting Vice Consul (as representative of H. M's Government) had voted, two protests (No 2 + 3) were presented to the meeting signed by several voters, against the above mentioned votes being received.

As on former occasions, the question was shortly discussed by the meeting, and the vote recorded by Bishop Corfe was allowed unanimously

unanimously and that of Mr Fox, by Messrs Nossé, Liu, and Wu.

The Ballot box was sealed up at 1. p. m. And reopened at 3. p.m. official members present as before.

At 3.15. the votes were counted the the result announced, as follows:-

Mr Woohtang 12

Mr Stripling 7

Mr Woolitang was therefore declared elected by a majority.

Election of one non official member, Dec. 6. 1893.

Order of Voting	Name	Lots
1.	C. Lührs	B 1 + 2
absent	J. Rogers	B 3
11	A. B. Stripling	B 4 D 24
absent	H. C. Meyer	C 1.2.3.4. D 25.26.27.28.37.
7	C. Wolter	C 5.6.7.8. D 1. 19. 33.
absent	Li Yim-Moon	C 9.
absent	Capt. F. Meyer	C. 10 + 11. D 42.
14	H. Rikitaki	C. 12.
absent	Kurikawa	C 13.
absent	Kumamoto	C 14.
15	S. Shindo	C 15 + 16.
19.	F. H. Mörsel	C 17. 20. 29. 30. 31. D 13.
13	Hori Kintaro	C 18, 26. 27.
16	S. Higuchi	C 19.
17.	I. Suyenaga	C. 21
9	Woolstand	C 23. 24. 28. 32. D 16. 17. 30.
5	C. Nishiwaki	C 25.
8	A. Gorschalki	D 3.
10	R. Brinckmeier	D 7. 8. 9.
4	L. A. Hopkins	D 10 + 12.
absent	W. Hutchison	D 11 + 12.
absent	S. Tomita	D 14.
18	T. Hollingsworth	D 15
3	R. Borioni	D 18.
absent	W. D. Townsend	D 21. 22. 23. 34. 35. 36.
absent	F. Allmacher	D 31 + 32.
6	H. B. M's Government	D 38.
2	Society for the Propagation of the Gospel.	D 43.
12.	Kimura	D 50.

Copy

No 1

Chemulpo.
5 December 1893.

The Election Committee
Chemulpo.

Gentlemen

Although having seen no circular notifying the Land owners the date of election, I been giving to understand the same to take place the 6th Instant, and that the Poll Box is to be only open from 10 a. m. till 1 p.m. as in previous years the Poll Box just to be open until 3 & 4 p. m. and I for one not able to attend during the above state time, but able to be present later on, and as I have some interest in the matter I protest against the shortness of time and request that the time as in previous years be extended to 3 or 4 O'clock.

I beg to remain &c.
(Sg.) F. H. Mörsel.

[Margin notes:]

[C]ircular sent round the Settlement twice (2.) then posted up at the municipal Buildings
(Sd) H. H. F.

[10] a. m. to 1 p.m. decided [a]t last meeting of Council.

Dec. 18. Ballot box open from 3 to 5, two hours only.-

Copy

No. 2.

We the undersigned registered land holders in the General Foreign Settlement of Chemulpo protest against Mr. H. H. Fox, H. B. M's Acting Vice Consul, who is not a registered land holder in the General Foreign Settlement, being allowed to cast his vote at this meeting for the election of a registered land holder in the Council.

Chemulpo, 6th December, 1893.

(sig.) C. Walter.
A. B. Stripling.
A. Gorschalki.
F. H. Morsel.
C. Lührs.

A similar protest was entered against Bishop Corfe, written by Mr Walter, but not signed by him or Mr Lührs.

Adjourned meeting of Dec 7 held at the Municipal Buildings on Dec 15 at 10.30. a.m.

Present; - Mr Nossé (in chair) Messrs Reinsdorf, Townsend, Wu, Nishiwaki, Stripling and Fox (Hon. Sec.)

A letter was read from Mr Krien informing the Council of his inability to attend the meeting and authorising Mr Reinsdorf to take his place.

The minutes of the last meeting were then read and confirmed.

Mr Stripling declined to take any part in the election of officers and appropriation of funds for the ensuing year on the grounds that the votes cast at the recent Election by H. B. M's Acting Vice Consul and Bishop Corfe were irregular.

Election of officials for 1894:-

Mr Townsend proposed, seconded by Mr Fox "that Mr Krien be re-elected President for the ensuing year. Carried unanimously.

Mr Fox proposed, seconded by Mr Townsend "the Mr Nossé be re-elected Vice President. Carried unanimously.

Mr Townsend having refused to serve again Treasurer, he proposed Mr Nishiwaki who was elected unanimously.

Mr

Mr Townsend proposed seconded by Mr Wu "that Mr Fox be re-elected Secretary, carried unanimously.

After a short discussion, the Executive Committee were unanimously elected as follows:-
Messrs Nossé Townsend & Fox.

Appropriations for 1894:-
Chief Constable's salary $900
On the motion to appropriation $960
wages for six police, Mr Fox moved seconded by Mr Nishiwaki "that the number of police be increased from 6 to 8 and that the appropriation be increased from $960 to $1272.
After some discussion the motion was put to the vote and carried by a Majority.
(Messrs Nossé Wu, Nishiwaki & Fox for:
Messrs Reinsdorf & Townsend against.)
Wages of Eight police — $1272.
Mr Nossé proposed that a sum of $300 be appropriated for police uniforms (including $50 for Chief Constables) Carried unanimously.
Police uniforms — $300.
Scavengers — 240.
Mr Nishiwaki proposed seconded by Mr Fox that 15 new lamps be set up in the Settlement at places to be fixed by the Executive Committee" Carried unanimously after a discussion.
Lamps (26) $200
Appropriation (cont.)
Repairs to Roads — $500
Contingent Expenses — $450
To

(To include 2 stores for Constables Quarters.)

Total, ordinary expenditure	$3862.
Grading new roads	500.
Making drains & walls	500.
Furniture for Municipal Building	100.
Trees	100.
Laying out cemetery	100.
Total Extraordinary expenditure	$1300.
Total appropriation of funds for 1894.	5162.

Agreed to unanimously.

Grading accounts: Mr Nossé asked Mr Wu to speak to the Kamni, and if possible obtain from him, the sum of $2100 due the Council for grading roads in the Settlement.

Mr Wu promised to do so.

Plan of Settlement: Mr Townsend said that it would be impossible to mark out the whole Settlement at present, a good many lots had been marked out and the Plan was now in Seoul with Mr Krien.

Mr Fox referring to the Kamni's despatch said the proper course would be to send up the Plan to Seoul through the Kamni, who would forward it to the Foreign Office, who in their turn would lay it before the Foreign Representatives for approval & signature.

Mr Stripling was of opinion

that the Plan belonged to the Council, as they had paid for it that the Council should send the plan to the Foreign Representatives and that if the Kamni wished for a plan he should pay for it.

After some discussion the Majority of Members agreed that the proper Course was to send the plan through the Kamni, but that under the circumstances (the plan being in Seoul), and with a view to save time, the Hon. Sec. should ask Mr Krien to send the plan to the Foreign Office and reply to the Kamni explaining the matter to him. It was further decided that the Hon. Sec. in his letter to Mr Krien, should ask him to inform the Representatives that it is the desire of the Council to make a road at some future date along the shore on the North West side of the Settlement, and although not marked now on the Plan that permission be reserved to do so.

The Hon Treasurer was asked, at the suggestion of Mr Stripling, to have the Accounts for 1892 + 1893 printed + published.

The meeting closed at 4.30 p.m. next meeting to be arranged by local members.

Extraordinary meeting held March 5th 1894.

Present Mr Krien (President) Mr Rosse, Mr Townsend, Mr Nishiwaki, Mr Woolitang, Mr Chow, Mr Wilkinson.

Mr Chow handed in a letter from Mr Lin, Chinese Consul, instructing him to act and vote for him at the meeting.
Mr Krien suggested that the views of the members should be taken as to Mr Chow's qualification to vote. An informal discussion followed in the course of which the precedent of Mr Reinsdorf being referred to Mr Krien explained that that gentleman held a commission as Vice Consul for the whole of Corea, but could only act in that capacity in his, Mr Krien's absence.
The question whether Mr Chow should be admitted to vote on this one occasion being put, it was carried.

Mr Wilkinson was asked to act temporarily as Secretary. The Minutes of the last meeting (Dec, 15th) were read and approved.

A letter from Mr Fox tendering his resignation as Secretary and member of the Executive Committee was read by the President.
Mr Wilkinson was proposed by Mr Krien as Secretary and Elected unanimously.
He was also elected in place of Mr Fox as a member of the Executive Committee.

Mr

Mr Krien handed in a letter (Dated Nov: 28. 1893.) from 3 landholders (Messrs Walter Townsend and Stripling) suggesting an alternative scheme to the proposal of the Corean Government for an enlarged Jetty. In answer to questions by members Mr Krien stated that the Corean Government's proposal had been accepted by four of the Foreign Representatives, but not by two others.

Mr Townsend pointed out the importance of doing something at once to repair and metal the approach to the existing Jetty. Mr Krien was of opinion that it would be best to go back to the old agreement and construct a road 8 metres wide.

Mr Townsend moved that

"In view of the urgent necessity for a metalled road in front of the Customs Godowns as far as the Jetty, the Secretary be requested to write to the Doyen of the Foreign Representatives to arrange with the Corean Government that the Municipal Council carry out at once, and at their, the Council's own expense, the metalling and draining of a road 15 metres wide from a point on the Bund opposite the Nippon Yusen Kaisha's Corner along the sea-wall, to the existing Jetty such road to be made without prejudice to any plan for filling in the fore-shore or the enlargement of the Jetty that may be agreed upon between the Foreign Representatives and the Corean Government." Carried unanimously.

In

In answer to a question respecting trees for the Settlement, Mr Nosse replied that he had written to Japan for them. The Council were of opinion that inexpensive trees such as Accacia are the most suitable.

On the subject of the Settlement Plan, Mr Krien explained that he found that the A lots had not been marked. He therefore asked the Surveyor to fill in those lots.
This had been done and the plan sent in to the President of the Foreign Office. Mr Krien stated that land within the limits of the Foreign Settlement not marked out in the Plan would continue to be saleable according to the practice hitherto observed.

Mr Nishiwaki, Hon. Treasurer, handed in Copies of the accounts for 1892) 3 printed in accordance with the resolution of last meeting.

Mr Nishiwaki giving notice that he would be absent from Chemulpo for a short period, it was agreed that the Hon. Secretary should be authorised to act also as Treasurer during his absence.

Mr Nosse proposed "That the Foreign Representatives be requested to obtain from the Corean Government repayment of the sum of $2,100. agreed upon between the Kamni of Inchiun and the Consular body at Chemulpo as the amount expended in grading roads in the General

General Foreign Settlement up to January 1st 1893.
Seconded by Mr Townsend. Carried unanimously.

Mr Krien stated that the German land renters had addressed a representation to him asking for a new election of a nonofficial member, maintaining that the election of the 5th Dec, 1893 was illegal on the ground that Mr Fox, H. B. M. Vice Consul, who voted on that occasion was not entitled to do so, because he was not a registered land holder and because he was not himself eligible for election as a Non official member being an official. Mr Krien added that he himself endorsed this opinion, and that he would oppose any voting by the British Vice-Consul in future.

It was arranged that the Executive Committee should draw up rules for the Cemetery and lay them before the next ordinary meeting.

Mr Woolhiting expressed a wish that the road adjoining his lot should be graded. Mr Townsend explained that the difficulty was connected with the incidence of cost of the necessary retaining walls, and referred to a discussion on the 6th and 20th Nov: 1891.

The next ordinary meeting will take place at a date to be fixed by the local members.

First Ordinary Meeting.

Present: Messrs Krien (President), Allen, Lin, Nosse, Wilkinson, Townsend, Woolitang.

The minutes of last meeting were read & approved

With reference to the grading of the road adjoining Mr Woolitangs lot, which had formed a subject of discussion at the last meeting, Mr Townsend explained that he had consulted Mr Lührs, the representative of Messrs Meyer & Co, owners of one of the lots abutting on the road, and that Mr Lührs had stated that he could not construct, or pay for the construction of a wall along Messrs Meyer's lot, unless and until the Corean Customs paid for the retaining wall built by the Council in 1891 opp D39. Mr Krien said that as long as this latter reimbursement was not made by the Customs he would not advise his countrymen to pay. Mr Townsend referred to the minutes of October 6, 1891, which showed that the wall opp D39 had been constructed in consequence of a resolution, one condition of which was that the question of liability for the cost be left to the meeting of the 20th October; and that at the latter meeting (Oct 20th) it was resolved that 'any walling required should be paid for by the lotholders affected'. Mr Wilkinson was of opinion that, apart from any question

question of the liability of the Customs for the wall erected in 1891, lotholders are liable for the erection of any retaining walls erected, or to be erected, since the date of the resolution of Oct. 20th of that year, off their respective lots.

With regard to the road in question (past lots D. 39. 40) Mr Lin, the Chinese Consul, observed that it was dug in 1891 without special official notification to the Chinese Consulate, and that to cut down the Chinese half of the road to the level of the Municipal portion would endanger the walls of that Consulate. He suggested that the Municipal Council should either pay for the necessary retaining wall, or should partially fill up their own portion of the road. Mr Krien proposed that the Council should proceed at the close of the meeting to examined the road.

The Hon. Secretary read the correspondence that had taken place since the date of the last meeting [Nos 1-4 received Nos 1-5 sent]. With reference to the Bund, Mr Krien stated the a meeting of the Foreign Representatives had been summoned, but had been postponed. With regard to the Kammis despatch of April 21st, forwarding $1,000 on account of the cost of grading roads, the Council were of opinion that the non-payment

of

of the rents for 1894 had nothing to do with the question. Dr Allen proposed, and Mr Krien seconded a resolution that "The Secretary be directed to reply to the "Kamni that as regards the balance "of $1,100, which is promised when the "1894 rents are paid, the Municipal "Council cannot allow that repay-"ment to be conditional upon payment "of rents, as the amount from the "latter source will be insufficient, and "moreover has nothing to do with the "grading of roads. The Council therefore "again request payment of this $1100 at "an early date". The resolution was carried.

The executive Committee submitted the draft of the Cemetery Regulations which it was agreed should be discussed seriatim at the next meeting.

Dr Allen moved that the Secretary be requested to procure from Messrs Waterlow and Sons two burial registers similar to those ordered for the Seoul Cemetery Committee.

Seconded by Mr Townsend, Carried unanimously.

The Secretary in his capacity of Acting Treasurer stated that the balance of funds in the Municipal Chest on April 23 was $5845.16.

Mr Krien gave notice of an appropriation of $200 for the fencing in of of the Municipal Lot and the Public Garden. This was unanimously approved. The Council were of opinion that the fencing should be by means of barbed wire.

A gratuity of $10 to Pang Kyenghi, Corean Writer at H. B. M. Vice Consulate was voted for the Clerical assistance given by him to the Hon. Secretary during the past Year.

Mr Townsend, on behalf of the Executive Committee, explained the system of half metalling adopted. Gravel was obtained from the islands, and was spread over the centre of the roads. On the top was placed disintegrated granite, and the whole was pressed by the stone roller kindly lent by the Japanese Settlement. The system had proved very successful. He drew attention to the condition of the road in front of the Customs, particularly from the Tidewaiters office to the Jetty. Owing to the impossibility of employing Carts, the carrying Coolies had put up rates and trade suffered. Moreover the space on which cargo was stored required to be drained; the lowermost tier of the rice bags had suffered seriously on this account. Space too was insufficient, the heaps of rice and other articles having in some cases left barely ten feet of passage way.

The

The Secretary read a letter received that morning from Mr Nosse, H.I.J.M. Consul, covering a petition from the Japanese lotholders asking that the roadway in question might be put into repair.
Mr Townsend proposed that a copy of the petition be sent to the Foreign Representatives for their consideration. This was seconded by Mr Woo Litang, and Carried.

It was agreed that the next ordinary meeting should take place on a date to be fixed by the local members.

The Council then proceeded to inspect the road adjoining Mr Woo Litang's premises. They were of opinion that the road should not be cut down at its junction with the Crossroad ("Ladder Lane").
They also examined the road by D 39, 40, and it was understood that Mr Xin should consult with the Chinese Resident with a view to the due grading of the Chinese half of this road.

Second Ordinary Meeting, June 25, 1894.

As only 4 members (Messrs Reinsdorf for Mr Krien; Townsend; Woo Litang & Wilkinson) attended, the meeting was adjourned till 10 a.m. on Tuesday June 25.

Adjourned Meeting, June 26, 1894.

Present: Mr Nossé (Vice President), Mr Reinsdorf [representing Mr Krien], Mr Lin [accompanied by Mr Chow as interpreter], Messrs Wilkinson, Townsend and Wooltang.

In the absence of Mr Krien, Mr Nossé took the Chair.

The Minutes of the last meeting were read and confirmed. The correspondence that had taken place since the date of the last meeting was read by the Hon. Secretary [No 6-10 received, 7-12 sent].

With reference to the further claim against the Corean Government for grading undertaken subsequent to the 31st Dec, 1892. Mr Wilkinson explained that he and Mr Townsend, on behalf of the Executive Committee, had entered into pourparlers with the Kamni, and that it was probable that the Claim of the Council might be settled for a payment of $550 [in addition to the $1100 yet unpaid] the Council agreeing to complete the grading of the two roads (a) to the North of the Municipal & E. C. Mission lots (b) between the Kamni's Yamen and the Settlement. The opinion of the meeting was that a settlement on the above basis would be satisfactory.

The draft of the Cemetery Regulations was again submitted, and Mr Townsend moved that: The words "five feet by 10 feet

feet" be substituted for the words "at least four feet by eight feet" in Regulation 4; and that the Regulations with this one amendment be passed as they stand. Seconded by Mr Wilkinson and carried unanimously.

A letter from Mr F. H. Mörsel complaining of the withdrawal of the Japanese troops from the houses occupied by his tenants, and declaring that if those tenants left in consequence he should object to pay ground rent, was read. It was decided that it was not necessary to answer it.

Mr Wilkinson moved and Mr Reinsdorf seconded, a resolution that: "The Council deprecate the stationing upon any of the settlements comprised in the port area of Chemulpo or their vicinity, of more armed men than may from time to time be absolutely necessary to maintain order, believing that the presence of any large number of troops in the near neighbourhood is in a high degree prejudicial to the peace and prosperity of the General Foreign Settlement, and a very possible source of danger to the lives and property of the residents". The resolution was carried unanimously and the Secretary was directed to forward a copy of it to the Doyen of the Diplomatic Body

Body, requesting him to be good enough to bring it to the notice of the Foreign Representatives.

A letter from Mr Kimura (dated June 23) was read, in which permission was asked to construct a second well in the projected road running east and west past the North of Lots D.67, 68. It was unanimously decided to grant the permission requested, on the conditions that all land renters in the General Foreign Settlement and their tenants shall have free access at any time to the well, and that should the Council hereafter decide that the well must be filled up it shall be filled up at Mr Kimura's expense.

The Secretary having drawn attention to the fact that although by the recent sale of land the Council received no less a sum than $3095, the auctioneer, had been paid only $2.27, or 2½% on the upset price, Mr Townsend moved that a present of $15 be made to Mr Myers, the auctioneer, for his services in connection with the sale of the five lots in question (D62, 63, 65, 67, 68.), carried unanimously.

Mr Reinsdorf moved the appropriation of $200 for fencing in the public garden and Municipal grounds. Carried unanimously.

Mr Townsend proposed that, in view

view of the approach of summer and the prevalence in the South of China of a form of plague, the Council should at once procure not less than 5 Cwt of Chloride of lime. Mr Wilkinson seconded the resolution, taking the opportunity to draw attention to the frequent stoppage of drains, especially in the east of the Settlement, by the carelessness of residents. The resolution was carried unanimously.

Mr Wilkinson proposed and Mr Townsend seconded; That a suitable portion of ground in the South east corner of Lot II 46 (which lot has not yet been sold) should be acquired by the Council and that upon it a public well should be sunk. Carried unanimously.

It was arranged that the next ordinary meeting should take place the first week in September.

(sd.) W. D. Townsend (sd.) W. H. Wilkinson.
Acting Chairman. Hon. Sec.

Third Ordinary Meeting Chemulpo 9th Nov; 1894.

Present; - Pak Syei Hoan, the Kamni (Mr Shim interpreting) Mr Eitaki Japanese Vice Consul (Mr Konishi interpreting), Mr Townsend, Mr Woo Litang, Mr Wilkinson

(Hon Sec.).

Mr Townsend having been requested to take the Chair, Mr Wilkinson explained that by a communication under date October 20th last the Kamni Bd stated that he was instructed by the Corean Foreign Office to himself fill the place as Corean Delegate in the Council lately held by Wu Kyong Son, and that Mr Nossé, the late Japanese Consul having been transferred else, Mr Eitaki, the Vice Consul and present Acting Consul, would succeed him as the Japanese official Member. The Kamni and Mr Eitaki then took their seats.

The minutes of the previous meeting were read and Confirmed and the correspondence since the date of that meeting was read (sent; Nov. 13 - 21; Received Nov. 13-17).

On behalf of the Executive Committee Mr Townsend stated that the number of Police in the employ of the Council had at one time dwindled down from 8 to 1; that there were now 4, but that it was intended to raise the number to 6 at least, as soon as suitable men could be obtained. The Chloride of lime and wire for fencing had been procured and were now in store on the Municipal Premises.

Mr Eitaki was elected a member of the Executive Committee in the place of Mr Nossé.

It was decided to postpone the fencing

fencing in of the Municipal Lot and of the Public Garden for the present.

Mr Woo Litang having drawn attention to the condition of the entrance to the Söul road abutting on the Western boarder of the Settlement, the Secretary was requested to write to the Kamni to ask that the obstruction existing there should be removed, and the ground kept open.

Mr Eitaki having pointed out the need for definite instructions to the Police, Mr Townsend explained that last spring when the force was more complete, Mr Nossi had been good enough to draw up a scheme. That scheme, however, as it presupposed 8 men to be in the force would not now be applicable. Mr Eitaki was requested to suggest a scheme for 4, with an alternative for 6 men; which he undertook to do.

The date of the next meeting will be fixed by the local members.

(sd.) F. Krien (sd.) W. H. Wilkinson.
President Hon Sec.

Fourth Ordinary Meeting Chemulpo 24th Nov: 1894.

Present:- Mr Krien (President); Mr Sill; the Kamni; Mr Eitaki; Mr Townsend; Mr Woo Litang; Mr Wilkinson (Hon Sec.) Mr Eitaki & the Kamni were accompanied by their interpreters.

The President welcomed Mr Sill

on

on taking his seat as U.S. official member.

The minutes of the meeting of Nov: 9th were read and confirmed, and the correspondence was read (Sent No 22, Received Nos 18-19)

With reference to the Corean Shanties at the entrance of the Seoul road and to the Kamni's suggestion (v. No 18 Received) that the squatters be permitted to remain till the spring, the Kamni undertook that the road should be clear of all obstructions by the close of the third moon of next year, Corean Calendar.

With regard to Mr Osborne's complaint (v. No 19 received), it was resolved to proceed at once to put the road in order and the Kamni undertook to warn the Transport Office of their liability to be fined under the byelaws, Mr Eitaki also promised to cause similar nuisances by Japanese Coolies on the public garden and its neighborhood to be abated, Mr Krien said that a complaint had been made by Mr Lührs of the absence of a bridge over a drain crossing the Ladder Lane near Mr Laporte's entrance. Resolved to direct Ragsdale to examine.

On behalf of the Executive Committee Mr Townsend stated that new overcoats being required for the Police, Mr Eitaki had undertaken to procure the necessary cloth from Japan. Mr Eitaki stated that he had prepared a scheme of duties for the Police, but that there

had

had not yet been time to translate it into English.

New plan of the Settlement, Mr Krien stated that he had, in accordance with the wishes of the Council, communicated the Plan to the President of the Corean Foreign Office. The President in a letter dated the 5th instant, had promised to convene a meeting of the Foreign Representatives at an early date for its consideration.

Mr Woo Li tang complained that Japanese coolies on Lot C 27 were in the habit of insulting him and other Chinese, and of throwing stones. Mr Eitaki undertook to see that the objectionable practice was discontinued. It was decided to hold the Election for an Elective Member in the place of Mr Nishiwaki (retiring on rotation) on Wednesday the 5th December, between the hours of 10 a.m. and 1 p.m.

The next meeting was fixed for the 6th December.

(Sd.) W. H. Wilkinson.
Hon. Sec.

Fifth Ordinary Meeting, Chemulpo Dec. 6th 1894.

Present; Mr Sill; the Kamni; Mr Eitaki; Mr Townsend, Mr Woo Li tang and Mr Wilkinson. The Kamni and Mr Eitaki were accompanied by their interpreters. In the absence of the President

President, Mr Sill was invited to take the Chair.

The Minutes of the previous meeting were read and confirmed, and the result of the election held on the 5th December was announced. [Mr Nishiwaki 12 votes, Mr Lührs 8 votes].

Mr Eitaki stated that he had taken measures to prevent the recurrence of the acts of Nuisance on the part of Japanese Coolies concerning which complaints had been made at the last meeting. He had not yet had time to have the scheme of police duties translated into English, but the order for the Cloth for police uniforms had gone to Japan.

Mr Wilkinson stated that the road leading past the Transport Office and Mr Osborne's house was in process of repair; and that a small bridge had been thrown over the drain in Ladder Lane.

Road in front of Customs Godowns. Mr Townsend drew the attention of the Council to the necessity for keeping open and properly metalling a road through the reclaimed land South of the Customs Godowns. In rain or snow the track was scarcely passible, and a heavy loss was inflicted on the trade of the Port not only by this circumstance, but also by the damage accruing through insufficient drainage, to the lower tiers of merchandise piled on the ground. It had been a subject

subject of Complaint for some years, but the Corean Government had done nothing.

Mr Wilkinson pointed out that last Spring the Corean Government had commenced to repair and enlarge the Jetty, and that in the scheme was to have been included the making of a road in front of the Godowns along the bund. This useful work had been unfortunately interrupted by political complications.

Mr Townsend observed that the work in question had been undertaken by the Customs without authority and against the protests of the President of the Council and of the landholders.

Mr Wilkinson ventured to correct what he felt to be a misapprehension. The scheme which embraced at once an extended Jetty and the bund-road had been approved in the Autumn of 1893 by all the Foreign Representatives with the exception of two. Of those two, one had left Corea and the other had since given in his adhesion to the scheme.

Mr Townsend then moved, and Mr Wilkinson seconded a resolution.

That the Secretary be requested to write to the Foreign Representatives requesting that they will, in concert with the Corean Government, have a road laid out from the end of the bund next to the Nippon Yusen Kaisha along

the

the bund to the Jetty, 15 metres wide, so that the Municipal Council can grade and metal this road early in March 1895.

Mr Eitaki asked what would be done with the Cargo on the 15 metre strip. It was replied that all such Cargo and stores, whether private or the property of any government, must be removed elsewhere, as the strip when metalled would be kept open as a thoroughfare. The resolution was then carried. Mr Wilkinson moved, as a corallary to the last resolution.

That the Foreign Representatives should be requested to confer with the Corean Government with a view the metalling and draining, as soon as possible, of all the cargo space between the 15 metre road referred to in the resolution just carried, and in front of the Customs' Godowns.

In answer to a question from the Kamni, it was explained that the resolution raised no question as to the persons in whom the ownership and control of the Cargo space are vested. The macadamizing of this ground and its proper drainage, would be of the greatest benefit to every one. Mr Townsend seconded the resolution, which was carried unanimously.

A letter from Mr Gorschalki was read requesting that the ground in front of the lots B1 and B2, with the two wells upon it, might be leased to him.

Mr Townsend

Mr Townsend pointed out that the ground in question was a roadway. The Council were of opinion that it was impossible to lease ground of such a character.

Mr Wilkinson observed that Mr Hori of Daibutsu's Hotel had laid down pipes along this land, and was selling water from the two public wells to to the shipping; he also drew attention to the fact that a quantity of merchandize had been piled on the ground. The Council, agreeing with the opinion of Mr Sill, held that it was improper for anyone landholder to sell to non residents water from a public well, and that merchandize could not be stacked on a public road. The owners of the merchandize should be required to remove it, and Mr Hori should be informed that the privilege of selling water from the General Foreign Settlement could only be granted on the terms given earlier to Mr Kimura.

The Executive Committee reported of two register book for the Cemetery.

With regard to the amount still due from the Corean Government on account of the grading of roads the Council were of opinion that the Kamni should be asked to pay as soon as possible the $1100, balance of the $2100 agreed upon in 1893, & in addition the sum of $550 for grading carried out between Jan 1st 1893 & Dec. 31st 1894, on

the

the Conditions recorded in the Minutes of the second Ordinary Meeting of this Year.

The following appropriations were unanimously passed:

Chief of the Police, Salary @ $75 –	$900
Policemen; 6 (to be added to in case of need) @ $15	1080
Uniforms	300
Scavengers; 4 @ $9	432
Lamps	200
Repairs to roads	500
Contingent expenses	450
	3,862
Extra Expenditure;	
Grading and draining new roads	500
	4,362

The following officers were unanimously elected for 1895.

President; Mr Sill.
Vice President; Mr Krien.
Secretary; Mr Wilkinson
Treasurer; Mr Nishiwaki
Executive Committee; Messrs Eilaki, Townsend & Wilkinson.

The next meeting will take place in February, on a day to be fixed by the local members.

(Sd) W. H. Wilkinson.
Hon Sec.

1895.

First ordinary meeting. Chemulpo March 7th 1895.

Present

Present: The Kamni, Messrs Chinda, Townsend, Wilkinson & Woolitang.

In the absence of both the President and the Vice President, Mr Townsend was invited to take the Chair.

Mr Chinda, who since the date of last meeting had been appointed H. I. J. M's Consul at Chemulpo, took his seat vice Mr Eitaki.

The Minutes of the previous meeting were read and confirmed and the Correspondence was read.

The meeting learnt with regret of Mr Sill's determination not to accept the post of President for which his doyennage in the Consular Body more particularly indicated him. It was pointed out that the functions of the President were, strictly speaking, confined to presiding at the meetings of the Council, and that he was not called upon to represent the Council outside the walls of the Municipal Buildings. It was, at the same time, convenient that he should be one who in some other capacity was in direct relations with the Corean Government at Seoul, although he could not, unless authorized ad hoc by the Council communicate with that Govt in the name of the Council. Mr Sill's time would not therefore be greatly infringed upon, while his acceptance of the post would be a convenience to the Council. Mr Townsend having assured the members that Mr Sill's decision was irrevocable, Mr Krien was unanimously elected President for the current year in his stead, with Mr Chinda as Vice President. Mr Chinda was also elected a member of the Executive Committee in the room of Mr Eitaki.

Bund road in front of Customs Godown.
It is understood that the Royal Corean Customs have entered into a contract with a Japanese for the repair and extension of the stone Jetty, the work to be completed in four months. The Council propose to proceed as soon as possible, meanwhile, with the 15 metre road, and it was arranged that Mr Chinda, as Japanese Consul, should give notice to any Japanese owner of goods in situ to prepare to remove them while the Executive Committee took steps to procure a supply of suitable metalling.

Mr Chinda drew attention to the need for a pest house, to which victims of infectious diseases of the more serious kind, such as smallpox, could be removed. It was agreed that the Secretary should write to Drs Landis & Kajima requesting them to be good enough to favor the Council with their views on this question. The Council was of opinion that the pesthouse when established should be under the joint conduct of the Settlements.

Accounts for 1894. A balance sheet was shown as follows:-

Date			
1894. Jan.		Balance from 1893	$1420.26
Apl. 11		Rents for 1893.	4457.84

Apl. 21

Apl. 21	Grading account, first instalment from Corean Govt.		1000.00
May 12	Sale of land (less auctioneer's fees)		3080.90
Dec. 31	Burial fees		35.00
" "	License "		170.00
" "	Interest on Current account		141.86
			10,305.86

Dec. 31	Police: Wages (less fines)	1870.74	$1870.74
	Clothing &c.		163.59
"	Roads Scavengers	278.13	
	Lamps &c	204.94	483.07
	Construction & repair	694.92	
	Trees	19.03	713.95
"	Printing & Stationery		14.73
"	Municipal Buildings Rent	75.60	
	Insurance	28.13	
	Coal	100.10	
	Miscellaneous	7.85	211.68
"	Cemetery; Registers 32.25 graves 6		38.25
"	Public Garden; Wire &c.		172.00
"	Clerical: gratuity Corean Writer		10.00
Dec. 31	Balance		6627.85
			10,305.86

New Plan of Settlement. Mr Chinda showed a tracing of the plan on which certain alteration were marked proposed by him after consultation with Mr Wilkinson and joint inspection of the ground. With regard to the more Northern part of the Settlement, it was pointed out that it was difficult to lay it out into lots pending a decision as to the course of

the projected Chemulpo-Seoul railway.
Mr Woo Litang drew attention to the circumstance that the snow that had fallen last month was allowed to remain in the streets instead of being promptly removed, with the consequence that it rendered the roads impossible. It was held that the Byelaws require each occupant to remove the snow from the foot walk abutting on his premises, but that the roads ought to be cleared by the Council's Scavengers.

Balance of grading account. The Kamni stated that he would reply to the Secretary's letter on this subject after obtaining obstructions from the Foreign Office.

The next meeting will be held in the first week in April on a day to be fixed by the local members.

LEGATION OF THE UNITED STATES SÖUL
No 229

FOURTH ORDINARY MEETING.

Sept. 21st. 1898.

PRESENT.- Messrs. Ishii, Reinsdorf, Sands, Ottewill, the Kamni, Wolter, Suzuki and Townsend, Hon. Secy.

In the absence of the President, Mr. Ishii was invited to take the chair.

The minutes of the Third Ordinary Meeting were read and confirmed

The correspondence was read by the Hon. Secy.

POLICE.-The meeting decided to increase wages of Police to following amounts, to begin September 1st, 1898.

Eklundh	Yen 80.00	per month.
Shimazaki	" 30.00	" "
Kitsuki	" 24.00	" "
Kijiyama	" 20.00	" "

Wages of Jail bay, lamplighter and scarvengers to remain as before, being deemed sufficient.

COMPLAINT read from Mr. Mondini regarding noise from adjoining tea house.

Mr. Ishii said he had warned the proprietor of tea-house, who had promised to observe the Municipal Regulations.

MADA.-Application received from Mada, requesting permission to store wood, etc. on Bund front of Lot B#1 on payment of rent for ground used.

NOT GRANTED.

FUJIWARA.-Application received from Fujiwara to lay down an iron water pipe under road between Lots C#4 & 5.

Permission granted on condition that road be put in good order after laying pipe, which must also be removed at any time when requested by the Municipal Council.

BAMBOOS, ETC. STORED ON BUND.-Chief of police reports obstruction of Bund by Bomboos, etc. stred there for long periods.

The Ex. Committee were asked to see that the Regulations be observed.

PUBLIC GARDEN.-Moved by Mr. Wolter seocnded by Mr. Townsend that a further sum of yen 100.00 be appropriated for the completion of Gardener's contract, which was laid before the meeting by the Ex. Committee. Carried U.

Moved by Mr. Ottewill.

Seconded by Mr. Suzuki.

That the Ex. Committee be empowered to spend a sum not exceeding yen 800.00 for a Gardener's and Gate Keepers house in the Public Garden. Carried U.

MR. SANDS requested loan of Municipal Jail, all expenses to be paid by him for prisoner and he to provide Chinese Police as watchman.

GRANTED.

BOUNDARY OF CHINESE SETTLEMENT.-

Moved by Mr. Ottewill.

Seconded by Mr. Ishii.

That the Ex. Committee be requested to define boundary line between the General Foreign Settlement and the Chinese Settlement. Carried U.

The Ex. Committee were also requested to fix boundary line of 15 metre road along the north shore to the Cemetery point.

PRESIDENT OF MUNICIPAL COUNCIL.

Moved by Mr. Townsend.

Seconded by Mr. Wolter.

That Mr. Ishii be elected President of the Chemulpo Municipal Council for the term ending Dec. 31st, 1898. Carried U.

The above election was held to fill the vacancy caused by the resignation of the Hon. H. N. Allen, received in his letter dated Sept. 17th 1898.

VICE PRESIDENT OF MUNICIPAL COUNCIL.

Moved by Mr. Reinsdorf

Seconded by Mr. Townsend.

That Mr. Ottewill be elected Vice President of the Chemulpo Municipal Council for the term ending Dec. 31st, 1898. Carried U.

The above election was held to fill the vacancy caused by the death of H. Bencraft Joly, Esq. late H.B.M.'s Vice-Consul.

THE MEETING THEN ADJOURNED to a date to be fixed by the Local Members.

(Copy of Minutes)

LEGATION OF THE UNITED STATES SEOUL
No. ____
Rec'd 12 I 1899
Ans'd ____ 18__

Municipal Council,

Chemulpo, Jan 4th 1899

First Ordinary Meeting 1899.

Present Mr. Reinsdorf President, Messrs Sands Shidehara Kammi, Walter & Townsend Hon. Secy.

Minutes of last meeting were read & confirmed

Discussion took place on the motion re collection of rents, moved at the meeting of Dec 20th 1898.

Messrs Shidehara & Townsend withdrew their motion of Dec 20th 98 and proposed the following motion.

That Consuls be requested to inform their Nationals, who are land renters in the Gen. Foreign Settlement that, unless rents are paid in Jan. of each year, legal proceedings will be instituted to enforce payment of the respective amounts with interest

Carried unanimously.

The Hon. Secy was requested to mention, as far as possible the subjects to be brought up at Meetings, when issuing the Notice.

Notice was given, that at the next meeting a Motion would be made to alter the Agreement as to taxes, making them payable in Gold Yen instead of Silver as at present.

Moved by Mr. Townsend, seconded by Mr Sands

That as rents for 1899 are payable in silver, that the Hon. Treasurer be be requested to receive same and change Silver into Gold yen to the best advantage possible, keeping his balance, as far as possible, in Gold yen.

Carried unanimously.

Moved by Mr. Walter, seconded by Mr. Sands

That in case of the Temporary absence of the Hon. Treasurer, the Hon. Secretary be empowered to sign checks and make payments

Carried unanimously.

The Meeting then adjourned, subject to the Call of the Local Members

(Signed) W. Townsend

Hon. Secretary

Second Ordinary Meeting Jan. 30th 1899.

No Quorum beeing present, the Meeting was adjourned to the 31st inst.

Jan. 31st- 1899

Present- Mr. Sundius, Vice President, in the chair,- Messrs Sands, Shidehara, Kamni, Wolter and Townsend, Hon.Secretary.

Moved by Mr. Sundius, 2 nd Mr. Sands, That the Agreement made with Mr Colbran, as per his letter of Jan.5th,having been accepted individually by the Members of the Mun.Council,be herely confirmed.

Carried unanimously.

Permission was granted by the Council to the Police,to have their families live at the Police Station.

Despatch was read from J.L. Chalmers Esq. Acting Commissioner of Customs, enclosing despatch from J.Mc Leavy Brown Esq. dated Jan. re. new North Bund Road and was laid on the Table for discussion at the next Meeting.

Taxes. The Kamni was requested by the Council to send letters to the Consuls, advising them of the Motion passed at 1st Ordinary Meeting re. Rents, that unless Rents were paid before Feb.28th 1899, legal proceedings would be taken to enforce payment with interest.

The Executive Committie were authrized by the Council to contract with Japanese Gardiner for 4oo trees to be planted in the streets of the General Foreign Settlement

Copy of Minutes Meeting
Jan 31st 1899
W.W. Townsend
Hon. Secy.

(Copy)

THIRD ORDINARY MEETING 21st FEB.1899

Present Mr. Reinsdorf , President

Messrs Sundius, Shidehare, Kamni, Wolter and Townsend , Hon. Secretary.
Minutes of the last meeting were read and confirmed.
Letter from the Commissioner of Customs was read, enclosing letter from J. McLeavy Brown Esq. Chief Commissioner of Customs, dated Jan.28th re New North Bund Road.

After discussion the fallowing motion was made by Mr. Townsend, seconded by Mr. Shidehare ;
That the Municipal Council is prepare to take over the 15metre Bund Road, as a part of the General Foreign Settlement and to preserve the same from being encroched upon for any private purpose
The Council will also proceed to metal the road, as soon as the Railway Co. shall have raised the road bed to the original level at which it stod stood before it was damaged by the recent storm.

While the Council will maintain the Surface of the Bund Road in a proper state of repair, it is cleady understood that no part ofthecost of restoring the Sea-wall from end to end and of maintaining it in repair is to be borne by the Council This woak, it is assumed ,will be done promtly, as required. by the Korean Govt; the Chinese Settlement Authorities and the Railway Company onthe Portion of the Wall which belong to them respectively or face their property and for which they are responsible. it is also understood that the Railway Company will fill in the ground behind the present breach, which breach was caused, as pointed out by the Mr. Brown in his letter of 28th Jan., by the absence of such filling. It is further taken by granted by the Council that all ground reclamed from the foreshore inside the new Bund Road shall pay Rent to the Municipal Council as C. Lots. being reclaimed foreshore ground, in accordance with Article 7 of the General Foreign Settlement Regulation and as arranged by the Chief Commissioner with American Syndicate. Until such rent shall have been paid the Council cannot bind itself to incur any expenditure in connextion with the Bund Road bed and attached grounds, etc, now taken over beyond the minimum amount required to guard such Road bed , etc, as an integral part of General Foreign Settlement. Carried unanimously.

The Hon. Secty was requested to Communicate the above motion to the Commissioner of Customs and to add the following motion which was moved by Mr. Sundius and secondedby Mr. Wolter and carried unanimously

In connection with my (Hon. Secy) letter of today and as the Municipal Council presumes that Title Deeds will be issued to the Seoul and Chemulpo Railway Company shortly, the Council begs to point out that the inside 15 metre Road should be laid out by joint Survey along the foreshore line according to the original plan of the Settlement and the Council request that you (Commr- of Customs) will make suitable arrangements to carry this into effect.

Discussion took place on the matter of a 15 Metre Road along the front of the New Japanese Bund extension.

Moved by Mr. Wolter
Secondedby Mr. Townsend

That the Hon. Secretary be requestedto write to the Doyen of the Diplomatic Corps asking him if possible to make arrangement for a 15 metre wide road instead of a 7 metre road, as at present, along the front of the New Japanese Bund Extension.

Carried unanimously.

The Meeting their adjourned subject to the Call of the Local Members

signed

Hon. Secretary.

W.D. Townsend

Copy of Minutes.

1
Dec. 7, 1900

Chemulpo, Korea, December 6th, 1900.

THIRD REGULAR MEETING.

Present -- Dr. Weipert, President, Messrs Allen, Ijuin, Goffe, the Kamni's Secretary, Messrs Odaka, Luhrs and Townsend, Hon. Secretary.

Moved by Mr. Goffe, seconded by Dr. Allen, That in view of no reply having been received from the Kamni, that Dr. Weipert be asked to communicate with the Foreign Office re Sanitation of the Corean Town. C.U.

Letter was read from Official Election Committee announcing that at the election held on Dec. 5th

Mr. Carl Luhrs had 12 votes.

Mr. G. Odaka had 9 votes

Mr. W.du F. Hutchinson had 6 votes.

Dr. Weipert, President of the Council, then declared that Mr. Carl Luhrs had been elected a member of the Municipal Council to serve three years from Jan. 1st, 1901, and Mr. G. Odaka to serve two years from Jan. 1901.

Moved by Dr. Allen, Seconded by Mr. Goffe, That 200 copies of the Election Rules be printed by the Council for distribution. C.U

Police Wages. Moved by Mr. Townsend, seconded by Mr. Ijuin, That Shimazaki be granted a gratuity of 25 Yen for

services

services up to Dec. 31st, 1900, and that the other policemen (2) be granted an increase of 2 Yen per month from Dec. 1st, 1900.

C.U.

R.R. Foreshore Taxes.

Dr. Weipert informed the Council that no answer had yet been received from the Japanese Minister at Seoul, but one was expected shortly.

Mr. Luhrs, Hon. Treasurer, presented a statement of Expenditures and Receipts by the Municipal Council up to Nov. 30th, 1900.

Moved by Mr. Townsend, seconded by Dr. Allen, That Messrs Goffe and Ijuin be appointed a Committee of 2 to audit the Hon. Treasurer's account at the end of the year.

Officers of the Council for 1901.

Moved by Dr. Allen, seconded by Mr. Ijuin, That the following Officers of the Council be elected for the year 1901.

Dr. Weipert -- President.

Mr. Goffe -- Hon. Secretary and Vice President.

Mr. Luhrs -- Hon. Treasurer.

C.U.

Moved by Dr. Allen, Seconded by Mr. Goffe, That the Executive Committee for 1901 consist of Messrs Ijuin, Luhrs and Townsend.

C.U.

Moved by Dr. Weipert, seconded by Mr. Luhrs, That the thanks of the Council be given to Mr. Townsend for his services as Hon. Secretary since Jan. 1897. C.U.

Appropriations for 1901.

Moved by Mr. Goffe, seconded by Mr. Ijuin, That the following amounts be appropriated for the year 1901.

Roads	Yen	3000.
Police	"	3500.
Uniforms	"	200,
Miscl.	"	500.
Coal	"	200.
Scavenging	"	1500.
Lighting	"	500.
Total	Yen	9400.

C.U.

The Council then adjourned, subject to the call of the Local Members.

(signed) W.D.Townsend.

Hon. Secretary.

MUNICIPAL COUNCIL,
GENERAL FOREIGN SETTLEMENT,
CHEMULPO.

Minutes

Chemulpo, 12th November 1913.

Fifth ordinary general meeting held at the Council Hall on Wednesday 12th November 1913 at 10.15 a.m.

Present Dr. Krüger, President in the Chair, and Messrs. Scidmore, Hisamidzu, Iwasaki, Baumann and Bennett.

Minutes of the previous meeting were read and approved.

House Cleaning. Correspondence between the Secreatry and the Prefect read by the Cairman; but no answer having yet been received from the Governor of the Province to whom the question was submitted, the matter must remain over in the meantime.

Abolition of General Foreign Settlements, Control of Cemeteries &c. Dr. Krüger reported to the Council that on the 30th of October an Order (Seirei) was promulgated regarding the new "Fu's" in Chosen, and in Article 34 it states that "the Laws and ordinaces with regard to the Japanese Municipalities, the General Foreign Settlements, and the Sanitary Association in Seoul will be abolished". Article 33 states that the time when this Seirei will be put into force will be decided by the Governor General. Article 35 states that all matters, rights, and obligations of the General Foreign Settlements with exception of Songchin will be taken over by the new "Fu" Prefectures, but that this will not be the case with regard to Cemeteries which are inside the boundaries of the General Foreign Settlements, and that with regard to the reserve fund of 20,000 Yen of the Municipal Council of the General Foreign Settlement of Chemulpo, a provision is made that this reserve fund is not to be handed over to the new Jinsen Fu Prefecture. In the protocols with regard to this reserve fund, at the Fifth meeting held on March, 17th 1913 Mr. Komatsu proposed that the existing public garden in the Foreign Settlement be maintained in good order and condition by the Authorities. Article 10 reads as follows:- "The existing Foreign

"Foreign Cemeteries in the Foreign Settlements shall be maintained
"by local Foreign Residents in conformity with the Laws and Ordinan-
"ces governing Cemeteries, Crematories, Burial, Cremation &c free
"of all taxes and rates. The sum of Yen 20,000- or so much
"thereof as may be necessary shall be appropriated for this purpose
"out of the property belonging to the Municipal Council of the
"General Foreign Settlement at Chemulpo."
In respect of this arrangement Dr Krüger suggested that the three
Trustees of the Cemetery-fund should jointly send in to our Council
their resignations and return to the Council the Trust-fund so that
by this action the Council would be subsequently enabled to handle
the fund in a way which they may deem expedient in order to fulfill
the above conditions.

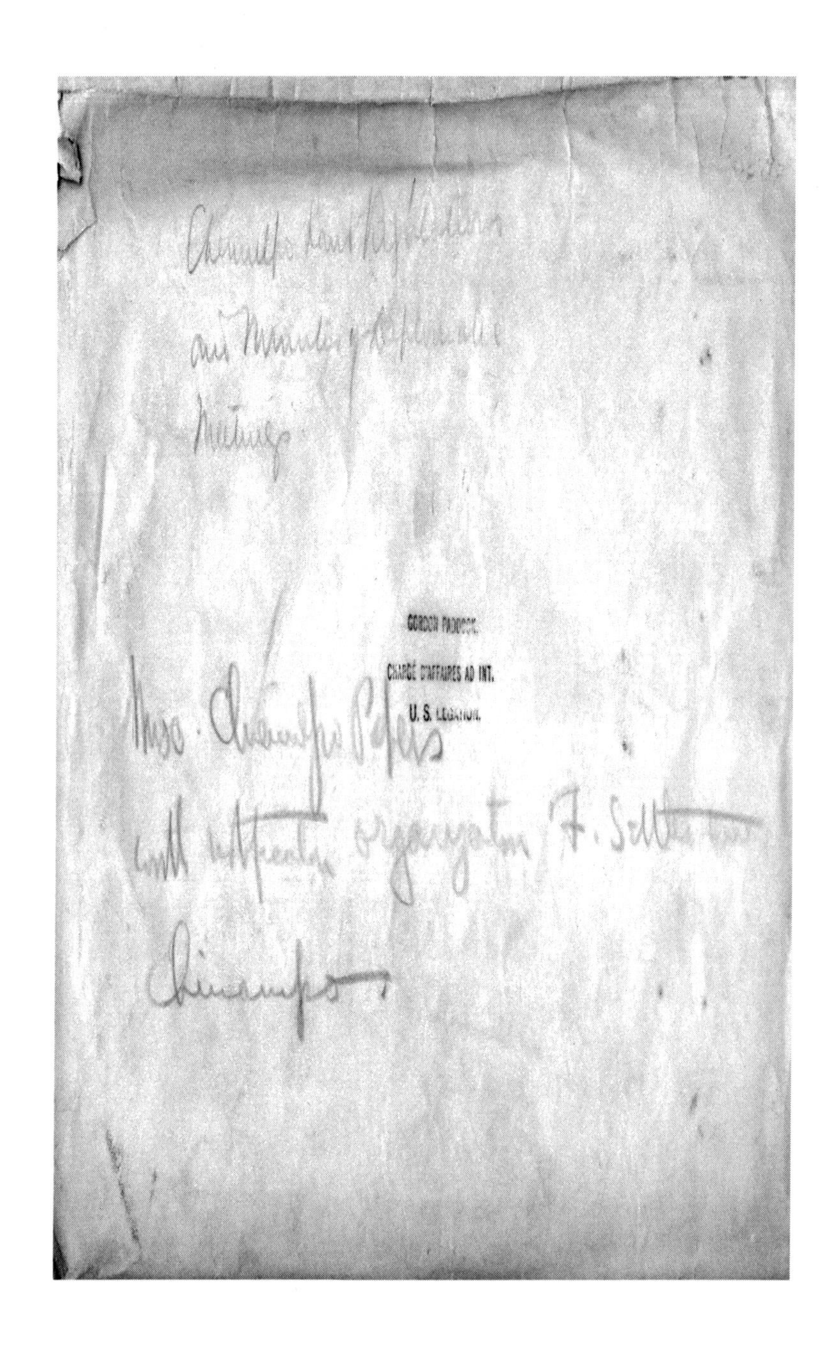
GORDON PADDOCK.
CHARGÉ D'AFFAIRES AD INT.
U. S. LEGATION.

10 May 1884.
16 d. 4 m. K.S.

Arrangements for the preparation of a General Settlement for all Foreigners at Chemulpo.

1 The ground in front of & lying to the South of Chinese Settlement will be filled in by the Korean Government within the limits shown by the red line on the annexed plan as a portion of the site of the General Foreign Settlement a road with a Seawall will be constructed in front of this ground and will be continued to the S. W. angle of the Chemulpo Bluff where a substantial jetty for the use of Cargo boats will be built This road will be two feet above the highest spring tides.

2. The above ground will afterwards be extended from time to time in a Southerly direction whenever more lots are required for General Foreign occupation by filling in the foreshore in front of the Japanese & so called General Settlement. The limit of this extension is the Bluff where the Japanese cemetery now is.

3. The ground north of the Chinese Settlement

Settlement as far as the red line shown on the annexed plan is also reserved for the purpose of a general Settlement for all Foreigners.

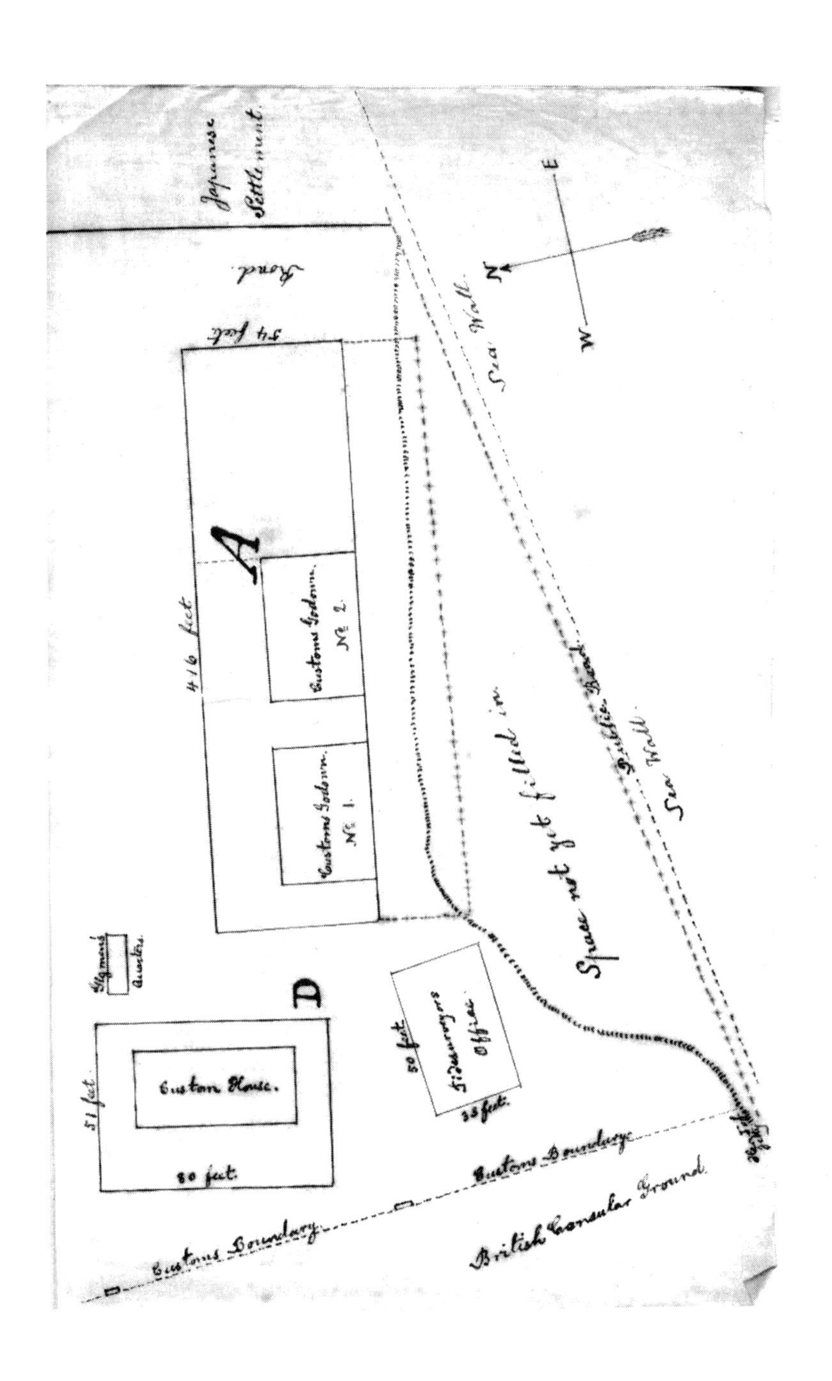
Japanese Settlement
Road
54 feet
416 feet
A
Customs Godown No 2
Customs Godown No 1
Sea Wall
Public Road
Sea Wall
Space not yet filled in
N
E
W
D
Custom House
51 feet
80 feet
Tidewaiters Office
50 feet
35 feet
Customs Boundary
Customs Boundary
British Consular Ground

Chemulpo General Foreign Settlement

List of Land renters etc. for 1 Jany. 1891

Holder	Nationality	Full tax $	c
J. Steinbeck	Aust.	120	90
H. B. M's Governmt.	Brit.	201	80
A. B. Stripling	"	487	98
T. Hollingsworth	"	26	24
W. D. F. Hutchison	"	44	54
Woo Li lang	Chin.	266	98
Li Pei-chien	"	55	14
Corean Customs	Corean	626	32
" Magistrate	"	22	44
E. Laporte	French	22	10
H. C. E. Meyer	German	597	12
C. Wolter	"	495	34
C. Lührs	"	40	14
A. Gorschalki	"	42	30
R. Brinkmeyer	"	47	70
F. M. Allmacher	"	171	00
F. H. Mörsel	"	347	70
Ota Richitaro	Jap.	60	90
Yenami Tetsuzo	"	125	22
S. Asa	"	54	00
K. Tosa	"	40	92
S. Shindo	"	46	20
Horikiri Taro	"	168	48
Shimanuchi Yoshio	"	60	12
Horiguchi Kayemon	"	34	00
Ohashi Taro	"	24	00
W. D. Townsend	Am.	72	90
Cooper's Executors	"	36	00
Total		4,358	48

Chemulpo General Foreign Settlement

List of lots of land sold etc up to 12th January, 1891.

Class	No	Date of purchase or Acquisition	Date of issue of Title deed	Title deed originally issued to whom	Nationality	Name of present holder (12 January 1891)	Nationality	Square Metres	Amount realized by sale $	¢	Upset price retained by Corean Govt $	¢	Balance handed to Municipality $	¢	Full rent due per annum $	¢	Crown tax to Government per annum 30 cents per 100 sq metres $	¢	Balance to Municipality per annum $	¢	Remarks
A.	1	No record sometime in 1884.	1888 Nov. 15	Corean Customs	Corean Govt	Corean Customs	Corean	682	654	72	654	72	"	"	136	40	2	05	134	35	
"	2		" " "	" "	" "	" "	"	705	676	80	676	80	"	"	141	00	2	11	138	89	
"	3		" " "	" "	" "	" "	"	674	647	04	647	04	"	"	134	80	2	02	132	78	
B	1+2	1884, Nov. 7.	1888, April 4.	Carl Wolter	German	Carl Luhrs	German	669	41	14	40	14	1	00	40	14	2	01	38	13	
"	4	1886 May 7.	1887 Dec. 2.	A. B. Stripling	British	A. B. Stripling	British	1,340	254	40	254	40	"	"	254	40	12	72	241	68	
C	1	1884 Nov. 7.	1888 April 4.	E. Meyer & Co	German	H. C. E. Meyer	German	1335	80	10	80	10	"	"	80	10	4	01	76	09	
"	2	" " "	" " "	"	"	"	"	1,305	78	30	78	30	"	"	78	30	3	92	74	38	
"	3	1886 July 15	" " "	"	"	"	"	1,350	122	17	81	00	41	17	81	00	4	05	76	95	
"	4	1886 Sept. 27	" " "	"	"	"	"	1,250	115	62	75	00	40	62	75	00	3	75	71	25	
"	5	1886 Oct. 5.	1884 April 4	" "	"	C. Wolter	"	1,410	142	41	84	60	57	81	84	60	4	23	80	37	
"	6	1889 March 11	1889 March 11	R. Seitz	"	C. Wolter	"	1,440	216	00	86	40	129	60	86	40	4	32	82	08	
"	7	1887 April 8	1889 April 8.	C. Wolter	"	"	"	1,320	300	30	79	20	221	10	79	20	3	96	75	24	
"	8	1889 April 8.	1889 April 8.	"	"	"	"	1,320	318	12	79	20	238	92	79	20	3	96	75	24	
"	9	1886 March 31	1887 Dec. 28.	C. H. Cooper	American	Li-Pei-chin	Chinese	919	172	31	55	14	117	17	55	14	2	76	52	38	
"	10+11	1884. Nov. 7.	1890, April 14	J. Steinbeck	Austrian	J. Steinbeck	Austrian	2,015	120	90	120	90	"	"	120	90	6	05	114	85	
								[illegible]													
								Carried over	3,940	33	3,092	94	847	39	1,526	58	61	92	1,464	66	

2\. Continued.

Class	No.	Date of purchase or acquisition	Date of issue of title deed	Title deed originally issued to whom	Nationality	Name of present holder (12th January, 1891)	Nationality	Square metres	Amount realized by sale $ ¢	Upset price retained by Corean Government $ ¢	Balance handed to Municipality $ ¢	Ground rent due per annum $ ¢	Crown Tax to Government per annum 30 cents per 100 sq. metres $ ¢	Balance to Municipality per annum $ ¢	Remarks
								Brought forward	3960 33	3092 94	847 39	1526 58	61 92	1464 66	
C	12	1888, May 16	1888, May 16	Kikitaki Heihachi	Japanese	Kikitaki Heihachi	Japanese	1,015	124 85	60 90	63 95	60 90	3 04	57 86	
"	13	" Sept. 3	" Sept. 7	Yenami Tetsuo	"	Yenami Tetsuo	"	1,020	714 00	61 20	652 80	61 20	3 06	58 14	
"	14	" " "	" " "	" "	"	" "	"	1,067	736 23	64 02	672 21	64 02	3 20	60 82	
"	15	" " "	" " "	" "	"	J. Yoshida	"	682	429 66	40 92	388 74	40 92	2 05	38 87	
"	16	1890, Dec. 12	1890, Dec. 12	S. Shindo	"	S. Shindo	"	770	2286 90	46 20	2,240 70	46 20	2 31	43 89	
"	17	1886, June 11	1888, April 4	F. H. Mörsel	German	F. H. Mörsel	German	900	54 45	54 00	. 45	54 00	2 70	51 30	
"	18	1888, May 17	1888, May 21	Horikin Taro	Japanese	Horikin Taro	Japanese	900	587 25	54 00	533 25	54 00	2 70	51 30	
"	19	" " "	" " "	Yenami Tetsuo	"	Shimouchi Yoshi	"	1002	672 84	60 12	612 72	60 12	3 01	57 11	
"	20	" " "	" " "	F. H. Mörsel	German	F. H. Mörsel	German	900	542 70	54 00	488 70	54 00	2 70	51 30	
"	21	" " "	" " "	Horiguchi Kayemon	Japanese	K. Wakai	Japanese	900	553 50	54 00	499 50	54 00	2 70	51 30	
"	22	1886, Nov. 7	" April 4	F. H. Mörsel	German	F. H. Mörsel	German	915	54 90	54 90	. .	54 90	2 75	52 15	
"	23	1888, May 19	" May 21	Woo Litang	Chinese	Woo Litang	Chinese	855	600 21	51 30	548 91	51 30	2 56	48 74	
"	24	" March 19	" April 4	"	"	"	"	408	67 32	24 48	42 84	24 48	1 22	23 26	
"	25	" May	" May 21	Yenami Tetsuo	Japanese	S. Aso	Japanese	900	342 00	54 00	288 00	54 00	2 70	51 30	
"	26	" " "	" " "	"	"	Horikin Taro	Japanese	900	297 00	54 00	243 00	54 00	2 70	51 30	
"	27	" " "	" " "	Horikin Taro	"	"	"	1,008	322 56	60 48	262 08	60 48	3 02	57 46	
"	28	1886, Nov. 7	" April 4	C. Wolter	German	Woo Litang	Chinese	900	54 00	54 00	. .	54 00	2 70	51 30	
"	29	1886, May 28	" " "	F. H. Mörsel	"	F. H. Mörsel	German	900	54 45	54 00	. 45	54 00	2 70	51 30	
"	30	" " "	" " "	"	"	"	"	915	55 36	54 90	. 46	54 90	2 74	52 16	
"	31	" " "	" " "	"	"	"	"	930	56 26	55 80	. 46	55 80	2 79	53 01	
								(17763)							
								Carried over	12,546 77	4160 16	8386 61	2,593 80	115 27	2,478 53	

3.

Continued.

Class	No	Date of purchase or acquisition	Date of issue of title deed	Title deed originally issued to whom	Nationality	Name of present holder (12th January 1891)	Nationality	Square Metres	Amount realized by Sale $ ¢	Upset price retained by Corean Government $ ¢	Balance handed to Municipality $ ¢	Full rent due per annum $ ¢	Crown Tax to Government per annum 30 cents per 100 sq metres $ ¢	Balance to Municipality per annum $ ¢	Remarks
								Brought forward	12,546 77	4,160 16	8,386 61	2,593 80	115 27	2,478 53	
C	32	1887 Dec. 5	1887 Dec. 20	Woo Litang	Chinese	Woo Litang	Chinese	810	648 00	48 60	599 40	48 60	2 43	46 17	
D	1	1886 Nov. 7	1888 April 4	C. Wolter	German	C. Wolter	German	4,300	129 00	129 00	. .	86 00	12 90	73 10	
"	2	1886 May 28	1887 Dec. 2	A. B. Stripling	British	A. B. Stripling	British	9,156	274 68	274 68	. .	183 12	27 47	155 65	
"	3	" April 6	1888 April 4	A. Gorschalki	German	A. Gorschalki	German	2,115	63 45	63 45	. .	42 30	6 34	35 96	
"	4	" May 7	1887 Dec 2	A. B. Stripling	British	A. B. Stripling	British	2,523	75 69	75 69	. .	50 46	7 57	42 89	
"	5	1887 April	1888 Nov. 15	Corean Customs	Corean	Corean Customs	Corean	6,344	190 32	190 32	. .	126 88	19 03	107 85	
"	6	{No record sometime in 1884}	. . .	"	"	"	"	1,497	44 91	44 91	. .	29 94	4 49	25 45	
"	7	1888 April 30	. . .	R. Brinckmeier	German	R. Brinckmeier	German	975	30 23	29 25	. 98	19 50	2 92	16 58	
"	8	" Sept 3	. . .	"	.	"	.	1,017	100 17	30 51	69 66	20 34	3 05	17 29	
"	9	1890 April 22	1890 April 22	"	.	.	.	393	11 79	11 79	. .	7 86	1 18	6 68	
"	10	" Oct. 28	" Oct. 28	L. A. Hopkins	British	L. A. Hopkins	British	656	33 46	19 68	13 78	13 12	1 97	11 15	
"	11&12	1886 May 28	1887 Dec. 2	W. D. F. Hutchison	British	W. D. F. Hutchison	.	2,227	69 04	66 81	2 23	44 54	6 68	37 86	
"	13	. . .	1888 April 4	F. H. Mörsel	German	F. H. Mörsel	German	1,005	31 16	30 15	1 01	20 10	3 01	17 09	
"	14	" April 19	1887 Dec 29	Ohashi Jan	Japanese	Ohashi Jan	Japanese	1,200	36 00	36 00	. :	24 00	3 60	20 40	
"	15	1888 April 11	1888 April 12	T. Hollingsworth	British	T. Hollingsworth	British	656	33 45	19 68	13 77	13 12	1 97	11 15	
"	16&17	1886 May 7	1887 Dec 20	Woo Litang	Chinese	Woo Litang	Chinese	1,790	107 40	53 70	53 70	35 80	5 37	30 43	
"	18	1886 Nov. 7	1888 April 4	C. Wolter	German	C. Wolter	German	1,207	36 21	36 21	. .	24 14	3 62	20 52	
"	19	. . .	. . .	"	. .	"	.	1,020	30 60	30 60	. .	20 40	3 06	17 34	
"	20	1887 Dec. 5	1887 Dec. 26	W. D. Townsend	American	W. D. Townsend	American	900	270 00	27 00	243 00	18 00	2 70	15 30	
"	21	" March 31	. . .	"	.	"	.	915	27 45	27 45	. .	18 30	2 74	15 56	
								40706							
								Carried over	14,789 78	5,405 64	9,384 14	3,440 32	237 37	3202 95	

4.

continued

Class	No	Date of purchase or acquisition	Date of issue of title deed	Title deed originally issued to whom	Nationality	Name of present holder (12th January, 1891.)	Nationality	Square metres	Amount realized by sale $	c	Upset price retained by Corean Government $	c	Balance handed to municipality $	c	Full rent due per annum $	c	Corean tax to Government per annum 30 cents per 100 sq. metres $	c	Balance to municipality per annum $	c	Remarks
								brought forward	14,789	78	5,405	64	9,384	14	3,440	32	237	37	3,202	95	
D	22	1884 Nov. 7	1887 Dec 26	W. D. Townsend	American	W. D. Townsend	American	930	27	90	27	90	"	"	18	60	2	79	15	81	
"	23	" " "	" " "	"	"	"	"	900	27	00	27	00	"	"	18	00	2	70	15	30	
"	24	1889 April 20	1889 April 20	E. Laporte	French	E. Laporte	French	1,105	33	26	33	15	"	11	22	10	3	32	18	78	
"	25	1884 Nov. 7	1888. " 6	E. Meyer & Co.	German	H. C. E. Meyer	German	885	26	55	26	55	"	"	17	70	2	66	15	04	
"	26	" " "	" " "	"	"	"	"	885	26	55	26	55	"	"	17	70	2	66	15	04	
"	27 & 28	" " "	" " "	"	"	"	"	2,962	88	86	88	86	"	"	59	24	8	89	50	35	
"	29	" " "	" " "	C. Wolter	"	C. Wolter	"	1,770	53	10	53	10	"	"	35	40	5	31	30	09	
"	30	" " "	" " "	"	"	Wo Litang	Chinese	2,640	79	20	79	20	"	"	52	80	7	92	44	88	
"	31	1888, May 14	1888, May 14	F. M. Altmacker	"	F. M. Altmacker	German	1,560	47	58	46	80	"	78	31	20	4	68	26	52	
"	32	" " "	" " "	"	"	"	"	1,500	45	15	45	00	"	15	30	00	4	50	25	50	
"	33	" Sept 3	" Sept. 13	"	"	"	"	1,800	177	30	54	00	123	30	36	00	5	40	30	60	
"	34	" " "	" " "	"	"	W. D. Townsend	American	1,830	183	00	54	90	128	10	36	60	5	49	31	11	
"	35	" " "	" " "	"	"	"	"	1,860	186	93	55	80	131	13	37	20	5	58	31	62	
"	36	" Dec 20	" Dec. 20	C. H. Cooper	American	"	"	1,800	54	00	54	00	"	"	36	00	5	40	30	60	
"	37	1887 June 17	" April 4	E. Meyer & Co.	German	H. C. E. Meyer	German	9,404	286	82	282	12	4	70	188	08	28	21	159	87	
"	38	1884 May 10	1887 Dec. 2	British Government	British	British Government	British	10,090	302	70	302	70	"	"	201	80	30	27	171	53	
"	39	1884 Oct 23	1887 Dec 28	C. H. Cooper	American	Corean Customs	Corean	2,865	85	95	85	95	"	"	57	30	8	59	48	71	
"	40	No record	None issued	None issued		Corean Magistrate	"	1,122	33	66	33	66			22	44	3	37	19	97	
								Grand Total	$16,553	29	$6,782	88	$9,772	41	$4,358	48	$375	11	$3,983	37	

Total Metres 125.035
3 [illegible] 13263
138.298

Held by Corean Govt 17.669

5 Continued

January 1892

Class	No	Date of Purchase	Title Deed Issued	Original Purchaser	Nationality	Present Owner	Nationality	Sq. Metres	Amt of Sale	Upset Price	Bal. to Council	Rent per An.	Consu Fee	Bal. to Municip.
II	42	24/3/91	25/3/91	Capt. F. Meyer	German	Capt. F. Meyer	German	7,700	$ 308 —	$ 231 —	$ 77 —	$ 154 —	$ 25 10	$ 130 90
II	43	3/4/91	9/4/91	Soc. Prop. Gaspel	British	S.P.G.	British	3,780	257 37	113 40	137 97	75 60	11 34	64 26
II	44	7/5/91	22/10/91	Municipal Council		M.C.		3,780	1082 97	113 40	969 57	75 60	11 34	64 26
II	45	1/7/91	18/11/91	Customs		Customs		3,266	96 68	97 68	— —	65 12	9 77	58 55
II	48	17/8/91	18/8/91	E Laporte	French	E Laporte	French	1,807	55 11	54 21	90	36 14	5 42	30 72
B	3	* 7/12/91	8/12/91	E Rogers	British	E Rogers	British	1,906	638 50	114 36	524 15	114 36	5 72	108 64
		* By arrangement M. C. gets all price.												
No														
C	12					H. Kikitaki	Japanese							
C	13/14					Kumamoto	"							
C	15					S. Shindo	"							
C	18					K. Hori	"							
C	19					S. Higuchi	"							
C	21					W. Nakai	"							
C	25					C. Nishinaki	"							
C	26					K. Hori	"							
II	14					W. Lührss	German							
II	18					R. Bonioni	Italian							
II	24					L.C. Hopkins	British							
II	29			to be transferred to		E Laporte	French							

General Account of Receipts and Expenditure
of
Municipal Council, General Foreign Settlement, Chemulpo.

Debt.

1891				
January	1	To Balance $ 6,658.55		
		Balance taxes „ 1,341.70		
		1890 $ 8,000.25		
		Gov't owing Council 1,400.00	$ 9,400	25
May	28	Interest on Deposit	216	00
June	17	„ „ „	54	00
August	8	Premium of $ 6,000. to Nagasaki	16	00
November	11	Net proceeds of Land Sales		
		of D 42. 43. 44 and 48.	1,185	44
December	31	Interest Current a/c F. N. Bk.	55	29
„	„	„ do		30
„	„	Balance Taxes for 1891		
		Taxes $ 1,871.23		
		Expenses of Policing„ 894.58		
		Balance	976	65
			$ 11,903	93

Cred't

1891				
January	1	By Corean Gov't owing to		
		Municipal Council,		
		Grading Streets in 1890	$ 1,400	00
August	29	Discount of draft of Shanghai	88	67
November	11	Cost price of M. C. Lot. D 44.	1,082	97
„	„	Rent for this lot. for 1891	24	65
December	31	Drains, Roads made in 91.	1,719	07
„	„	Corean Gov't owing to		
		Municipal Council,		
		Grading Streets in 1891	1,156	22
„	„	Taxes for 1891 on Lots		
		B 4. D 2. 4. not yet		
		Received $ 243.99—$ 47.76	196	23
„	„	Deposit, Hongkong and Shanghai		
		Bank Corp. Shanghai	5,911	33
„	,	In hand of Police Sup't	1	37
„	„	Bank balance 1st national		
		Bank, Chemulpo	323	42
			$ 11,903	93

Chemulpo, 1st January 1892

Carl Wolter

Hon. Treasurer

朝鮮旬報第二十一号附録

明治廿四年度仁川各國居留地會收支決算報告

收入ノ部		
前年度越高	六、六五八 五五	
仝　税金餘剩越高	一、三四一 七〇	
小計	八、〇〇〇 二五	
朝鮮政府勘定越高	一、四〇〇 〇〇	
		九、四〇〇 二五
各銀行預ケ金利息		三二五 五九
長崎為替打歩		一六 〇〇
土地賣却代金		一、一八五 四四
但D第四十二号四十三号四十四号四十八号分		
本年度税金殘高		
本年度税金	一、八七一 二三	
警察諸費	八七四 五八	
		九七六 六五
合計		一一、九〇三 九三
支出ノ部		
朝鮮政府勘定		一、四〇〇 〇〇
但前年度中道路償還分		
上海為替引料		八八 六七
各國居留地會所有地所代金		一、〇八二 九七
但D第四十四号分		
仝上　本年度地税金		二四 六五
本年度道路溝渠修繕費		一、七一九 〇七
朝鮮政府勘定		一、一五六 二二
但本年度中道路償還分		
本年度未納税金		一九六 二三
香港上海銀行預ケ金		五、九一一 三三
警察署手許有金		一 三七
第一國立銀行當座預ケ金		三二三 四二
合計		一一、九〇三 九三

右之通相違無之候也

明治廿五年一月

仁川港各國居留地議會
名譽會計役
シー、ウォルター

H. I. J. M.'s Legation,
Seoul, Corea.

12 May 1892

Hon. Mr. Heard

I have with pleasure received your note of yesterday's date inquiring me about what I have said in the last diplomatic meeting on the subject of Japanese foreshore. I remember I have expressed at that time my conviction & of my government that by our Chemulpo treaty Japanese foreshore belongs naturally to Japanese settlement; I also stated that in fact the Corean Government have assented to our views. As to the suggestion & proposal of Mr. Hilker, I simply said that I had no objection; I did mention nothing about the decision of the different Governments by which I would be willing to abide.

Yours Truly
T. Kajiyama.

Chemulpo
[illegible] copy of map

Seoul 15th Sept 1893

To the

Honorable P. A. Dmitrevsky,
H. I. R. M's Chargé d'Affaires
&c. &c. &c.

Dear Mr Dmitrevsky,

I send you herewith a copy of a plan that has been prepared by the Customs to show the limit to which, in the opinion of very competent Engineers, filling in of the foreshore at Chemulpo can be safely carried without danger of injury to the Inner Harbour.

Of course you will understand that it is not necessary to fill in all, or any part of the foreshore within the line, but that filling in beyond it is considered, will most certainly restrain and diminish the tide forces it is desired to utilize in order to keep the very limited

anchorage

2

anchorage free from the sand-banks which are encroaching on it; and it is possible that experience may yet show that some slight modification of this line may become advisable in the interest of the Port.

It is hardly necessary for me to add that no agreement as to filling in is implied by anything delineated on the plan.

Yours very Sincerely
F. A. Morgan

Chemulpo

No 22.

28th day, 3rd Moon, 503 yr.
May 3 - 1894.

Sir,

I have the honor to inform you that I am in receipt of a despatch from the Japanese Consul, stating that the Japanese Merchants asking for sale of 5 pieces of Lots on the West-North side of D lot which situated in the General Foreign Settlement at Chemulpo and also he sent me a plan for the said 5 lots drawn out according to the new plan which made by the Municipal Council.

I have measured the said 5 lots and erected boundary stones on each lot as following:

D. lot No 65 - 1,080 sq Metres, this lot is on the South side of D. lot No 50.
D. lots No 62 - 1,100 sq. M. No 63 - 1,020 sq. M., No 67 - 880 sq. M. and No 68 - 1,050 sq. M, these 4 lots are on the

North

2.

North side of D. Lot No. 50.

I have now to inform you that the above 5 lots shall be sold by public auction at the Tidesurveyor's office on the 8th of 4th Moon at 2. P. M. (May 12.), therefore the notice for sale has put up at the gate of Tidesurveyor's office. And I would request you will notify the American Citizens who would purchase the said lots, in order that they may present at auction at certain time.

I have &c.

Yun Kiang Hwan,
Acting Superintendent of Trade
Jenchuan.

Honorable,
John M. B. Sill
U.S. Consul General.

四等五十號地南邊其第四等六十二號地一千一百丁方米突第四等六十三
號地一千二十丁方米突第四等六十七號地八百八十丁方米突第四等六十八
號地一千五十丁方米突此四址均在第四等五十號地北邊茲擇於我曆本年 西曆本年
四月初八 五月十二 日午後二點鍾時在海關理船廳內將該五址照章公拍除出
示於理船廳及公司兩門前俾衆咸知外相應備文照會
貴總領事請煩查照傳知貴商欲租賃該地者卽於屆期隨帶
銀元到理船廳聽拍出價永租可也須至照會者
右 照 會

照

會

大朝鮮署理監理仁川港通商事務俞 為

照會事照得接准 日本領事照會以日商大谷正誠等請將仁

川濟物浦各國租界第四等西北邊之基地五址照章拍租并按公

司新繪之圖繪送該五址圖前來本監理照章勘明該五址地丈量

清晰各竪界石其第四等六十五號地一千八十丁方米突此一址係在第

大美欽命駐劄朝鮮總領事施
開國五百二年三月二十八日
美第二十二号

Municipal Council,

Chemulpo, May 4th 1894

Chemulpo

THE UNITED ... No 2 May 4 1894 ... 7 ... SOUL

Sir,

The Acting Superintendent of Trade at this Port has sent to me a Notice of Auction of Five Lots in the General Foreign Settlement, to be held on the 12th instant.

This Notice, of which I have the honour to enclose a translation, I have caused to be posted at the Municipal Buildings

I have the honour to be
Sir,
Your obedient servant
W. H. Wilkinson
Hon Secretary

Hon. Jno. M. B. Sill
etc etc etc
Doyen of the Foreign Representatives
Söul

Chemulpo
3

Proposed Resolution

Whereas the Japanese Authorities have, in spite of the urgent representations made to them, refused or neglected to withdraw the troops stationed in the Jap. Settlmt & upon the Bund of the G.F.S.; and whereas certain recent occurrences have shown the grave danger to the lives & persons of residents on the G.F.S. arising from the presence of those troops in the port area and their practice of moving freely about it carrying arms;

The Council do request ~~the For Repts. to ask the~~ Comm'rs of the vessels of war now in the port to ~~land a sufficient number of men to~~ take such measures as shall prevent persons equipped with weapons of any description from passing through the General F.S. unless provided with a permit issued by this Council & stamped with its seal.

Chemulpo

Municipal Council.
Chemulpo, December 7th 1894.

Sir;

I have the honor to request that Your Excellency will be good enough to bring before the Foreign Representatives the two following resolutions, passed by the Council at its meeting of yesterday:

(1) That the Foreign Representatives be requested in concert with the Corean government, to have a road laid out from the end of the bund next to the Nippon Yusen Kaisha, along the bund to the jetty, 15 metres wide so that the Municipal Council can metal and grade this road early in March 1895.

(2) That the Foreign Representatives be requested to confer with the Corean Government with a view to the metalling and draining as soon as possible, of all the Cargo space between 15 metre road referred to in the resolution just carried, and the front of

2.

of the Customs Godowns.

I have the honor to be

Sir,

Your Excellency's

Most obedient servant.

W. H. Wilkinson

Hon. Secretary.

His Excellency

Count Inouye

Doyen of the Foreign Representatives.

Seoul

H. I. J. M's Legation.
Seoul, December 19, 1894.

Sirs;

I have the honor to lay before you a copy of a communication which I have received from W. H. Wilkinson Esq, Honorary Secretary of the Municipal Council of Chemulpo regarding the resolutions passed by the Council meeting of December 6, 1894, with the desire that you will be good enough to give full consideration to the questions therein contained and inform me of the views that you entertain respecting them, so as to enable me to make proper disposition of this affair.

I avail myself of this occasion to renew to you the assurances of my highest consideration.

K. Inouye.

Hon. J. M. B. Sill.
Minister Resident and Consul General of the United States.

C. Waeber Esq.
H. I. R. M's Chargé d'Affaires.

W. C. Hillier Esq.
H. B. M's Consul general.
F. Krien Esq.
H. I. G. M's Consul with functions of Imperial Commissioner.
G. Lefèvre Esq.
Gérant du Commissariat de France.
Seoul

Chemulpo

Circular

Gentlemen and Colleagues;-

As President of the Municipal Council of the General Foreign Settlement of Chemulpo, I have been asked by that body to propose to the Minister for Foreign Affairs and to the Foreign Representatives, that said Council be allowed, temporarily, to police, light and scavenger the Chinese Settlement at that place, the expense of this work to be born by the Chinese Residents. The absence of any such provision at present is a menace to the health and

peace

peace of every resident of C:
Chemulpo.

I may add that the Minister for Foreign Affairs agrees to this proposition and it now awaits your individual sanction.

Will you kindly suggest your approval or disapproval hereupon.

I have the honor to be
Your obedient servant

Seoul April 19. 1895 John M. B. Sill.

To
His Excellency Count Inouye — I fully approve K. Inouye
Honorable C. Waeber — I fully agree [illegible]

W. C. Hillier Esquire I entirely approve
W.C.Hillier

F. Krien Esquire. I agree Kr

G. Lefevre Esquire. approved G.L.

Municipal Council,

Chemulpo, April 24 1894

Chemulpo

THE UNITED STATES LEGATION SÖUL
No. 6
Rec'd Ap 25 1894
Ans'd 18

Sir,

I have the honour to acknowledge receipt of your Despatch of the 22nd instant informing me that the Minister for Foreign Affairs and all the Foreign Representatives at Söul heartily approve of the proposal that this Council should temporarily police, light, and scavenger the Chinese Settlement at Chemulpo.

I have laid your Despatch before the

Hon. J. M. B. Sill
United States Minister
etc etc etc

the Executive Committee of the Council,
who are today commencing to put in
order the streets and drains of that
Settlement.

I have the honour to be,

Sir,

Your obedient servant,

W. H. Wilkinson

Hon. Secretary

No 7

~~Municipal Council,~~

Mayor's Office Chemulpo, April 30th 1895

Copy

Sir,

I have the honor to acknowledge the receipt of your letter of the 5th inst. in which you request us to co-operate with you in filling up the ground in front of Nippon Yusen Kaisha's office, so as to properly connect with the road you are constructing along the bund. I called an extraordinary meeting of the Council of our Settlement and submitted for consideration the subject of your communication under reply.

The meeting, actuated by the desire of promoting

To W. J. Wilkinson Esq
Hon. Secretary, the Municipal Council of the General Foreign Settlement, Chemulpo

promoting the convenience of the public in general, resolved that the Settlement shall undertake the work of not only filling up the ground as requested by you, but also of extending the width of the road all along the bund. The bund, being the most level passage between the two Settlements and the Customs' jetty, is the busiest place, where men and cargoes pass most frequently. But the width of the street, which according to the regulation should be 12 metres, as is the case with other streets, is really not more than 6. As the consequence, the public has always been subjected to the inconvenience of obstructions, which will be felt more

Keenly

keenly after the construction of the road near the Customs Godowns.

In order to meet with these exigencies, the Municipal Council has resolved to extend the road in question to a width somewhat more spacious compared with other streets, and I fully trust that the work, when completed, will greatly promote the mutual convenience of the two Settlements. In consequence, however, of the extension of the plan, you will please understand that more or less time will be required for the preparation of the work.

In conclusion, I beg to state that, for want of the quorum in the Council owing to

the

the absence of many members, I have not been able to reply to your communication as promptly as I ought to have done.

I have, etc

(Signed) J. Furuta,

Mayor of Japanese Settlement.

Municipal Council,

Chemulpo, May 2nd 1895

Dear Mr. Sill,

I received yesterday from the Japanese Municipal Council the enclosed reply to our letter of the 5th ultimo.

I have shown the despatch to Mr. Townsend, and we are both agreed that in itself the proposal of the Japanese Council is excellent. There would seem, however, one point, or rather two, to be considered.

In the autumn of 1893 the Corean Government officially informed the Foreign Representatives that all the foreshore

south

south of the General Foreign and the Japanese Settlements appertained [or would when filled in appertain] to the General Settlement. The Japanese therefore are, strictly speaking, only entitled to fill in to the width of the 12 metres mentioned in Mr. Furuta's despatch. All ground beyond [that is, south] of that appertains to us.

In agreeing unconditionally, therefore, to the Japanese proposal we might seem to be giving away certain prospective rights: on the other hand, a 15-metre road from the jetty right through to Coreatown would be a public boon.

Would it be possible, do you think, to arrange that in consideration of the increase of 3 metres [or whatever it is to be] acceded by the General Settlement to the Japanese, the latter agree under no circumstances to close the road? — I ought to have brought in first my second point, which is, that the Japanese are apt when there is any suspicion of an epidemic, to endeavour to enforce quarantine regulations, one of which on the

the last occasion (as I am informed) consisted in stopping some, or all, of their streets, & forcibly disinfecting passers-by.

Yours very truly
W H Wilkinson

Municipal Council,

Chemulpo, Dec: 9th 1895

Sir,

At a meeting of the Council held on the 6th instant the following resolution was passed without a dissentient vote:

"This Council believing it to have been the intention of the signatories to the Chemulpo Land Regulations that the 'Consuls of the Treaty Powers' referred to in §6 should be Consular Officers actually resident in Chemulpo, and recognizing the many inconveniences that have arisen from the

same

Hon. J.M.B. Sill

Doyen of the Foreign Representatives

Söul

same persons acting both as Official Members of the Council and as Foreign Representatives at Söul, respectfully requests, through the several Representatives, the attention of the Governments of the Treaty Powers to this matter, to the end that in each case a special Officer, not being the Representative of the Government at the Corean Court, may be appointed to attend the meetings of the Council".

I have accordingly the honour to respectfully request that you will be good enough to communicate the above

resolution

resolution to the Foreign Representatives.

I have the honour to be,

Sir,

Your most obedient

humble servant,

W. H. Wilkinson

Hon. Secretary

Dear Colleague,

I will be happy to meet with you in my private office at 3 P.M. on Monday the 30th instant, to discuss the matter mentioned in the enclosed letter from the Honorary Secretary of the Chemulpo Municipal Council, if convenient and agreeable to you.

Yours

very sincerely

JOHN M. B. SILL

U.S. Legation. Dec. 27/95.

Please indicate approval or otherwise

Cr. Lefèvre

yes Hillier

yes Waeber

yes Kr.

yes Komura

Municipal Council,

Chemulpo, January 20 1896

Sir,

With reference to my letter of the 9th ultimo submitting a resolution of the Council in regard to Official Members, I have had the honour to receive your Despatch of the 30th December informing me that the Foreign Representatives had decided that the resolution in question was invalid because, in contravention of Sect. B § 12 of the Rules for regulating the Council's Proceedings,

no

Hon. J.M.B. Sill

Doyen of the Foreign Representatives

Söul

Circulated & seen by all the Representatives Jan 21. 22.

no notice of the motion had been given in the circular convening the meeting.

This Despatch I laid before an extraordinary meeting of the Council on the 16th instant, when the following resolution was passed:

"The Council respectfully demurs to any infringement of the privilege, reserved to it under Section 1 § 2 (a), of determining all questions arising under the Rules appertaining to the deliberations of the Council".

I have

I have the honour to be,

Sir,

Your most obedient servant

W. H. Wilkinson

Hon. Secretary

Chemulpo 10
17/2 97

Jenchuan 15th Feb. 1897

Superintendent of Trade
Ye Chai Chung to Mr. Sill
U.S. Minister & President of the
Chemulpo Municipal Council

Sir,

I have the honour to inform you that I have sent a letter to the Secretary of the Municipal Council on the date of 23rd Ult. with the enclosures of a check of sum $802.90 which was extracted from the rent of 1895 paid by the four land holders of the Chemulpo Foreign Settlement and $54.50, the interests of one year last for all the rents which was deposited at the Japanese Bank, for the fund of the Municipal Council; and also sent him the original and duplicate copies of said Check's receipt which were provided by my office in need of his signature and to be sent back to my office.

In

In further I beg to inform you that I have received an answer from him written by English, but without the signed receipt. So I returned the same English letter to him as I had no translator, and requested him to communicate with me hereafter in accompany of a translation as usual.

I trust your Excellency will kindly instruct the Secretary to have the said receipt to be signed and send back to me and then I will deliver, to the Municipal Council, the certain amount for the Municipal funds which are extracted from the annual rents of last year to settle that accounts.

I have &c.

(Sig.) Ye Chao Chung (official seal)

Interpreters had great difficulty in translating this letter. The form of expression not being as usual with Koreans. It may have been written by a foreigner.

照會第二号

大朝鮮仁川港監理李

爲照會事照得本年正月二十三日本監理備函附送紳董公司文案本

港各國租界內四租户未完已繳到一千八百九十五年之年税欵內公司應存備金八百二元九

角並自一千八百九十六年正月初一日起至十二月三十一日止之陸續繳到各年税収存日本第一銀

行之利息銀內公司應得銀五十四元五角合共銀八百五十七元四角銀票一張連代繕収到該

銀正副収單二張等因嗣於正月二十五日接到紳董公司文案送來洋文書函一

件而収到該銀之正副収单未見盖印畫押送還本署因無繙譯之員是以當將

該洋文書函備文送還一面請該紳董公司文案以後凡有於本署文件仍請照

舊以英漢二文合璧自公司之設迄今既將已九載之久紳董公司文案向用英漢

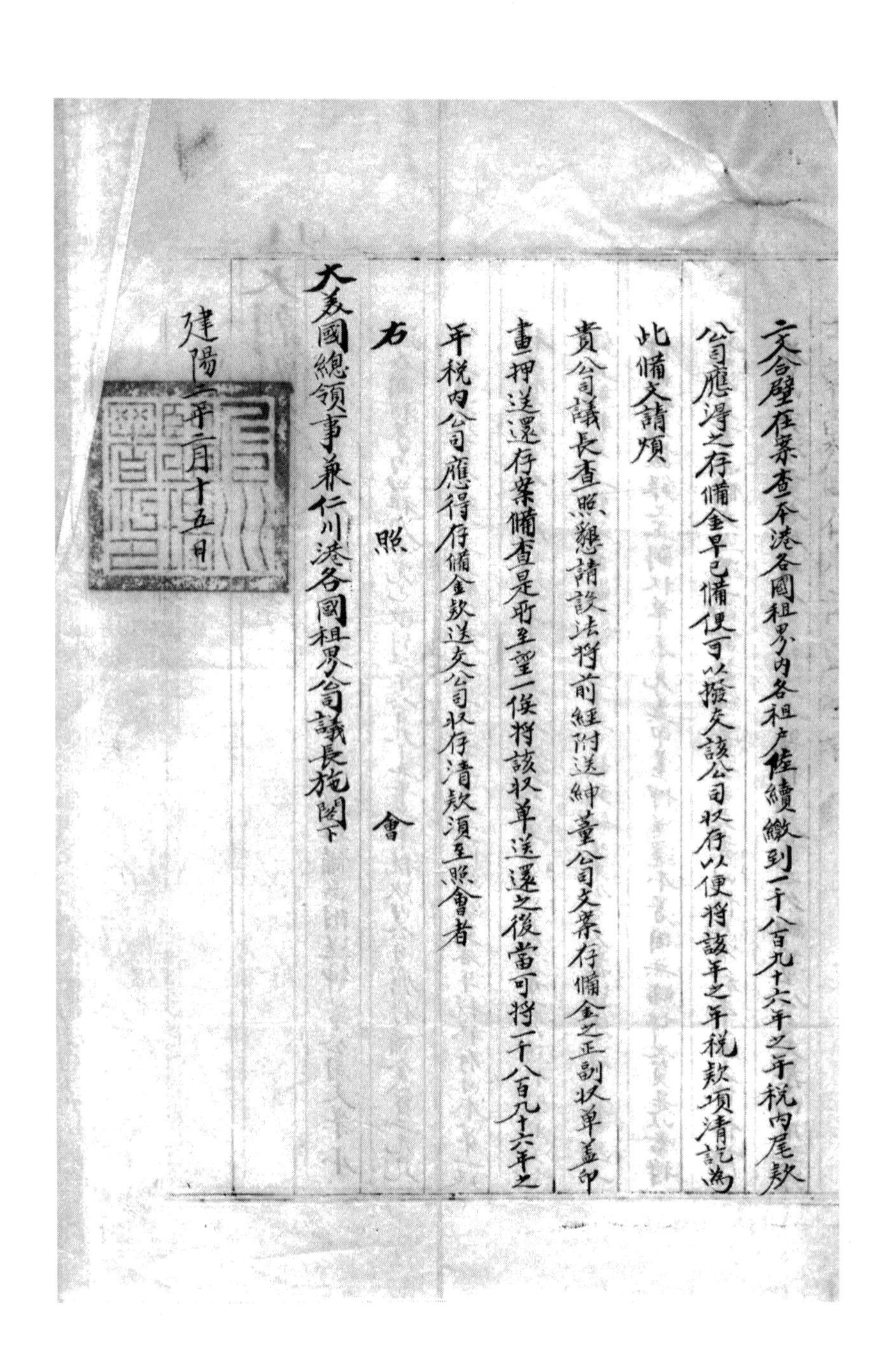

文合璧在案查本港各國租界內各租戶陸續繳到一千八百九十六年之年稅內尾款
公司應得之存備金早已備便可以撥交該公司收存以便將該年之年稅款項清訖為
此備文請煩
貴公司議長查照、懇請設法將前經附送紳董公司文案存備金之正副收單蓋印
畫押送還存案備查是所至望一俟將該收單送還之後當可將一千八百九十六年之
年稅內公司應得存備金款送交公司收存清款須至照會者
右 照 會
大義國總領事兼仁川港各國租界公司議長施閣下
建陽二年二月十五日

Municipal Council's Office.
Chinnampo. 22nd August 98.

LEGATION OF THE UNITED STATES. SÖUL.
No. ....
Rec'd 26. 8. 1898
Ans'd .... 18..

Sir

I have the honour to inform Your Excellency, that at a meeting held to-day, that the Municipal Council for the Foreign Settlement of Chinnampo, has been inaugurated, and that the following officers have been elected, Eugene Peugnet, President, and Yasunosuke Ohki Honorary Treasurer.

I am
Sir
Your Excellency's obedient servant.

Eug. Peugnet.

To His Excellency
Horace N. Allen
Minister Resident and Consul General of the United States of America.
&c. &c. &c.
Seoul

Chemulpo File No. 166 L.C.

Söul, Sept. 20th 1900

UNITED STATES ... SÖUL

Dear Dr. Allen,

this morning I asked Mr. Hayashi about the present condition of the Chemulpo-Railway-Station-Rent-question. He said that by pointing out the 6th paragraph of the Title-deed form, which according to his opinion was in favour of our demand, he had succeeded in persuading his Government that something had to be done in order to arrive at a compromise. He would therefore very soon lay the proposals of the Railway-Company before the meeting of the Representatives. The chief features of these proposals would be, that the Company was willing to pay the tax, provided that a proper title deed would be issued in the name of the Company and that the whole ground in question would be classed as D lots. This would mean a reduction of the rent to 1/3 of the rent paid by C lots and demanded hitherto in view of Art. 7 of the Land-Regulations.

As to the title deed, it will have to be issued by the Corean authorities and ought to be limited by the same conditions as to its termination, as the Railway concession itself.

Mr. Hayashi said he would communicate to us a detailed statement before having the meeting, but I thought it would be better to inform you about the main features at once because you may perhaps have an opportunity

now in Chemulpo to speak
about the matter with Mr.
Townsend and other parties
interested.

Hoping that you and Mrs.
Allen are in good health
I am with kind regards

Yours

very sincerely

H. Beipert.

60 pcs Metres @ D $1,200 per year
" " @ C 3,600 " "
" " Less 30% per 100 sq m
Dec Grant $ 180.

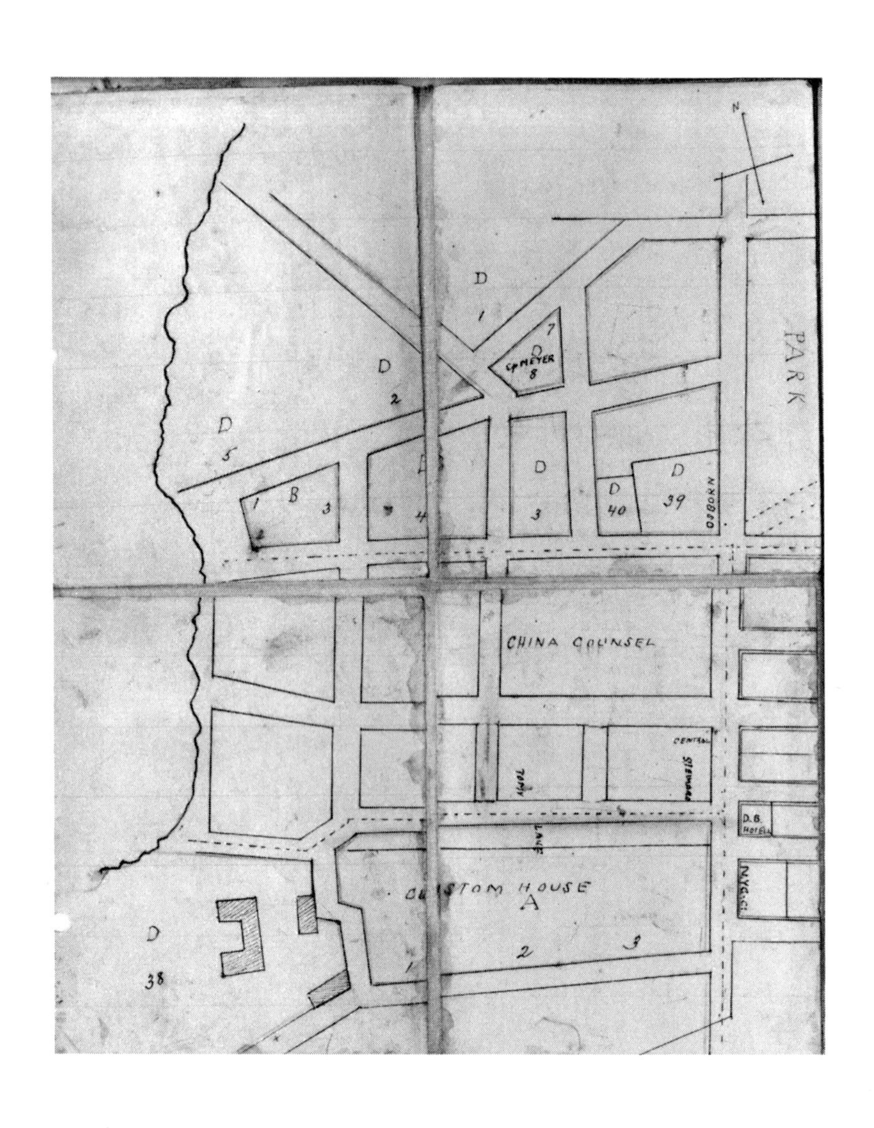
N
PARK
D
1
7
D
MEYER
8
D
2
D
5
1 B 3
4
D
3
D
40
D
39
OSBORN
CHINA COUNSEL
CENTRAL
LANE
D.B.
HOTEL
CUSTOM HOUSE
A
1
2
3
D
38

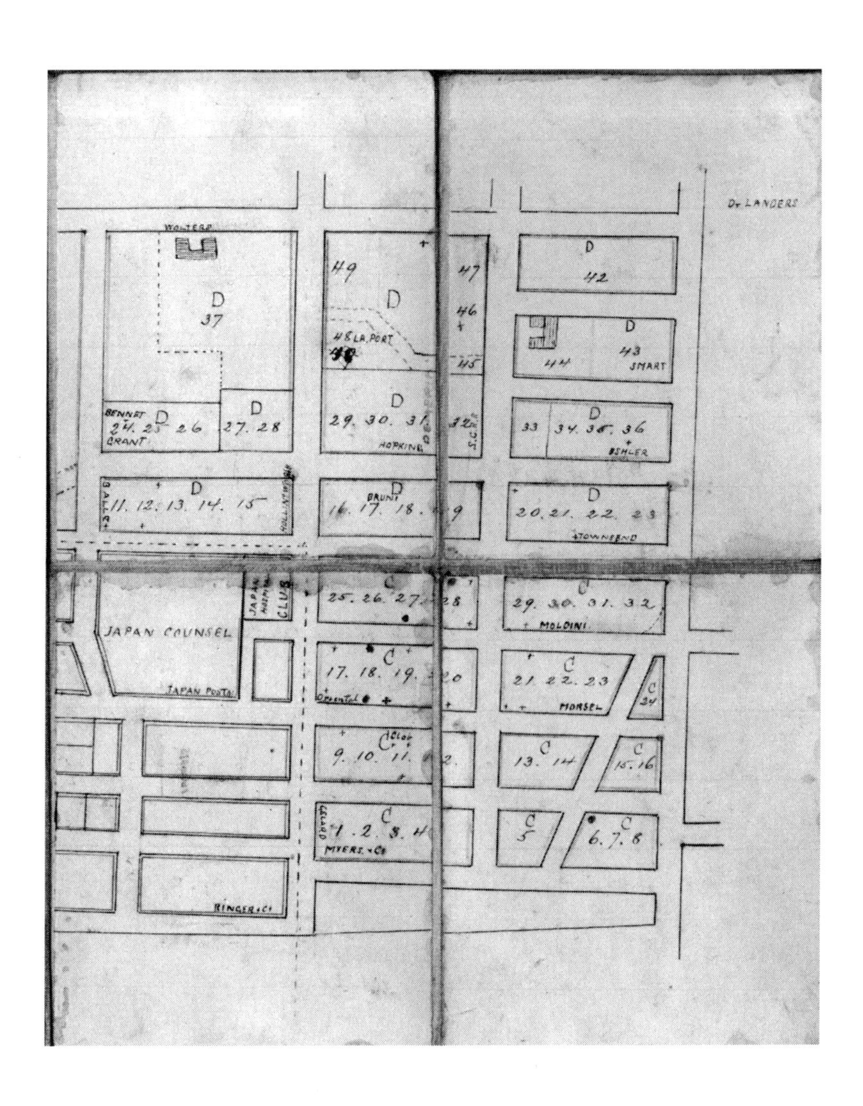
Dr LANDERS
D
37
BENNET
GRANT
24. 25 26
27. 28
49
D
48 LA PORT
47
46
45
29. 30. 31.
HOPKINS
D
42
D
43
44
SMART
33
34. 35. 36
ESHLER
11. 12. 13. 14. 15
BRUNI
16. 17. 18.
20. 21. 22. 23
TOWNSEND
JAPAN COUNSEL
CLUB
JAPAN POST
25. 26. 27.
28
29. 30. 31. 32
MOLDINI
17. 18. 19.
21. 22. 23
MORSEL
24
9. 10. 11.
13. 14
15. 16
1. 2. 3. 4
MYERS & Co
5
6. 7. 8
RINGER & Co

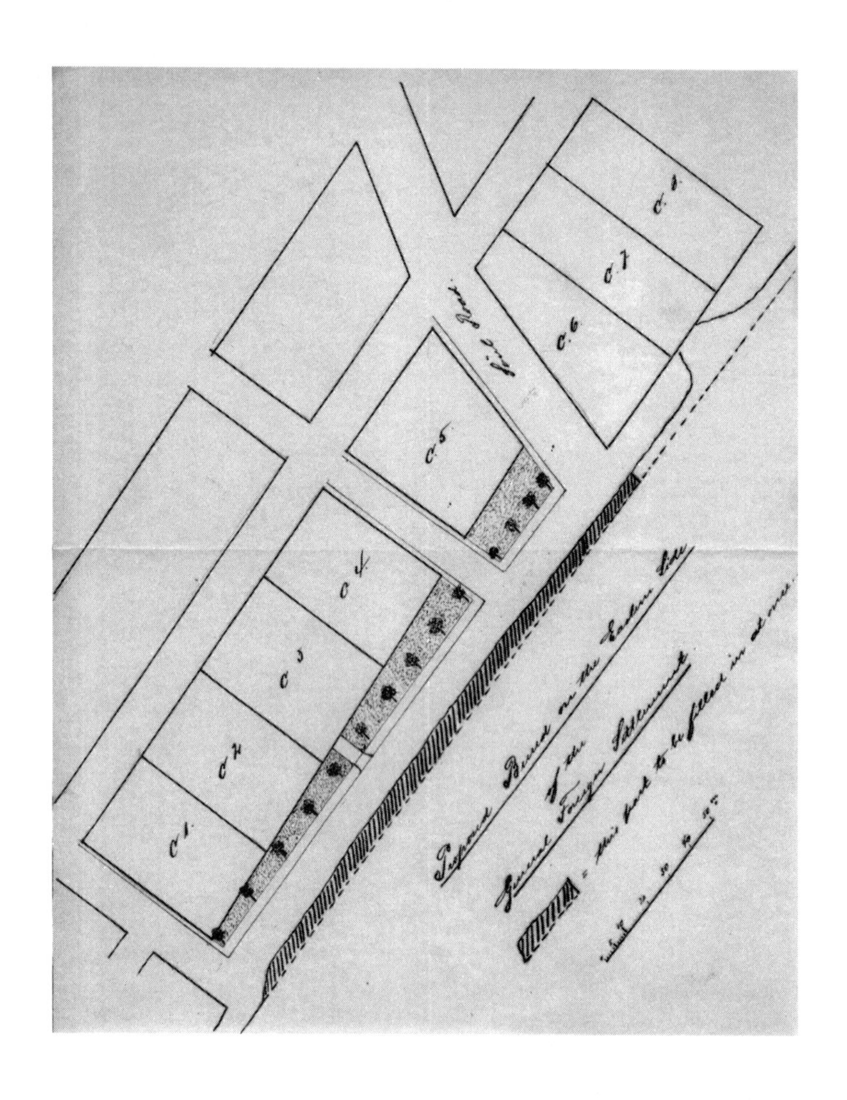
C.5
C.6
Proposed Bund on the Eastern Side
of the
General Foreign Settlement
= this bank to be filled in at once.

Suggestions for a new agree-
-ment and Land Regulations
for the General Foreign Settlement
of Chemulpo

---

1. The old Regulations are hereby
abolished, excepting in so far
as they are embodied in the
present agreement and Regu-
-lations

2 The Municipal Council shall
consist of the Consuls of the
Treaty Powers, whose subjects or ci-
-tizens hold land in the settle-
-ment, the chief officer of the
Royal Customs at Chemulpo
and three land-holders.

3- A court shall be established,
consisting of the Consuls, or

Representatives of all the Treaty Powers, before which it may be sued.

4 - The Korean Government shall lease in perpetuity to the Municipal Council the land known as the General Foreign Settlement, which shall be newly defined and which shall include the foreshore North and South.

The Korean Government will undertake to remove the Korean dwellings and graves within the limits of the Settlement as speedily as possible and certainly before the expiration of
from the date hereof.

5 - The Municipal Council shall pay as rent on the 1st of February of each year a sum equal to 30 cents per 100 square metres upon all lots sold to that date.

6 - Rents shall be payable on

1st of January of each year at half the present rates (to be previously specified) which may be increased at the discretion of the Foreign Representatives. In case of neglect or refusal to pay, they may be collected by summary process before the Consul of the Delinquent.

7 - Title deeds shall be issued by the Municipal Council in the form attached.

8 - The Korean Government may hold the lots of which it is now in possession, and may acquire other lots by purchase, but only for strictly official purposes.* Such lots shall be subjected to taxation, municipal regulation and control, precisely as other lots in the settlement.

* Connected with the settlement

이영미

인하대학교 인문학부를 졸업하고 동 대학원에서 석사 및 박사 학위를 취득한 한국근대사 연구자로, 주요 관심사는 개항기와 일제강점기 한국에서 활동하였거나 한국 관련 저술을 남긴 서양인들이다. 2016~2019년 건양대학교 충남지역문화연구소에서 '근대전환기 〈알렌 문서〉 정리·해제 및 DB화'를 수행하였으며, 현재는 인하대학교 한국학연구소에서 서구 세계에서 성립된 한국학을 정리 및 심화하는 작업을 추진하고 있다.

인천학자료총서 25

제물포 각국 조계지 회의록 2

2020년 2월 28일 초판 1쇄 펴냄

기　획 인천대학교 인천학연구원
역　자 이영미
펴낸이 김흥국
펴낸곳 보고사

등록 1990년 12월 13일 제6-0429호
주소 경기도 파주시 회동길 337-15 2층
전화 031-955-9797(대표)
02-922-5120~1(편집), 02-922-2246(영업)
팩스 02-922-6990
메일 kanapub3@naver.com / bogosabooks@naver.com
http://www.bogosabooks.co.kr

ISBN 979-11-5516-966-7 94300
979-11-5516-520-1 (세트)

정가 28,000원